THE ECONOMIC LIVES OF PLATFORMS

Rethinking the Political Economy
of Digital Markets

Edited by
Anne Mette Thorhauge, Andreas Lindegaard
Gregersen, Eva Iris Otto, Jacob Ørmen
and Morten Axel Pedersen

First published in Great Britain in 2024 by

Bristol University Press
University of Bristol
1–9 Old Park Hill
Bristol
BS2 8BB
UK
t: +44 (0)117 374 6645
e: bup-info@bristol.ac.uk

Details of international sales and distribution partners are available at bristoluniversitypress.co.uk

© Bristol University Press 2024

British Library Cataloguing in Publication Data
A catalogue record for this book is available from the British Library

ISBN 978-1-5292-3749-8 hardcover
ISBN 978-1-5292-3750-4 ePub
ISBN 978-1-5292-3751-1 ePdf

The right of Anne Mette Thorhauge, Andreas Lindegaard Gregersen, Eva Iris Otto, Jacob Ørmen and Morten Axel Pedersen to be identified as editors of this work has been asserted by them in accordance with the Copyright, Designs and Patents Act 1988.

All rights reserved: no part of this publication may be reproduced, stored in a retrieval system, or transmitted in any form or by any means, electronic, mechanical, photocopying, recording, or otherwise without the prior permission of Bristol University Press.

Every reasonable effort has been made to obtain permission to reproduce copyrighted material. If, however, anyone knows of an oversight, please contact the publisher.

The statements and opinions contained within this publication are solely those of the editors and contributors and not of the University of Bristol or Bristol University Press. The University of Bristol and Bristol University Press disclaim responsibility for any injury to persons or property resulting from any material published in this publication.

Bristol University Press works to counter discrimination on grounds of gender, race, disability, age and sexuality.

Cover design: Liam Roberts Design
Front cover image: stocksy/CACTUS Creative Studio
Bristol University Press uses environmentally responsible print partners.
Printed and bound in Great Britain by CPI Group (UK) Ltd, Croydon, CR0 4YY

Contents

Acknowledgements		iv
1	Rethinking the Political Economy of Digital Markets *Andreas Lindegaard Gregersen, Eva Iris Otto, Morten Axel Pedersen, Anne Mette Thorhauge and Jacob Ørmen*	1
2	Modes of Connectivity: On the Economic Ontology of Platforms *Vincent Manzerolle*	17
3	Platforms and the Social Imaginary of Ordinary Life *Juan M. del Nido*	37
4	Burdens of Legacy: Enumerative Accountability in Digital Markets *Vibodh Parthasarathi*	53
5	Voice Intelligence and the Future of Engagement Metrics on Commercial Platforms *Joseph Turow*	73
6	Brokering Data Markets: The Agentive Power of App Builders at the Edge of Platforms *Eva Iris Otto*	88
7	The Political Economic Process of 'Platformization': The Historical Trajectory of Alibaba *Elaine J. Yuan and Lin Zhang*	108
8	Efficient and Illegitimate: Legitimacy Problems in the Platform Model *Andreas Gregersen and Jacob Ørmen*	127
9	Player-Driven Economies and 'Money at the Margins': Game Items as Contingent Commodity Money *Anne Mette Thorhauge*	140
10	After the Attention Economy: A Postdigital Anthropology of the Future *Morten Axel Pedersen*	153
References		163
Index		189

Acknowledgements

We would like to thank the following organizations and individuals for supporting the activities that have contributed to the making of this book. With thanks to the European Research Foundation as part of the project: 'The Political Economy of Distraction in Digitized Denmark' (DISTRACT) (grant number 834540)), and The Carlsberg Foundation for a donation to run two workshops during 2021 (Grant number CF21-0703).

We would also like to thank Marion Fourcade and Natasha Dow-Schüll for their generous and extensive feedback, and extremely helpful comments on paper drafts and workshop presentations. Many thanks also to all participants during the workshops and subsequent revision of manuscript for their critical and constructive work with draft manuscripts, and for the administrative and practical assistance from Maya Møller Nielsen, Emilie Munch Gregersen, Asger Hans Thomsen and Sofie Læbo Astrupgaard.

We are also grateful to the peer reviewers and manuscript proposal reviewers recruited by BUP for highly useful comments during the editing process, and to our editors at BUP for their diligence, competence, professionalism, and patience.

1

Rethinking the Political Economy of Digital Markets

Andreas Lindegaard Gregersen, Eva Iris Otto, Morten Axel Pedersen, Anne Mette Thorhauge and Jacob Ørmen

Over recent decades, discussions about 'digital markets', 'data capitalism' and 'attention economy' have become ubiquitous among academics, policy makers, and thought leaders. In many ways, 'platform' has emerged as the master concept capturing what supposedly is novel about this new form of capitalism (Helmond, 2015; Srnicek, 2017; Nieborg and Poell, 2018; van Dijck, Poell and de Waal, 2018). For example, prominent scholars have invoked this concept to suggest that digitized forms of data collection and analyses have heralded an era of 'surveillance capitalism' (Zuboff, 2019) or 'attentional serfdom' (Williams, 2018), where algorithmically generated segmentation, profiling and manipulation of users delivers ever more granular and precise behavioural blueprints to advertisers (Fourcade and Healy, 2017). Yet, while this business model has succeeded to an unprecedented degree in the digital age, it hardly represents a new kind of market capitalism. The notion that 'if the product is free, then you are the product' has undergirded commercial media for more than a century (Gorman and McLean, 2003; Webster, 2014; Wu, 2016), and the tendency for dominant companies to monopolize markets (for example, Google Play) and infrastructures (for example, Amazon Web Services) has an even longer tradition in the history of capitalism (see, for example, Braudel, 1992). Furthermore, the platform is not a uniform model diffused throughout societies worldwide but rather an organizational form shaped by and embedded in local contexts (see, for example, Davis and Xiao, 2021; Langley and Rodima-Taylor, 2022). The platform is at once a continuation of societal developments over time and an instantiation of a particular organizational form in space.

Against this background our ambition in this volume is to rethink the political economy of digital market by asking what came before platforms and what might come after them. As we have just indicated, the platform literature may at times seem blind to its placement in time as well as lacking spatial breath. Where work on platforms has been done in non-Western contexts, it has typically focused on utopian/dystopian exemplars of the digital age, such as 'data-driven authoritarianism' in Communist China (Lee, 2019) or 'techno-animism' in Japan (Jensen and Blok, 2013). As soon as one moves away from the hubs that are home to Big Tech and their most important costumer (and thus user-data) bases into the digital and data-economic margins, one is faced with a multitude of entanglements between these global infrastructures and local concerns and constraints (Hobbis and Hobbis, 2022). By unpacking the otherwise generic concept of 'platform economies' into locally embedded variations of concrete digital markets, our ambition in this book is to lift discussions about the economic and political implications of digital technologies away from its sometimes-ephemeral theoretical abstractions and lofty claims, and instead focus on how this concept can best be operationalized in contexts cutting across both space (geography) and time (history).

By doing so, we propose, it will be possible to critically access the enormous popularity that the concept of the platform has gained over the last decade among scholars and in the public, by asking question such as, what does the platform notion do for us? What are its empirical boundaries and its theoretical blind spots? As such, while we acknowledge the contribution of existing research on platform capitalism, we believe that a thorough investigation is needed of the deeper temporal and the wider spatial dynamics that undergird emerging reconfigurations and negotiations between technology, information, society and markets.

This is not to deny the challenges platforms pose to contemporary societies, quite the opposite. The increasing concentration of financial power surely pose a threat to the global economy and so does the monopolization of communication and news to democracies. However, an important question is whether this threat derives from the involved actors' status as platforms or merely from their status as companies that have managed to grow to an unreasonable size due to a political environment favouring deregulation and concentration of money on private hands in the wake of the financial crisis (Srnicek, 2017; Frenken and Fuenfschilling, 2020). That is, their power may be due to wider economic and historical factors and a general capitalistic strive toward monopoly. From this perspective contemporary platforms' path to monopoly status may as well pass though their ability to attract venture capital (Langley and Leyshon, 2017) as it may pass through ingenious and superior platform architectures holding every user and complementor in a firm grip, the typical explanation of platforms' power base.

With the ambition to rethink the political economy of digital markets, we have invited a selected group of established and upcoming researchers from media studies, anthropology and sociology to explore one or more of the following questions: To what extent can classical political economic approaches shed new light on prevailing paradigms in media studies, digital anthropology, digital sociology, and science and technology studies (STS)? How does material infrastructures inform our understanding of 'the digital' in digital markets and the 'platform' in platform economies? Will the materiality and the imaginary of the platform remain applicable in future imbrications between digital technology and market capitalism? Can a focus on the concept of money, as a historically and culturally contingent phenomenon, inform the study of cryptocurrencies and other digitized forms of capital? It is our contention that, as the contributors to this volume seek to address these and cognate questions, we will all need to rethink and reassemble the concept of 'the platform'.

In what remains of this introduction, we begin by unpacking how the concept is used in current platform studies by identifying and critically discussing four general themes in platform studies. After this, we address the geographical and historical specificity of platforms with a view to substantiate and further specify their place in time and space. Finally, we introduce each of the eight individual chapters that make up the bulk of this volume, discussing and comparing how they offer different takes on the above questions as well as the wider concerns and themes raised in this introduction.

Four overarching themes in platform studies

Marxist-inspired analyses of digital labour (that is, Daubs and Manzerolle, 2016; Srnicek, 2017; Morozov, 2019; Fuchs, 2022) have forcefully shown how Big Tech extends the extractive logic of pre-digital capitalism to exploit its users, developers and other actors. Within digital sociology, media studies and anthropology, several volumes have explored the data revolution from a political economic perspective, with reference to concepts such as 'surveillance capitalism' (Zuboff, 2019), 'media infrastructures' (Plantin and Punathambekar, 2019), and 'attention economy' (Pedersen et al, 2021). However, one of the biggest shortcomings to such political economical perspectives on platforms is its focus on global systems and large-scale structures at the expense of local variations and negotiations. We need to turn our attention to more local and embedded[1] understandings of 'customer or brand loyalty', 'safety of data' and 'professional practices', to explore not only how hegemonic systems of digital and data reproduce but also how differently situated actors re-imagine and rework their scope for action and for change in specific situations. To begin this necessary interrogation of the platform concept, we present four themes cutting through the literature: materiality, ownership and agency and organization, economic frameworks and strategic discourse. These themes are overlapping but separated out here for analytical purposes.

Our first theme is materiality and structure. In Montfort and Bogost's work, which offers an early, influential programmatic formulation of platform studies, platforms are conceptualized as 'the hardware and software design of standardized computing systems' (Montfort and Bogost, 2009: 2) with the goal of understanding such design structures as fundamental conditions for computational creativity. Within this perspective, the prototypical example of a platform would be the Atari VCS. Much of this work focuses on games, and the perspective could thus be widened to such software as the game developer middleware platform Unity; Poell and Nieborg (2018) include such a perspective under their umbrella of software studies (see also Fuller, 2008), which forms one arm of their own combined approach to platforms. A related strand of platform studies has explored 'how computing devices (such as Intel-chip-based PCs) and software environments (such as gaming systems) affect the characteristics of application software built upon them' (Plantin et al, 2018: 294). This strand focuses on software as well as larger infrastructural components (Blanke and Pybus, 2020), and it leads to establishing the boundaries of the platform at the wider level of hardware-software integration, such as the use of APIs, technical integrations and so on. Within this lens, Google Cloud Platform is (also) a platform, since it is a hardware and software structure integrated into a set of productivity tools available for the end-user through a variety of APIs and interfaces; this would lead logically to inclusion of software such as Microsoft Office or Adobe Creative Suite as productivity platforms. One problem with Montfort and Bogost's specific variant of platform studies, however, is not so much their idea that work of this kind 'must be technically rigorous' (Montfort and Bogost, 2009: 1) but rather that 'only the serious investigation of computing systems as specific machines can reveal the relationships between these systems and creativity, design, expression and culture' (Montfort and Bogost, 2009: 3–4). We agree that serious investigation of a range of specific properties and relationships is crucial for understanding platforms, but this endeavour should not be shackled to 'machines' – or anything else for that matter. Matter still matters, and we do not naïvely argue that the 'bare metal' of hardware offers no resistance. However, we find this call for monolithic attention to computation unproductive.

Our second theme is the operations of platforms. If platforms consist, so to speak, primarily of software and hardware, how are these matters organized to serve particular operations? Here, the literature seems to have converged on the notion of two-sided and multi-sided markets as the dominant organizational form: Platform companies operate multi-sided markets – and if you have not already reorganized your business along such lines, you should, seems to be the mantra of Parker et al (Parker et al, 2016). This lens, however, is applied somewhat inconsistently even by its proponents, and it is evident that a software studies productivity platform such as Microsoft Office is captured less well within this perspective. One solution is to distinguish between different types of platforms incorporating different operations and structures, such as Srnicek's distinction between five different types of platforms: advertising, cloud, industrial, product, and lean platforms (Srnicek, 2017). Alternative distinctions could be that of Van Dijck et al's between sectorial and infrastructural platforms (Van Dijck et al, 2018) or Kenney and Zysman's (2016) between platforms for platforms, platforms that make digital tools available online, platforms that mediate work, retail platforms and service-providing platforms. These various attempts at categorizing platforms all build on the idea that platforms may be grouped based on differences in organizations and operations. However, the resulting distinctions also indicate that platforms as such cannot be distinguished by a single business model such as 'multisided markets'.

Another theme is the overall economic framing. Here, the question is whether these manifold platforms embody a new type of capitalism or whether they merely instantiate more of the same? And, relatedly, what kind of framework should we deploy to understand the types of economic actors and economic action? Here, one might invoke various incarnations of Marxist and Polanyian analysis, where the platform literature arguably has been dominated by the former. This has led to a series of astute analyses of commodification (see, for example, Fuchs, 2022) but has also tended towards a type of monolithic and totalizing conceptualizing already hinted at in the previous sections. One remedy might be a renewed interest in the work of Fernand Braudel (1982, 1992), whose notion of the anti-market seems to have found resonance among those interested in the way tech giants seek competitive advantage (see, for example, Peck and Phillips, 2021). To see why, it is obvious that the critical stance of standard issue Marxism is opposed to the laudatory business manual aspects of platform hype, but a Braudelian criticism offers a more fundamental critique of the validity of the model of matchmaking neutrality. What if platform operators merely masquerade as matchmakers, but in reality, are in the business of operating anti-markets? Another position keeps the notion of platforms as two-sided or multi-sided markets but couples it to the idea that they accumulate value through gathering and using big data (Birch et al, 2020; Fourcade and Kluttz, 2020; Kenney and Zysman, 2020). Platforms are defined economically as a 'new regime of accumulation' (Kenney and Zysman, 2020: 57) and such an approach would lead us to ask who participates, understood in empirical terms, in this 'new regime' and which actions form part of the regime of accumulation in the localized practices in different places.

Our final theme is that of governance and strategic discourse. To some extent a meta-theme, this theme targets the reasons various actors and stakeholders might have for using the term platform – however ill defined – to describe a set of interconnected properties and operations. The very idea of the platform as a neutral piece of scaffolding for user agency holds considerable metaphorical power, leading to a notion of disinterested facilitation and propping up of creativity and productivity (Gillespie, 2010). At the same time, this power is not purely metaphorical but also serves as capital ready to be deployed in battles of public affairs, most prominently when platform companies seek to define themselves as operators of platforms, not owners of media companies. If they were recognized as the latter, specific responsibilities and regulation would follow immediately (Khan, 2018; Gorwa, 2019). This discursive meta-perspective has the advantage of drawing upon and bringing together several of the other strands of thought, since it to a large extent depends upon being able to draw connections between them. The discourses around platforms and the entailed issues will probably to some extent remain unresolved, however many themes or typologies we conjure up. We should also recognize that all academics have some skin in this strategic game of definitions. Hesmondhalgh (2019) thus offers a concise overview of the issues involved in strategic deployment of the platform term (which includes academic jockeying for position). His stance is that 'it is pointless to resist the widespread usage of the term 'platform' – it is clearly here to stay in spite of the confusing discrepancies and clashes between different uses of the term' (2019: 209).

Historicizing 'the platform'

Having outlined parts of the wider thematic and theoretical landscape of current platform studies, we can now turn to the first of the two proposed dimensions through which we wish to resituate the platform phenomenon and concept, namely by unearthing its historical predecessors. Indeed, most of the digital platforms that dominate our everyday usage of the internet are barely of age. Platforms like Meta/Facebook (founded 2004), YouTube (2005) and Twitter (2006) are just entering adulthood, Airbnb (2008), Uber (2009), WhatsApp (2009) and Instagram (2010) are venturing into teenage life, while Toutiao and Musical.ly (the predecessors of TikTok, launched in 2012 and 2014) are merely kids. Nonetheless, their popularity has skyrocketed worldwide based on an organizational form, the platform, which is at once novel in its technical capacity and age old in the economic operations. In short, we need to put the platform in historical perspective. But which perspective, precisely? The historian Fernand Braudel (Braudel, 1982; Hufton, 1986) offered a framework to understand history through different perspectives on time: the *longue durée* (the longest timespan encompassing centuries or even millennia), the *moyenne durée* (covering societal developments and cycles, *conjecture*) and the *courte durée* (the shortest time span, focused on events and experience of everyday life). If we borrow this taxonomy from Braudel, we can identify historical antecedents and continuities of platforms on these three scales.

On the grandest scale, the history of capitalism provides an important background. Braudel saw the tension between a market economy (competition and exchange) and capitalism (domination and power) as a central driver of the economy in Europe since the Middle Ages (Braudel, 1992). Braudel saw the capitalist sector as inherently *anti-market*, in that a few large corporations seek to control price-setting mechanisms through monopolization and extract value from different areas, while operating outside the legal and normative grounds of the market. This has perhaps been most clearly demonstrated for the large industrialist corporation in the nineteenth and twentieth century, but recently scholars have shown how platforms have utilized the legal void in the regulation of digital markets to assert market dominance either through acquisition of competitors or aggressive lobbying (Culpepper and Thelen, 2019; Peck and Phillips, 2021). The tendency not to specialize in select markets but to invest in activities where profits are to be found has been especially clear with the diversification of platform business. Amazon has broadened its portfolio from selling books online to selling everything online (including storage) as well as offering streaming and advertisement services. In the longue durée the platform model represents a continuation of anti-market practices from the early modern merchants to industrialist capitalists.

As concerns the Moyenne durée, this can be associated with the emergence of organizational forms that predate yet are quite comparable to that of digital platforms. The previous century saw the emergence of an organizational form distinct from the integrated firm. The two-sided platform model originates in advertisement-based media (such as newspapers and commercial television) and credit card systems (Parker et al, 2016). This type of organization brings together distinct types of actors (commonly referred to as 'sides' in the market) such as viewers and advertisers or consumers and merchants and derives revenue from the resulting interactions. Typically, one side functions as the payment side subsidizing access for the other side; advertisers pay for the attention of viewers that then gain access to media content for free or at a discount. This creates *indirect network effects*, where the activities of one side on the platform affect the activities of the other side, for example, the more attractive viewers a TV network can draw in the more advertisers are willing to spend, or the more users of a certain credit card there are the more shops are willing to accept the card as a payment method (Rochet and Tirole, 2003). Thus, in contrast to the supply-side economies of scale that dominated the industrial firm with a focus on reducing cost per unit, the two-sided platform model introduced demand side economies of scale (winner-takes-all mechanisms) as the primary determinant of success.

In the shortest time scale, we can see the conditions for the rise of platforms in the beginning of the twenty-first century. First, the development of social technologies for the web (encompassed by the term Web 2.0) as well as technologies to access the internet (notably smartphones) and increase the usability of the internet (through stronger connections such as broadband and mobile data) provided the technical infrastructure for digital platforms to take off. Second, the financial world was ready for the platform model at the turn of the century. After the bursting of the dotcom bubble, governments incentivized investments through low interest rates which created fertile ground for the risky investments in upcoming platforms (Srnicek, 2017). As many platforms operate on a subsidy model where the service is offered free to users, continuous influx of capital is necessary to survive the early growth years until the business turns a profit. Amazon, again, illustrates this process well. Founded in 1994, the company managed to operate through the 1990s, be listed as a public company and survive the dotcom crash without being profitable. When Amazon managed to corner the market for online retail by outspending competitors (Stone, 2013), it became one of the world's most valuable brands – a position that has only grown during the COVID-19 pandemic. Taken together, from the vantage of this the shortest of Braudel's timescales, then, the rise of platforms is the result of, among other factors, a technical momentum, a regulatory vacuum, and financial opportunities without which the platform model would have taken a different form.

By way of closing the present discussion of how best to historicize 'the platform' as an empirical phenomenon and an analytical concept, let us present some preliminary reflections on the future sense (or tense) of this question. Braudel's model takes us some way in terms of answering what came before platforms. But we also need to ask what might come after. By posing and exploring this inevitably speculative question, we should be placed in an even better position to put the finger on what, if anything, might be distinct about platform capitalism and its forms of production, circulation and consumption. A possible answer to these questions can be found in recent discussions of the 'postdigital' (Jandrić et al, 2018). As Cramer writes in one of the first uses of this concept, it 'describes an approach to digital media that no longer seeks technical innovation or improvement but considers digitization as something that has already happened and thus might be further reconfigured' (2015: 20). Often, and with good reasons, social scientists are sceptical towards 'post-concepts', which tend to be tied to periodizing logics positing bounded and homogeneous intervals in time and space (for example, 'modernism'), which are demarcated from and in opposition to what comes before and after (for example, 'postmodernism').

However, for Cramer at least (although not necessarily other scholars of the so-called postdigital condition), the postdigital:

> should ... be understood here ... in the sense of post-punk (a continuation of punk culture in ways which are somehow still punk, yet also beyond punk); post-communism (as the ongoing social-political reality in former Eastern Bloc countries); post-feminism ... [and] postcolonialism ... as postcolonial practices in a communications world taken over by a military-industrial complex made up of only a handful of global players. (2015: 13, 21)

This is the lesson we want to heed here – that far from representing concepts imprisoned within a specific historical moment, the prefix 'post' instead holds the potential to complicate overly easy periodization. Much like, say, postmodernist art represented an intensification of certain stylistic traits that were already present or dormant in modern art, so also the postdigital may be theorized as the product of a simultaneous transformation, where certain features and dynamics that have become closely associated with 'the digital' shall undergo a further intensification, acceleration and radicalization, whereas others will contract, slow down, or wither away. Where we will go from this will be a question of the post-digital, or maybe post-platform – order. Having ceased being defined as a historical concept in a simple linear sense – viz. as denoting a unique period ontologically distinct from others, the postdigital now emerges as historical in a non-linear sense, whose value lies in its capacity to temporalize hitherto overly presentist conceptions of platform capitalism.

Provincializing 'the platform'

Let us now turn to the second dimension in our process of resituating the platform, namely the lacking concern with the spatial situatedness of concrete cases of platform capitalism. Put differently, our ambition here is to provincialize the platform as an empirical phenomenon and theoretical concept. In borrowing this phrase from anthropology, where it has played an important role in attempts to decolonize and de-essentialize central discussions in this discipline (Chakrabarty, 2007), we wish to critically recontextualize and re-theorize actually existing platforms within the concrete specific societal, cultural and economic settings and situations in which they are irreducibly embedded. Thus understood, the problem is not that 'the platform' is provincial in having a certain discursive genealogy and a certain material and economic situatedness – this, after all, is a predicament that it shares with all other concepts. It is instead, again, an opening to attend to the specificities of platforms in their context – in fact, it is an insistence on the importance of embedding within contexts. With this follows the need to make explicit and carefully reflect upon the analytical challenges as well as the opportunities pertaining to this state of affairs – the need, in short, to provincialize the platform.[2]

It is true that the importance and need for 'context' is emphasized within parts of the existing literature. For instance, recent platform scholarship has attended to the physical location of platform companies in the US with easy access to venture capital focused on 'doing first, and saying sorry later' (for instance, keeping a hand under Amazon during the dot.com bubble until it became profitable) and the celebration of a Silicon Valley-related type of business ethics focused on 'moving fast and breaking things'. The conflux of particular legal, social and cultural factors in and around Silicon Valley seems to have created a situation of opportunity leading to some of the largest and most influential American platform companies (for example, Birch et al, 2020; Kenney and Zysman, 2020). Yet, it seems to us, the relation between platform and societal context in current platform studies needs to be further specified and further theorized to fully fulfil its analytical promise and purpose.

Analyses from this Silicon Valley-dominated perspective, we argue, place considerable emphasis on platforms' data collecting powers within a framework of advertising and consumer capitalism, and as a consequence disregard other contexts and thus explanations of platforms' power in society. Current work on platform society (Van Dijck et al, 2018) surely brings forth important and rigorous analyses of the way big tech has risen to unprecedented size and power and transformed societies in the process. Moreover, the position of big tech corporates among the most valuable companies in the world[3] speaks its own language as concerns the strategic power of platform ownership in today's global economy. Yet, this strategic power is very often explained quite narrowly with platforms' access to large amounts of data and superior data processing techniques, that is, platforms' ability to monopolize, extract, analyse, and use increasing amounts of data (Srnicek, 2017: 43) bringing about a new era of 'surveillance capitalism' (Zuboff, 2019). In extension of this, platforms are attributed with an almost supernatural ability to track individual users' whereabouts, actions, tastes and political beliefs with the aims of segmentation, prediction and value extraction. Indeed, it has become a common-sense trope that platforms 'know us better than we know ourselves' and are able to predict our future life circumstances in ways unavailable to us. Yet, this strand of analysis builds on an underlying conceptualization of unbroken lines of power extending from the economic clout of 'big tech' corporations to every corner of everyday platform use, with severe limitations of conceptualizing actual contexts of use. This perspective, we posit, contrasts with several contributions in this volume, which emphasize the fundamental messiness of platform use and data collection which obstructs any clear-cut relationship between centre and periphery. Western middle-class consumption is an overarching yet implicit scheme running through this entire line of argumentation. For example, the literature on the commercialization of user data seems to assume a one-to-one relationship between the communication device and the individual, which makes the relationship between data and the individual rather straightforward (see for instance Fourcade and Healy, 2017). While this may certainly be a norm and a reasonable expectation within certain subsets of society, the assumption disregards all the contexts where devices are for economic or other reasons shared by entire households or groups, such as families and peers. Similarly, much of this literature assumes that all users represent value as potential consumers in a value extraction scheme based on advertisement. Yet, users may represent little or no value as consumers due to lack of economic means (Ørmen and Gregersen, 2022) or they may be positioned entirely outside the relationships that characterize market society and consumer capitalism (see, for instance, Kusimba et al, 2018). Indeed, the narrative about platforms' extraordinary power to track individual users to sell their attention to advertisers can be seen as just another instance of the previously mentioned strategic discourse or platform rhetoric (Gillespie, 2010) manufactured to convince advertisers and users alike and to cover up all the messiness and inconsistency that characterize platform use and data collection in practice.

Accordingly, another key aim of this volume is to exit the 'fishbowl' of platforms and platform studies to watch it from the outside. By contrasting current notions of platform society with a set of alternatives, it becomes possible to inquire in a more rigorous manner what are truly characteristics of platform society and what should rather be attributed to wider differences between societies and economies. Moreover, it becomes possible to ask whether we are talking about one or several 'platform societies' with different working logics. Further, as a complimentary way to step outside the fishbowl, we propose to pay attention to the analytical possibilities of centre–periphery relations, emphasizing both the empirical and conceptual boundaries of platforms. One way to operationalize this is by asking precisely what might not be a platform. Instead of committing to one of the four themes we have described previously – and therefore pre-define which type of platform boundary we should look at – we wish to take a step sideways in our attempt to provincialize the platform and instead suggest two different approaches, which draw on a radical embedding of platforms into their contexts.

The first approach we propose are studies from regions considered periphery (from the view of both industry and traditional digital scholarship) in relation to digital development, in which what is platform and what is not, is not theoretically pre-decided but traced out through attention to local negotiations. In this we consider space in a geographical manner.

While attention to the embeddedness of platforms in legal, cultural and social contexts is tentatively increasing within platform studies (for instance, Birch et al, 2020), there is still a great need to do the same for platforms not in the context of Silicon Valley. Through their tendency towards tacit universalism, platform studies and public discourse around platforms at the same time both over and under recognize the importance of platforms in other contexts, hence the need to look towards the peripheries and centres of platforms. The second approach in turn broadly considers the social and material practices of (trans-geographic) digital communities at the mainstream periphery in which platforms play varying roles. By this approach we consider space relationally. By shifting our focus to the type of practices and translations across the community, the platform is again set into context to the broader social and material processes, highlighting how communities engage in practices that can be seen to contribute to a platform while also causing frictions and multiple orders of meaning and value-creations.

If we position ourselves at the margins with a 'peripheral vision' (Nash, 2001) this refracts the platform from a different embedded context. This peripheral vision emphasizes how the aims and practices of platforms are not imposed from the centres directly. Instead, one effect of platforms seems to be the ability to translate into a variety of local economic, legal and social contexts. But this again, never frictionless, leads to important qualifications and re-evaluations of what platforms are and are capable of. For instance, the close conceptual affinity between capitalism, platforms logics and digital markets might need to be rethought as they give surprising insights into how platforms can be transformed in local settings and subsumed under other types of economic structures (Hobbis and Hobbis, 2022). But the peripheral position also comes with a second critical aim: to question how certain parts are made periphery and others centre in study of, and self-representations of, platforms. A thoroughly contextual approach should therefore also critically access how the particular places, communities and practices are made marginal by both platforms (who have had a large success with exactly this in legal and social terms, helping them gather large wealth without taking much social responsibility) but also by scholarship. The need to provincialize the platform is therefore a call to attend both the boundaries of mainstream platform geographies, and to attend to the conceptual universalization of platforms, where any grounding quickly fades away.

Rethinking platform capitalism

In the previous sections we have questioned the status of the platforms as trans-historical and trans-spatial and introduced a set of analytical perspectives aimed at contextualizing platforms within their wider economic, historical, and spatial contexts. Platforms should be analysed in accordance with their specific operations and structures, as well as their embedding in the overall economy. We have argued that the 'longue durée' of capitalism, the more recent history of precursory organizational forms and most recent past with the dot.com bubble, and the financial crisis should all be included when explaining current platforms' specific paths via economic growth to near-monopoly status. We have also suggested that, concurrently with this focus on the past political-economic phenomena and forms that predate and, perhaps, gave rise to platform capitalism, additional analytical mileage can be gained by asking what might come after 'the platform' as a hegemonic vehicle of capitalist exploitation and political domination. Without such a multilayered and non-linear conception of what platforms have been, are and could be in their past, present and future instantiations, we risk operating with simplistic, teleological and deterministic explanations of the rise of contemporary platforms. Similarly, to further decentre 'the platform' as both a phenomenon and a concept, we have argued that a tacit centre-periphery model of Western consumer societies undergirds current accounts of the relationship between platforms as hubs of economic power and norms for user behaviour. To counter this bias, we see a need to explicitly provincialize the platform and focus on the conceptual and geographical boundaries of platforms to investigate critically and cogently what might be truly distinct about platforms and the wider ecosystem of digital markets and data materialities within which they are embedded.

To re-situate the platform, then, we must reinstate it into the broader economic, historical, and geographic context within which it operates. We must disassemble the notion of platforms into its individual components to identify what is new about contemporary platforms and what are characteristics of wider historical, social, and economic currents. The contributors to this volume approach this disassembling from different analytical angles. Ranging from detailed ethnographic accounts of how platform potentials and perils are negotiated in everyday digital market practices among app developers in Copenhagen (Otto), to sweeping theorizations of the emerging voice intelligence industry (Turow), the eight chapters that follow rethink the relationship between digital markets and platform capitalism from an interdisciplinary perspective.

First media scholar Vincent Manzerolle situates platforms within the wider history of media and capitalism. He points out that media play a key role in terms of connecting the moment of production, circulation, and exchange in time and space. Using the platform as an entry point, Manzerolle reflects on the relationship between capitalism and connectivity – drawing on the work of Sohn-Rethel, Kittler and Innis – and identifies in this process four coordinative abstractions: money, price, derivative, and affordances.

Next anthropologist Juan M. del Nido similarly addresses contemporary platforms as both building upon and reworking older conceptualizations. He points out that while platforms did not invent the moral legitimacy entailed in the figure 'ordinary individuals' and 'ordinary life', they successfully built and utilized a specific moral legitimization related to the imaginary of 'ordinary life' that developed from European history. Conceptualizations such as 'ordinary life' are invoked as the moral justifications underpinning modern institutions such as representative democracy. The idea of the ordinary life gains a new material iteration through the workings of platforms and, in doing so, intensify a particular moral order.

From a different geographical perspective media scholar Vibodh Parthasarathi attends to the stakes of audience measurements in legacy news markets in India. Parthasarathi recounts the importance of making any subject visible in order to engage in processes of enumeration. As he carefully analyses through attending to the 'history of media markets, the trajectory of the business of audience measurement and specific contexts in which media platform are studied', current media platforms reconfigure market systems through processes of enumeration. In a historical study of these partially path-dependent processes, Parthasarathi shows how audience measurement has been a 'persistent and thorny issue in the long history of media governance'. This persistence, in turn, makes for a situation where many of the anxieties associated with these processes are carried over to the present state of media platform operations in India – and possibly elsewhere, given the centrality of audience enumeration for digital platforms.

In a similar vein, media scholar Joseph Turow focuses on emerging developments within industry of voice speaker systems and turns our attention to the increasing use of voice with speaker platforms. Detailing the ambitions and efforts of speaker-platforms to capture as much of the person as possible, Turow theorizes the logics by which these specific platforms attempt to gain market success. Focusing critically on an aspect of what might come next with the (post-)platform, media systems scholar Turow's chapter helps us conceptualize a plausible future of a 'personalized biometric engagement', based in equal parts on the seductiveness of the spoils of surveillance and widespread resignation caused by a lingering awareness of the tendrils of corporations reaching ever deeper into our private lives.

Focusing on what might, surprisingly, also be considered a periphery of platforms within capitalist society, anthropologist Eva Iris Otto attends to the relations and gaps between transnational platforms and local Danish app and data markets. By an ethnographic study of app-developers, designers and salespeople in Denmark, Otto shows the labour that actors, what she calls the 'middle men', do in order to align platforms and local markets. As the ones materially building the links between platform and local market interests and concerns, middle men such as app developers, play a crucial brokerage role. Attending ethnographically to their work complicates traditional narratives of the power and reach of platforms into local markets.

Like Otto, media scholars Elaine J. Yuan and Lin Zhang explore what platform capitalism looks like from a geographical or conceptual periphery vis-à-vis the Silicon Valley centre, namely by tracking the emergence of digital markets at the intersection between platforms and state in China. They show how the history of the platform Alibaba is intimately intertwined with both regulatory and state affairs, while not simplifying this into an argument about Chinese authoritarianism. The events surrounding the Chinese platform Alibaba have often been portrayed rather unilaterally as related to an authoritarian regimes' control over the free market, in opposition to US free market values. In fact, as the chapter shows, there are many similarities between the relation between the platform Alibaba and the Chinese state and the relation between the US government and the big American platform companies. By their careful analysis of Alibaba's relations to local market practices and state regulations, Yuan and Zhang contribute to the tempering of our claims about the organizational powers of platforms.

Taking another global platform, YouTube, as a case in point, Andreas Gregersen and Jacob Ørmen offer a temporal displacement of platform scholarship by applying central tenets of resource dependence theory (RDT) to the notion of multisided markets – a 'blast from the past' of organizational theory, as it were, to interrogate the relationship between platform companies and their environments. The central business model and resulting organization of digital media platforms have led to market dominance but also to substantive problems of legitimacy for the companies operating these platforms. Such problems of legitimacy are central to the survival of organizations, and RDT posed the dichotomy of efficiency and effectiveness to unpack this problem, with the latter term standing in for organizational legitimacy. Thus, organizations can be highly efficient and still be considered ineffective, that is, illegitimate, by their environment. The chapter argues, in a nutshell, that dominant platforms may have been highly cost efficient, but the result has been a lack of effectiveness, evidenced through a series of legitimacy crises for platforms.

Anne Mette Thorhauge analyses how economic practices originating in games on Steam, the dominant platform in the domain of PC gaming, travel beyond the platform as emergent monetary networks. Virtual items obtained in Steam-based games are integrated into economic transactions on and beyond the platform in a range of ways that consolidate their status as money, that is, units of transaction and means of payment. She applies Nigel Dodd's (1994) concept of monetary network to identify if and how these economic practices differ from pre-digital and pre-platform examples of 'local monies' and contends that the primary difference concerns the way game items remain tied to the platform, as the key transaction mechanism and store of value.

In his epilogue, Morten Axel Pedersen offers a postdigital anthropology of the future. He reflects on the concept of the postdigital as an intensification of the digital and on the possible future directions of the digital attention economy as artificial intelligence is changing the game.

Together, the chapters provide new perspectives on 'the platform' as a theoretical concept, an organizational form, and as lived practice. The volume hopefully inspires and provokes readers to further question the taken-for-granted concepts and ideas in related fields.

Notes

1. Partly overlapping with the political economical in the study of digital capitalism, there has been a renewed scholarly interest in the concept of 'embeddedness' as it originally theorized by Polanyi (1944) and subsequently refined by sociologists (Granovetter, 1985; 2017; see Krippner and Alvarez, 2007) and anthropologists (Gregory, 1982; Strathern, 1988) in their analyses of digital markets (Fligstein, 2001; Beckert, 2009), money (Ingham, 2013; Dodd, 2014) and, indeed, platforms (Tubaro, 2021).

2. As Chakrabarty explains, her project about provincializing Europe is not as such concerned with 'the region of the world we call "Europe." That Europe, one could say, has already been provincialized by history' (2007: 3). Rather, as she goes on to explain 'the Europe I seek to provincialize or decenter is an imaginary figure that remains deeply embedded in clichéd and shorthand forms in some everyday habits of thought ... in the social sciences' (2007: 3–4; emphasis original).

3. Apple, Alphabet, Microsoft, Amazon and Meta make up the top five on Forbes Magazine's list of the most valuable brands in 2020 (www.forbes.com/the-worlds-most-valuable-brands/). The picture is slightly different if we look at the Forbes list of the most valuable public companies in the world in 2023 as measured by assets, market value, sales and profit. Here traditional industrialist and financial behemoths dominate but several of the platform companies are still featured in the top 30 (www.forbes.com/lists/global2000/).

2

Modes of Connectivity: On the Economic Ontology of Platforms

Vincent Manzerolle

The task of investigating the many *economic* lives of platforms also compels a concurrent search for a common underlying thread, a mode of existence that is shared across these iterations. What exactly are the shared economic qualities upon which a great variety of case studies depend? This chapter provides a framework for examining the 'economic ontology' (Mäki, 2001) of contemporary platforms through a historical and conceptual lens. In doing this, it integrates concepts from media theory and Marxist political economy, emphasizing the connective and coordinative function that platforms play in mediating transactions. The chapter's overarching goal is to contribute to a more general history of the relationship between media and capitalist accumulation. To do this, the chapter foregrounds 'connectivity' as a core theme for understanding the recurrent intertwining of profound changes in media and markets, culminating in contemporary forms of platform-centric strategies of accumulation; where the proliferation of 'transactional affordances' (Manzerolle and Daubs, 2021) ensures we are, in some way, 'always already inside the market' (McGuigan and Manzerolle, 2015).

What I want to highlight in this contribution is that the questionable resemblance between platforms and markets reflects underlying modes of connectivity used to facilitate transactions. By 'mode of connectivity' I here refer to the specific combination of technological, economic and epistemic factors that coordinate agents and affordances in time and space. In this respect, platforms, beyond what they signify as a set of interrelated discourses about the state of information technologies and their political and economic importance, are instrumental in enabling a very specific space–time coordination that links individuals, interfaces and information through the capacities of an underlying infrastructure. A platform is merely the most recent iteration of the mediated way that markets exist and in which transactional affordances can be embedded. The chapter argues that a focus on the modern platform's coordinative and connective capacities – epitomized by the transactional affordance – not only extrapolates its core infrastructural role in modern capitalism but, by extension, also establishes a longer historical progression that reveals the intellectual intertwining of Western metaphysics and economics.

Outline of chapter

The outline for this chapter is as follows: the first two sections elaborate on the relationship between capitalism and connectivity, looking at the concept of the platform as an entry point. In the second section, I introduce two concepts from Alfred Sohn-Rethel's recently republished text *Intellectual and Manual Labor: A Critique of Epistemology* (2021): his concept of 'social synthesis' and the 'exchange abstraction'. The chapter will then examine the implications of Sohn-Rethel's argument by using the works of media theorists Friedrich Kittler (2009), Harold Innis (1995, 2008) and Randy Martin (2015) to better interrogate how modern markets, transactions and consumption practices are embedded in digital media and vice versa. Though not exhaustive, the chapter identifies and discusses four coordinative abstractions: money, price, derivative and affordance. In taking this approach, this chapter outlines some key ways that platforms are, at their core, a specific mode of connectivity subsumed, though not exhausted, by the circulatory needs of capitalism in its search to reduce barriers and facilitate transactions ubiquitously.

The many economic lives of platforms

As the theme of this collection suggests, the economic roles platforms play in modern political economies are diverse and heteronomous. I want to add that platforms play an infrastructural role in modern capitalism, but they do so within a longer historical trajectory that links together the ontological and economic presuppositions of Western capitalism itself. That is, to investigate the economic lives of platforms is to also identify what specific features they articulate to become so widely and rapidly indispensable, and arguably transformative, so much so that some identify 'platform capitalism' (Srnicek, 2017) or 'platform accumulation' (Meier and Manzerolle, 2019) as a relatively new era of capitalist accumulation. Without denying the important newness at hand, this chapter will thread together a historical narrative to support an analysis of the many economic lives of modern platforms. I here employ the term 'economic ontology' (Mäki, 2001), an analytical approach used to uncover the 'ontological presuppositions of economic theories' (p 10). For example, economist James Buchanan (1991) argues that, generally speaking, modern economics presupposes 'methodological individualism' whereby individual autonomy and choice is conceptually disconnected or isolated from non-market forces like community (p 14). He later states that the creation of patterns resulting in a particular 'economic order' presupposes 'spontaneous coordination' as '*the* principle of our discipline [economics]' (p 22). In this presupposition, a whole range of coordinative and connective media are made invisible, leading to a more general neglect of media in economic theory (see Babe, 2018). In this chapter I want to expand this programme to consider the ontological presupposition of economic media as they contribute to the larger analysis of platform capitalism.

A brief historical prelude to this discussion will set the tone. In 1685 London printer William Leybourn published *A Platform for Purchasers, a Guide for Builders, a Mate for Measurers*. The book is an example of a largely forgotten, and wholly understudied, genre of commercial publication known as 'ready reckoners' – printed aids that 'contained tables of precalculated results of all kinds of multiplication useful for commerce' (Williams and Johnson, 2005: 64). Leybourn intended this text to provide 'tables ready calculated for those that either sell or purchase land or houses' as well as 'rules and tables for measuring work of various descriptions' (Murray, 1930: 299). According to Williams and Johnson (2005), this genre originated in the mid-sixteenth century, becoming essential texts needed to calculate the value of commercial transactions as they became more sophisticated and abstract. The ready reckoner was indeed an analogue platform – meaning, an infrastructural medium – for the human computational infrastructure of an emerging mercantile class in Western Europe:

> Most seventeenth-century tradesmen were heavily dependent on the tables and ready reckoners which poured out in profusion, enabling the user to look up rates of simple compound interest or to work out the price of some commodity. Such devices were essential for people whose arithmetical skill was rudimentary. (Thomas, 1987: 117)

I begin with this specific example for three reasons: the first is, most obviously, the explicit use of the word 'platform' in the title. Although uncommon for the time, it suggests that even in the seventeenth century the word platform was understood as a metaphor for the growing intellectual complexity of an emerging commercial 'way of knowing', one that relied on newly introduced Arabic numerals used to calculate by 'algorism', a synonym for what we today call 'arithmetic' (Thomas, 1987: 106). Indeed, an etymological dictionary from the eighteenth century includes four definitions for the word 'platform', one of which was simply a 'model or pattern of a thing' (Bailey, 1759). In the context of the ready reckoner, market transactions were already understood as virtual and computational. The second reason is to note the coincidence of an expanded commercial printing industry that supported the development of a more sophisticated, and abstract, understanding of 'the market'. In the pages of the ready reckoner, the market is understood primarily as an accumulation of prices in the tables and charts contained therein.

Finally, *Platform for Purchasers*, specifically emphasized the importance of new forms of calculation in the growing market for land purchasing and development. The year, 1685, is significant in expansion of the British Empire into North America and the Caribbean, which opened markets, including land, for which new types of calculation were needed (Nettles, 1933). In fact, Leybourn was producing these texts as the term 'British Empire' was beginning to be used more widely (Adams, 1922). Leybourn's *Platform for Purchasers* is the product of converging transformations of media and markets, it provides a way to link the situated merchant within a wider set of connections that expanded the possibilities for market transactions in an era where the availability of information, and the growing need to calculate and compute pricing information, was growing in lockstep with European colonialism.

Although set in the seemingly distant past, what this anecdote does provide is a set of essential processes and abstractions that are now deeply associated with contemporary digital platforms and platform capitalism more generally. Namely, that platforms represent market mediators, or makers, that they provide mechanisms for calculating and facilitating market transactions, and by their very interfacial logic, are instrumental in populating our media with a multitude of transactional affordances. To put more simply: in so far as platforms may lead multiple economic lives, there are some underlying 'essential' features that unify this diversity, and moreover, that these essential features are part of a historical/genealogical trajectory that can be traced into the past, analysed in the present, and projected into the future.

Connectivity and capitalism

In its most simple diagrammatic presentation, capitalism is defined by the interconnection of at least three moments in its circuitous reproduction: production, circulation and exchange (see Kjøsen, 2016 for a thorough explication). Although there is great variety in the nature, types, and formal qualities of specific capital formations, these moments share a need to be connected in time and space. That is, capitalism is itself dependent on media of connectivity to reproduce itself as a circuit of interconnected moments (Kjøsen, 2016). The circuit culminates in the moment of exchange (for example, market transaction) which signals that the circuit may begin anew. Within this Marxist framework, I would therefore like to consider the market itself as comprising an evolving, and layered mode of connectivity; that is, as a set of media-dependent ways in which the 'moment of exchange' is produced through the coordination (that is, mediation) of social actors and economic institutions. Connectivity is also another way to think about the ontological and epistemic, as well as cultural and economic, implications of media; to paraphrase media theorist Friedrich Kittler, today, it seems, from the perspective of capital's reproduction, only that which can be connected 'exists at all' (in Peters, 2015: 320). Yet the forces working to make this kind of connectivity an ontological presupposition are political and economic, not metaphysical. Insofar as they are highly capitalized, the connective capacities of modern platforms reflect a longer historical process of reshaping life itself according to the territorializing function of capital's circulation (Garnham, 1990; Mattelart, 1996, 2000).

Taking a media theoretical perspective in developing this line of analysis entails treating media as infrastructural, often invisible, or highly embedded, forgotten or ignored, particularly in the seamless integration of transactional features in digital media. Dominant media often produce 'habits of thought', creating abstractions that conceal their operations and effects. Arguably the term 'platform' itself could be considered such an obscuring term. Concern over the shaping impact of economic media on cognitive and communicative capacities is one of the core issues that animated Canadian media theorist Harold Innis' history of communications work (1995, 2007, 2008). Innis' work was an attempt to provide a grounded understanding of economic thought, indicating that such thought was invisibly supported by the materiality, and scarcity, of information. Media of information storage and transmission created material limits on what could be known about, and acted upon in, the world. Hence the production of abstractions that purport to describe, rather than manifest, economic phenomena (Mackenzie, 2006).

For Innis, economic thought was shaped by the biases of dominant media, and economists themselves were blinded by the seeming autonomy and spontaneity of markets. However, if we focus on the mediating functions enacted, a market is, at least nominally, defined according to the media by which a transaction can occur. For example, prices exist as statistical abstractions unless and until there is some transactional affordance that can facilitate the exchange such as a platform like Robinhood that allows the realization of prices through consumer/user actions. I think this is particularly true when we specifically think about 'The Market' – an embedded abstraction, primarily subsumed within the ubiquitous digital platforms and devices upon which we depend. Indeed, thinking markets as separate from media seems virtually impossible under contemporary platform capitalism. Consequently, platforms provide the sinews of modern capitalism by stabilizing the modes of connectivity that link participants in time and space – they offer techniques and technologies that 'sustain interactions' as well as 'epistemological frameworks' (Apperley and Parikka, 2015: 5), harmonizing abstractions among market participants. Olma goes even further in making the connection between platforms and markets, noting that, 'While marketplaces connect supply and demand between customers and companies, digital platforms connect customers to whatever. The platform is a generic "ecosystem" able to link potential customers to anything and anyone, from private individuals to multinational corporations' (Olma, 2014).

In this sense the platform allows its controller to reduce the diversity of potential into a standardized, singular 'user/buyer'; that is, the only buyer available is the one provided by the platform and within the affordances provided by the platform controller. This seemingly ontological effect is made more valuable because transactional data can be paired with highly detailed personal data created as a pre-requisite for using the platform. Platforms offer a 'way of knowing' and a 'way of being' that aligns with the material conditions of connectivity afforded by modern capitalism. I am here referring to the media capacities and potentialities that contain 'biases' (to use Harold Innis' term) that shape and constrain the actions and habits of thought of individuals and institutions alike (Comor, 2001; Babe and Comor, 2018). In considering contemporary platform capitalism within a larger historical context, we might find it helpful to consider the ways that media forms and intellectual abstractions are drawn together – interconnected – within the moment of exchange.

In the context of capitalist modes of production, modern platforms might be described in terms of what Marxist philosopher Alfred Sohn-Rethel calls a specific type of 'social synthesis', or in the media-centric focus of this chapter, what I refer to as a 'mode of connectivity'. This concept is useful in specifying that capital has its own specific connective needs, hence it draws in historically important ways of coordinating market activities, maintained by the production and reproduction of transactions, mediated in a material sense by money, but also intellectually by what he calls the 'exchange abstraction'. For Sohn-Rethel, the social synthesis is 'the network of relations by which society forms a coherent whole ... As social forms develop and change, so also does the synthesis which holds together the multiplicity of links operating between men according to the division of labour' (Sohn-Rethel, 2021: 4). For example, we can think of Amazon as a platform that generates a particular social synthesis that links together production, distribution and consumption in order to produce a coherent whole. Not only does Amazon supply the connective elements that coordinate these various moments of the circuit of capital, but it also supplies the underlying infrastructure through its Amazon Web Services (AWS) business. The social synthesis is a way of understanding how specific forms of connectivity support and coordinate disparate individuals in time and space, and thereby reproduce the larger social totality. In this respect, the Marxist analysis of modes of production confronts the mediating effects of concurrent modes of connectivity.

What brings these actors together is a shared habit of thought, a shared epistemic space or intellectual capacity, opened, according to Sohn-Rethel, by the intellectual aspects associated with the commodity itself. Hence his contention that, 'the socially necessary forms of thinking of an epoch are those in conformity with the socially synthetic functions of that epoch' (Sohn-Rethel, 2021: 5). In commodity producing societies, transactions between individuals requires an epistemic correlation, what he calls the 'exchange abstraction'. This is needed because in commodity producing societies, and specifically, in the transactional moments needed for commodity exchange, time and space are conceptualized separately to account for the tension between the use value and exchange value of the commodity. To continue using Amazon as an example, the purchase of a product using its platform (whether physical or digital) necessarily demands a delay between the moment of purchase and subsequent consumption. In the case of physical products, the delay may be several days. However, in this case, the exchange abstraction provides an epistemic link to the user/consumer. One purchases on Amazon knowing, abstractly, that, at some point in the future, the product will be delivered, and satisfaction thereby fulfilled. The enactment of the moment of exchange, presupposes a way of thinking about future fulfilment, this is the core of the exchange abstraction.

What I argue is that Sohn-Rethel's analysis holds much for thinking about both the novelty and historicity of platform capitalism particularly given its dependence on a proliferation of transactional affordances and the convergence of social and financial media. Recent arguments about the convergence of social media and payment technologies (Manzerolle and Wiseman, 2016; Swartz, 2020) have stressed the essentially communicative nature of money as a core medium with implications for culture, identity and community as well as finance. As Swartz (2020) explains:

> Cash, cards, checks, and apps do more than transmit value. Our credit card, for example, says something about how we see ourselves and how powerful institutions see us. It says something about the nature of the transaction and the relationship between the parties involved. Transactions are embedded in and reflective of social, cultural, and relational meanings. These meanings shape and are shaped by the communication and media technologies – whether paper or electronic – that perform the transaction. (p 4)

Swartz makes a compelling case, building on James Carey's work, that money reflects the communicative goal of the 'maintenance of society in time; not the act of imparting information but the representation of shared beliefs' (p. 7). Hence money, in addition to its core economic function, is both ontological and epistemic in nature as well.

Swartz's argument about the centrality of payment media to the production of transactional communities – communities bound and reproduced by transactional media – echoes Sohn-Rethel's emphasis on the 'social synthesis', but as a Marxist the latter specifies that it is in specifically commodity producing societies (as opposed to, for example, feudal societies) that 'the social synthesis is centred on the functions of money as the "universal equivalent"' (Sohn-Rethel, 2021: 6). This distinction is important because of the way the commodity form requires a universal equivalent (that is, money) to represent the value of abstract labour, concealed in the commodity form. Unlike other modes of production, capitalism must 'realize' the abstract labour surplus in terms of money to accumulate, expand, and generally reproduce, its necessary social relations.

Sohn-Rethel's argument about the centrality of the exchange abstraction as a product of the specific social synthesis of commodity producing societies is an argument about the structuring economic ontology of capitalism itself, but it still lacks an awareness of the specific media forms and effects supporting this synthesis. In the next section, I work through four core coordinative abstractions that constitute the transactional life of contemporary platforms and situate them within a longer historical and conceptual history of markets and media. I have selected these, not as an exhaustive list of features but as phenomena that are central to understanding the contemporary economic life of platforms. Further, these coordinative abstractions also help historicize the much longer history of media and the emergence of capitalist accumulation strategies. Put more simply, I argue these are necessary features of platform capitalism.

On the economic ontology of platforms: money, price, derivative, affordance

Money

Money offers an essential starting point in critically evaluating the economic ontology of platforms. Money, as Beverungen explains, is a 'prerequisite medium' that 'provides the general equivalent by which commodities can be exchanged' (Beverungen, 2019: 13). Treated as a core medium, 'Money points us beyond markets, since as a medium it determines our situation and precedes other media, and it points to capital accumulation, which depends on it and which is historically shaped by different kinds of money' (Beverungen, 2019: 1). Yet there is more at stake intellectually in foregrounding money as an ontological presupposition of capitalist markets:

> Money ... is the potential link between a theory of media and a theory of capital; it becomes central to making media studies critical and to a media theoretical contribution to the critique of capital. Money offers itself up as the capitalist medium, as a medium that makes capital possible and potentially makes all other media capitalist. (Beverungen, 2019: 13)

Moreover, money offers the calculative and mathematical basis for both markets and computing innovations (both of which can be, and have been, understood as information processors, see Mirowski and Somefun, 1998; Bowles et al, 2017), culminating in the development of universal computing machines that now largely underpin market activities. As Schröter explains:

> Whatever else money may be, it is a medium that makes it possible to attach countable numbers ('prices') to concrete objects or processes, ... The 'mathematization of production' is implicit in capitalism from its very beginning, insofar as value (however it is derived) is expressed, measured, and accumulated in the abstract form of exchange value, which finally finds its embodiment in digital, countable, and therefore mathematically describable money (and even the most complex 'derivates' traded at stock markets today stem from this basic mathematical logic of money). (Schröter, 2019: 81)

Friedrich Kittler's argument (2009) about the media a priori foundations of Western intellectual and scientific thought, could be usefully expanded to include money in order to engage with the relationship more directly between media capacities and the transactional functions of the market. Indeed, Schröter makes such a point when he writes, 'All media (at least in capitalism) presuppose money for their technological infrastructure, their skilled workers, the production of their content' (Schröter, 2019: 99).

Money, in the senses described by Schroter and Beverungen, does not emerge alongside capitalism, but is, as Marx (1976: 188–244) identified, more foundational in supporting the coordinative function of markets themselves. Too much of the ancient and early modern world was stunted by the slave-based mode of production, forms of primitive accumulation that overly fetishized the spontaneity of markets in realizing wealth, until Marx intervenes by drawing us into the 'hidden abode' of production (Marx, 1976: 279).[1]

It is a far remove from the high-tech wizardry of modern platforms, but history is sedimented in our most important infrastructure. What is new today is often the culmination of underlying historical forces. Although it is widely understood that the intellectual foundations of Western science and philosophy can be traced back to the ancient Greeks (Innis, 2008), as Sohn-Rethel notes, ancient Greece was also 'the first to be based on a monetary economy' (p 98). The argument, not unlike like Kittler's (2009), revolves around a particular a priori, whose impact and significance on Greek intellectual life is not fully examined.

'Social synthesis' and 'exchange abstraction' are the core concepts that first emerge, for Sohn-Rethel, when we consider intellectual impact of the widespread adoption of coined money on the minds of primarily aristocratic Greek philosophers, products of an emerging merchant class, whose material conditions were defined by a separation between intellectual labour (for example, science, philosophy) and manual labour (for example, material production driven by a slave economy). 'The significance of this development has seldom been appreciated' (Sohn-Rethel, 2021: 98), largely because, 'in contrast to the ancient Near East ... the Greeks develop a notion of (monetary) currency' but, crucially, also 'produce thoughts about it' (Seaford, 2004: 143). This is particularly noteworthy given that 'coins are among the first mass produced objects in history' (Seaford, 2004: 122–3). In more contemporary terms, as already discussed, this constitutes the emergence of a foundational transactional community (Swartz, 2020).

The Greeks were the first to develop, adopt, and truly embrace a modern sense of money, that is, as medium exchange, measure of value, store of value, means of payment. This adoption of coined money at precisely the same time that Greek idealism – for example geometry, arithmetic, and metaphysics – begins to define the ancient world of the Mediterranean. According to historians David Schaps (2004) and Richard Seaford (2004), coins used as money first emerge in Lydia (current Turkey), sometime in the early-mid seventh or early sixth century. The adoption of money by the Greeks rapidly transformed various facets of ancient Greek life:

> The monetization of the marketplace appears to have been immediate (a matter of decades at the most) and total. Nowhere in the historical record after coins have been invented do we find local markets being run by barter. Everything sold in the marketplace was sold for a price, and the price was expressed and expected in coins. (Schaps, 2004: 111)

Moreover, the adoption of coinage by the Greeks is combined with another critical, parallel medium, the alphabet. Taken together they offer the materialist underpinnings of the forms of social synthesis defined by market exchange in commodity-producing societies:

> Coinage and the alphabet each constitute a system of all-embracing equivalence or reference that is, through deployment of an intermediary (value, sound), reduced to a minimum of components (the types and sizes of coins, letters). And they are each radical developments of

Near-Eastern practice that have their first widespread use among the Greeks, and will be united, in a sense, in the logos of Heraclitus, which combines the meanings of verbal and monetary account. (Seaford, 2004: 122)

One of the more critical connections that Sohn-Rethel makes, is to the specific rise of Pythagoreanism as a dominant force in Greek intellectual life. Although shrouded in mystery, the figure of Pythagoras is often claimed to be the foundational thinker of Western philosophy, and the proponent of a form of philosophical idealism that united math, music and mysticism. But as Sohn-Rethel, and the Marxist historian George Thomson (1972) note, the rise of Pythagoreanism, particularly towards the end of the sixth century, is deeply implicated with the widespread adoption of coined money (incuse coins in particular). The simultaneous adoption of coined money and the spread of Pythagorean idealism appears to be one of the great under examined connections of the ancient world. As Seaford elaborates, the Pythagorean interest in coinage was important, not only for economic reasons but also intellectual ones too, 'By providing a universal measure, money permits a universe of controlled peaceful transactions' (Seaford, 2004: 204). This is reflected in a quote by Pythagorean statesman and philosopher Archytas who purportedly said that 'The discovery of calculation (logismos) ended civil conflict and increased concord. For when there is calculation there is no unfair advantage, and there is equality, for it is by calculation that we come to agreement in our transactions' (quoted in Seaford, 2004: 204). The coin offered a form of idealism in which number permeated all physical reality, enabling a universal connectivity among all things, where difference and sameness could be recognized and reconciled. It also concealed the true source of value – socially necessary labour time. For the ancient Greeks, and Pythagoreans in particular, the coin was not only a transactional medium, but it also expressed an entire cosmology. In the coordinative features of the coin, providing the basis for a particular type of social synthesis, the intellectual capacity for abstract considerations about value and exchange emerge. The material media of transactions, give way to the coordinative abstractions that establish the virtual world of markets, and later platforms, more generally.

Price

The second abstraction I want to highlight, and the advancement of both social synthesis and the exchange abstraction, is the emergence of what Harold Innis calls the 'price system' (1995: 66–87). In the adoption of coins, as noted above, the concept of price becomes a core habit of thought, but its tendency towards systemic development was stunted by the limits of available media (coins, papyrus, parchment and so on). Anticipating more recent scholarship (for example, Swartz, 2020), Innis considered the price system to be 'a significant medium of communication and of political economic power' (Babe and Comor, 2018: xvi) but also a way of knowing that contributed to a 'neglect of the technological conditions under which prices operate' (quoted in Babe and Comor, 2018: XVII) – that is, it offered a form of abstract thought that concealed its material foundations. Harold Innis was specifically cognizant of the role that prices played within, and because of, larger transformations in the dominant media of communication. For example, Innis interrogated the way that innovations in the printing press, including related policies and regulations, seemed to underpin the spread of the price system. As Tom Easterbrook writes, Innis realized that the 'key to economic change and much of its dynamic must be sought in changes in communications, for the penetrative power of the pricing system is but one aspect of the penetrative power of systems of communication' (quoted in Babe and Comor, 2018: XII). The price is a medium of information that reduces the complexity of a commodity to its numerical/monetary value (see Babe, 1995).

The price system emerges, as Innis correctly noted, from a very particular media transformation that underpinned wider political economic shifts. Indeed, some historians describe the rise of prices as a 'revolution' that began in the sixteenth and seventeenth centuries (Vilar, 2011: 76; Braudel, 1992: 468). The price revolution was, in many descriptions, considered a product of the massive injection of newly coined bullion extracted from Spanish colonies in the New World (see Vilar, 2011); the wide availability of precious metals in the form of coins made pricing mechanisms both more widely used and more volatile. Innis notes that the price system spread rapidly 'into the economy of Europe and into economic thought' stimulating 'the flow of trade from Europe to the new world and to the old world, from the West Indies to the East Indies' (Innis, 2018: 145). So, although the use of prices as an informational tool in localized markets is an ancient practice (see Schaps, 2004), in this context the price system involved a totalizing view of the world in which prices came to represent, not only products available at a local market, but a mechanism expanding markets across both space and time in an era where European colonialism set up strong incentives to link markets together. The price increasingly becomes a mechanism not only for connecting spatially and temporally disparate actors, institutions, indeed, markets, but it also works to convey 'a sense of relative value to entire populations' (Babe and Comor, 2018: XVII). As already noted, transformations in the epistemology of the market give way to particular 'habits of thought' or 'mindsets' that discourage 'critical appraisal of the values instantiated through money prices' and 'sweeps aside all awareness of the technological and historical conditions under which the price system operates' (Babe and Comor, 2018: LXXIV). As a specific example, Innis was concerned about the spread of an extreme 'present mindedness' that seemed to follow the spread of the price system. This especially pernicious habit of thought emphasized short-term thinking and planning, significantly undermining the ability for individuals and institutions to reckon with longer-term issues – perhaps epitomized by the contemporary inability to deal with climate change in any substantive way. Innis, however, is a significant thinker in this regard because he always foregrounds the materiality of information as a constraining factor in the decision-making processes of individuals and organizations. For example, if we consider price formation in contemporary markets, it is difficult to do so without understanding the specific infrastructure of information transmission and processing that underpins high-frequency algorithmic trading. In this context, the materiality of information – that is, the fact that information is bound by the carrying capacity of underlying infrastructure (in this case, the use of microwave transmission networks) – confers specific advantages to those who have access to the networks, while it confers disadvantages to those who do not.

Yet the price system itself, as Innis has demonstrated, was profoundly linked to the introduction of paper and the development of printing press in the fifteenth and sixteenth centuries (see Eisenstein, 1983; Innis, 2015). The introduction of paper and printing specifically made commercial data and calculations (as the ready reckoner demonstrates) more widely available; opening the scope of the exchange abstraction to include globally integrated markets. The accumulation of pricing data, available widely through printed texts (for example, ready reckoners) that could circulate spatially between localized markets, provided a powerful data set upon which the discipline of economics itself could be developed.

As information, the price does not exist outside of some media or channel of information that can be disseminated to multiple participants in the market, even if the price varies between the channels themselves. As the introductory example of the ready reckoners suggests, the expansion of market transactions was also highly dependent on a print culture that could disseminate, and enable the calculations of, pricing information. That is, the price, as information, is also shaped in the first instance by the available media, and likewise changes the social synthesis to incorporate greater informational inputs and computational resources. Commercial literacy and numeracy were both greatly expanded by the printing press and enabled the spatial-temporal coordination – connectivity – that supported European colonialism and mercantilism. But more contemporaneously, pricing information is implicated in complex ways by which platforms create 'transactional communities' because the price system must be accepted by the participants themselves. Prices, however, are not the static entities they may have appeared to be in a print culture with circulatory delays. In the era of digital media platforms, prices, like all information, are subject to a steady flow, and as such have both a spatial and temporal quality. As I will discuss next, derivatives provide a mode of connectivity that 'binds' the past, present and future together, at the same time that it 'blends' together 'different forms of capital into a single unit of measure' (Bryan and Rafferty, 2006: 12); for example, derivatives connect 'assets in the present to prices in the future' (p 10).

Derivative

The domination of the price system following the media transformations associated with paper and printing, sets up the emergence of another coordinative abstraction involving, at first, the electric telegraph and the beginning of the 'financialization' of the economy through the creation of derivative markets. The long history of the derivative is thousands of years in the making, and in so far as it is implicated in transformation in media forms, it is evidence of the significance of space-time binding technologies like writing (see Sumerian cuneiform derivative contracts in Swan, 2000). Randy Martin (2015) has written brilliantly in *Knowledge LTD* about the 'social logic' of the derivative, indicating that its significance extends beyond financial markets. A derivative is, very simply, a contract for 'securing the price of a commodity whose production, like a crop, will be delivered at some point in the future' (Martin, 2015: 60). However, Martin notes that its more contemporary significance is in providing an 'anchor to render all exchange transactions across the globe commensurate with one another' (Martin, 2015: 60). Yet, as a social logic, the derivate is a template for a range of knowledge commodities and connectivities. As Martin explains:

> the core operation of derivatives is to bind the future to the present through a range of contractual opportunities and to make all manner of capital across disparate spheres of place, sector, and characteristic commensurate with one another ... [and] introduce a highly dynamic but comprehensively convertible measure of prices across time and space. (Martin, 2015: 60)

The derivative extends the homogenizing power of money and prices into the future. In this exchange abstraction, information itself is also reshaped as a continuous flow, a stochastic time sequence of data upon which speculations about the future can be made. Because derivatives are performance based, they require a steady stream of information about changes in prices, or other significant indicators, that can produce a data set useful for speculation.

The data stream allows for the uncertainty of some future state to become a speculative 'bet' on particular outcomes.

Derivatives markets, such as futures, rely on tracking the time sequence associated with fluctuating prices, and they presume that global markets are connected enough, and the pricing information widely disseminated and sufficiently available, as to make statistical assumptions about future behaviour. Seen through the conceptual framework outlined by Sohn-Rethel, here we see more explicitly the exchange abstraction and social synthesis exacerbating processes of disembedding, a point made by media theorist James Carey (1988) regarding the development of futures markets in the wake of the electric telegraph. Carey observed that the (still dominant) futures markets in Chicago emerged in the same year as the arrival of the telegraph (Carey, 1988: 168). Carey's argument can be understood retrospectively as a moment in which the electric telegraph catalyses the flows of information necessary for linking markets together:

> before the telegraph, markets were independent of one another … the prices of commodities were largely determined by local conditions of supply and demand … The telegraph removed markets from the particular context in which they were historically located and concentrated on them forces emanating from any place and any time … they became everywhere markets and every time markets and thus less apprehensible at the very moment they became more powerful. (Carey, 1988: 167–9)

The rise of futures trading extends and deepens the spatial-temporal connectivity of the exchange abstraction, moving from tangible goods to receipts as representations of goods (Carey, 1988: 169–70). The contractual basis of the derivative also mirrors the now commonly experienced contractual aspect of using digital media platforms, each with their own 'Terms and Conditions' or 'Terms of Service' that must be agreed to, even if the user does not read or understand the implications of the contract but legally binding and shaping future usage. In this respect, the user, through their data exhaust, is open to the social logic of derivatives. The derivative binds space and time contractually, and as a factor in the market, ensures that 'no transaction is final' and that 'there is always a globally realizable potential for improved performance' (Martin, 2015: 62).

What Carey identified as a core technical feature of the telegraph and its impact on the market for futures contracts, Martin expands to reflect its current role in the global market for speculation; 'For all their powers of integrating an ever-enlarging conception of what can be considered a source of value and how price can be represented across wide spans of time and space, derivatives deliver neither equilibrium of value nor stability of price' (Martin, 2015: 62). The harmonization of prices between markets 'opened up, because of improvements in communication, *the uncertainty of time*' (emphasis added, Carey, 1988: 168); or as Randy Martin has elaborated, they introduce a situation of strategic 'nonknowledge' or of asymmetrical knowledge that supports expanded speculation (or outright gambling) on future prices, or any other uncertain future state. Perhaps the best evidence has been the explosion of sports gambling platforms (for example, FanDuel, DraftKings, Caesars and so on) that allow users to bet on virtually any aspect of a competition, indeed these same platforms can make almost any future uncertainty the object of a 'prop' bet such as betting on 'the color of Gatorade that will be dumped on the winning coach' of the Superbowl (Platana and Pempus, 2023). The potential to create novel prop bets using these platforms is seemingly endless, constrained only by regulatory interventions. In a related way, Thorhauge and Nielsen (2021) have detailed how in-game virtual goods of online video games like *Counter-Strike* and *Fortnite* have led to the development of 'skin-betting' where 'acquiring, exchanging, gambling with, and speculating in skins [cosmetic game items] have become a game in its own right and show clear similarities with traditional gambling' (p 53). The casino of the digital world is wholly based on the social logic of the derivative, where any future data point can be made the object of a speculative bet. The social logic of derivatives, Martin explains:

> make available to capital accumulation what would be considered new materialities of ideas and perceptions, weather and war, bits of code stripped from tele-technology or DNA, the microscopic and cosmic. If once derivatives required some underlying source of value ... now such instruments could be cooked up out of a singer's potential future earnings, or a slew of tornados that might never make landfall, or a new medicine that might never get approved for patients' use. (Martin, 2015: 61–2)

Yet what Carey identified as being a unique contribution of the telegraph to the development of futures markets in the United States, might equally hold for the broader financialization of the global economy. As Vogl points out, 'Financial markets have always been structured by the close connection between price formation on stock exchanges and innovations in media technology, which since the nineteenth century have included the introduction of the telegraph, the use of transatlantic cables, and the accelerated communication of market information via ticker tape' (Vogl, 2014: 143). The impact is not merely an economic one but as Martin suggests has profound implications for the epistemic and ontological core of contemporary capitalist cultures; 'Derivatives are now increasingly orienting production and exchange; they are also reorienting how we understand our sense of belonging together and the wealth that issues from our common labors' (Martin, 2015: 78). We can see the derivative as an underlying structure of emerging digital markets, including those in speculative virtual goods and currencies. Any system that provides consistent data inputs over time can become the underlying asset of a derivative. Derivatives as an embedded part of modern platforms are more widely associated with the spread of speculation and gambling – crypto currencies, video games, professional sports, almost any and all aspects of future events can be turned into a derivative. Any possible future state whose outcome is uncertain but for which time-based data exists can be subject to the social logic of derivatives. This is important because the growing transactional component of platforms expands the range of potential purchases to include items real, virtual, or speculative. This phenomenon is seen in the rise of 'gamble-play' across digital and mobile platforms (see Albarrán-Torres and Goggin, 2014; Albarrán-Torres, 2018; Ross and Nieborg, 2021).

Affordance

The economic life of modern platforms is, however, experienced largely in terms of a user's encounter with the design features of the interface. We do not see the platform; we see the interface and its affordances which guided navigation. It is at the interface point, the outer skin of the onion, that users find their ability to enact the moment of exchange; to realize what was previously a potentiality. Abstractions of thought are materialized in the affordances provided by the platform. In this final section, I want to briefly suggest that the newest addition to the layers of connectivities I have discussed is the 'transactional affordance' – the embedded opportunity to transact that now populates all facets of platformatized media (Manzerolle and Daubs, 2021; see also Swartz, 2020).

> In the context of digital social media, a transactional affordance refers to how the technical features enabling an economic exchange are realized through the contextual awareness and opportunities for specific types of action afforded to individual users. These new consumer-focused affordances are symptomatic of wider logics in the operations of largely monopolistic digital platforms, which some refer to as 'platform capitalism' (see, for example, Srnicek, 2017). The production of data – particularly transactional data and metadata – is increasingly a central business model of digital platforms. (Manzerolle and Daubs, 2021: 1281)

Two contemporary cases that I want to briefly discuss in this regard: the incorporation of transactional affordances in mobile social media; the second, is the transactional-focus animating investment in blockchain cryptocurrencies and decentralized finance, where 'coined' money returns as pure exchange abstraction. Because the 'salient aspect of a disembedded economy is anonymity' (Schaps, 2004: 32) a platform-based economy, in which the transactional affordance is the critical interface of exchange, suggests a new form of embedding in which the identity of the user is reinscribed in numerous ways.

It seems that everywhere we look we find new opportunities to buy, to transact, to produce the moment of exchange ubiquitously, the mobile phone being the key 'instrument of exchange' that we have available. The process by which the colonization of our digital media by transactional affordances proceeds is by no means even or assured but does in fact signal a core goal of platform companies themselves – to control all contexts in which transactions occur, and to exploit any residual data that might be generated. Social media platforms, indeed, platforms of all kinds, have increasingly re-oriented their operations to embrace various types of transactional affordances. Content producers, such as influencers or advertisers and marketers, are orienting themselves around funnelling behaviour into discrete transactions of one sort or another; I have explored this theme elsewhere (Manzerolle and Kjøsen, 2012; McGuigan and Manzerolle, 2015; Manzerolle and Wiseman, 2016; Manzerolle and Daubs, 2021), and so will avoid delving too deeply here. Only to suggest that what we consider to be social media platforms, are really platforms for the (re)embedding of transactional affordances, now ubiquitously available in various flavours, enabling any number of types of commodities or services. The rise of transactional logics throughout the modern digital ecosystem is testament to the real incentives that ultimately support the commercial operation of these systems – cheap money, speculative investments, attention markets, advertising or direct subscription fees – to participate in platform capitalism means to navigate the primacy of transactional affordances as gateways into the social/cultural/political digital ecosystem. Swartz summarizes the overarching logic.

> Silicon Valley is attempting to build money technologies that create transactional communities that work for our social media lives; they are doing so according to social media business logics. Many companies are hoping to harness the promise of transactional 'big data' and put it into conversation with other 'social' data sets. These new systems are governed according to practices native to Silicon Valley, such as click-through 'terms of service' agreements. They are organized according to economic arrangements also native to Silicon Valley, such as venture capitalism. The goal of fin-tech is to 'disrupt' payment by redirecting the flow of payment revenue and data through Silicon Valley's digital warehouses and toll roads. (Swartz, 2020: 20–21)

Crypto currencies and decentralized finance services (DeFi) are explicitly a technological and political movement to mobilize and subordinate digital infrastructure in service of a 'right to transact'; hence, the redeployment of digital infrastructure and material resources to produce a new set of transactional affordances equipped to deal with a new commercial abstraction. Indeed, the entire purpose, and end goal, of the proponents of commercial blockchain technologies is to subordinate all digital infrastructure to the transactional affordance. One can barely read a sentence describing any new blockchain technology without seeing the word 'transaction' looming large as the purported use-case/value. In the original bitcoin proof of concept, Satoshi Nakamoto (2008) uses the word 'transaction' almost 70 times in 9 pages. Indeed, the entirety of the crypto market, and much of its mythology, rests on a particular fetish over transactional affordances that blockchain technologies provide. The volatile world of the crypto market – infested with Ponzi schemes and distorted, paranoid economic theories – is the result of a computational infrastructure, a network of computers connected to facilitate a purportedly non-hierarchical transactional system. It aspires to money-like functionality, a market defined by price movements ('number goes up') but is itself simply a sophisticated casino, a derivatives market in which the social synthesis and exchange abstraction take on their most absurd form.

Conclusion

In this chapter I have taken an oblique approach to examining the economic lives of platforms with a goal of expanding the conceptual frameworks by which we can undertake this type of examination. In a broader sense, this chapter uses the contemporary dependence on platforms to understand the longer historical relationship between media and markets – considering a particular genealogy of the 'moment of exchange' as the teleological endpoint of highly capitalized, consumer-facing platforms – a moment now made into an imminent potentiality seemingly everywhere. As such, there are three core takeaways that I want to reiterate:

1. The analysis of platform capitalism reveals a longer historical link between media and capitalist development.
2. The term 'platform' is itself a coordinative abstraction that reflects the particular mode(s) of connectivity necessary for contemporary capitalism.
3. The economic ontology of platforms presupposes a media analysis of capitalism as a diagrammatic circuit linking specific moments in time and space.
4. The analysis of abstractions reveals the media materiality that supports particular modes of connectivity and related habits of thought.

I have made the case for thinking about 'connectivity' as a core theme in the development of modern digital markets, and of historicizing contemporary discussions of the economic impact of platforms. In considering contemporary platform capitalism within a larger historical context, we might find it helpful to consider the ways that media forms and intellectual abstractions are drawn together – interconnected – within the moment of exchange. I have selected four abstractions – money, price, derivative and affordance – in order to investigate the connection between media and platform capitalism as a historically contingent, yet necessary, relationship. These terms have allowed me to drill into the economic ontology of platforms in order to highlight their connective and coordinative dimensions. Moreover, I have made a preliminary case that evolving modes of connectivity create their own abstractions supporting the development of transactional media, or the transactional function of media. My approach has been to think through this process at the intersection of media theory and Marxist political economy.

I also want to note that the approach I have taken here has its own presupposition for the role that capital plays in developing these modes of connectivity, but as I have noted it is but one set of modalities, albeit one whose connection to the broader circulatory rhythms of capitalism itself is a saturating force. I want to acknowledge that the economic and cultural significance of platforms is not exhausted or fully contained by this logic; the creation of specific capacities does not over-determine them, hence the potential for unforeseen, novel, revolutionary or creative developments to emerge. However, in this chapter I focus on an economic ontology around which capitalist mode of production must circulate. That does not mean that connectivity is ubiquitous in the same way, but rather the axiomatics of capitalism and its historical connection to the media forms of Western science and philosophy have established the abstract basis for the transactional communities and cultures emerging across the various digital platforms. The economic lives of platforms are bound up with the social lives of individuals and communities.

Acknowledgement
The author wishes to thank Atle Kjøsen, Edward Comor, and the editors for providing valuable feedback on earlier drafts of this chapter.

Note
[1] Many recent authors have also noted how, beyond the coordinative function discussed in this chapter, digital platforms conceal new 'hidden abodes' of exploitation, whether the 'new economy' (Böhm and Land, 2012), the 'gig economy' (Doorn and Badger, 2020) or 'platform work' (Moore and Joyce, 2020).

3

Platforms and the Social Imaginary of Ordinary Life

Juan M. del Nido

One of the goals of this volume is to think about platforms as things and the platform as a notion in *historical* terms, against the grain of the prevailing presentism the editors discussed in the introduction. One way of attempting this exercise is to ask whether platforms represent a radical break from social relations as we knew them or whether they are simply extensions or variations of things we already know. Thinking with two of the themes the editors proposed, 'overall economic framing' and 'strategic discourse', and complementing Manzerolle's work in this volume, in this chapter I will historicize the notion of platform obliquely, by asking a different question: how do the universalizing discourses around platforms *still* retain some sort of validity? And, paraphrasing the editor's introduction, its obverse question: what kind of work is the notion of the platform doing to further, sustain, or reproduce that universalism?

This chapter will argue one of the reasons this universalism persists is that platforms are only a particularly literal, intense and absolute embodiment of a social imaginary that we have known for centuries, secular but mystical, premised on the exaltation of ordinary life. This ordinary life, that is, the life the vast majority of us cannot help but lead (Taylor, 2004: 73), carries with it a moral order we understand intuitively and take as common sense, where it is rightful that each of us tends to their own needs as they see fit; where we extol the ways of knowing ordinary experience provides; and where popular choice is the seat of the ultimate, and ultimately only, legitimacy.

For centuries and still today, the exaltation of this ordinary life served as general guidance and foundational myth to imagine and legitimize things such as representative democracy, the ethics of revolutions, neoliberal philosophy, political legitimacy and more. It was also, however, always hedged by institutions, ritual and other extra-ordinary brakes funnelling its intensity and mediating our experience of it. Yet, recently, this social imaginary has come to present more, more extensive and more intractable demands on our relations, demanding we realize it in more literal and fuller ways. Social scientists and public discourse associate this increase with a much decried and often poorly understood 'neoliberalism'. This is, surely, part of the story; still, in examining the moral order inside this social imaginary born centuries before neoliberalism was even conceived, my argument in this chapter is that platforms magnify, concretize and give rhetorical currency to an ethical project at the heart of western and westernized political and social intuition. This is a project concerned with the epic of a life, any life, contingent and individual and in a way sublime precisely for being so.

Theoretical and methodological considerations

Research into platform economies is increasingly concerned with a particular kind of masking, duping and concealing: 'Uber's unique brand allows it to constantly *mask* its manipulative activities' (Rosenblat, 2018: 115); 'YouTube and its competitors *claim* to empower the individual to speak' (Gillespie, 2010: 352); 'Uber, despite *presenting* itself as an empty vessel for market forces, shapes the appearance of a market' (Srnicek, 2017: 47); '(Google works) to *downplay* its role, as merely an intermediary, to limit its liability (Gillespie, 2010: 356); 'for social media companies, the term (platform) is appealing because it allows them to *portray* their relationship to content as agnostic' (Lingel, 2020: 2); 'Airbnb *argues* that it is not just resurrecting the tradition of hospitality as practiced over the centuries, but qualitatively improving upon these forms of sociality' (Stabrowski, 2017: 332, all emphasis mine). These 'framings' happen through PR, marketing and legal strategies, software terminologies, and Twitter trending topics, sustaining various promises of 'empowerment', 'openness' and 'freedom', and positioning companies in specific ways with respect to publics and governmental authorities. Broadly speaking, this literature seeks to unmask and reveal the real, or effective, workings of these platforms, of social relations through them, and how, in real life, such promises are unsustainable, illusory or flat out lies (for further examples see Srnicek, 2017; Thelen, 2018; Culpepper and Thelen, 2019; Ravenelle, 2019; van Doorn, 2020; Schor, 2021; Walsh, 2021; Yates, 2021).

This chapter shares this critical orientation, but rather than examining how these utopias do not work, I follow recent writings in technoutopianism (Sims, 2017; Ames, 2019) to ask, rather, why this utopia still manages to persuade, beyond obvious economic necessity. Emergent work in platform studies is showing how, for example, delivery drivers in Belgium actively embrace the moral economy of a self-reliant, not self-sufficient, self (Duus,

2022), and how Indian gig economy drivers develop an ethical horizon with reasons to enter, stay in and defend the platforms even if they are in conditions of precarity (Medappa, 2022). Here I will examine the affects and intuitions of the moral order within which this utopia makes sense. Empowerment, freedom, openness are notoriously abstract notions: how has, for example, 'empowerment' become such an obvious virtue and so intuitively imagined in individual terms (instead of generated, for example, by institutions and regulations) as to be unworthy of attention? What are the conditions of possibility of 'empowerment', or 'freedom', or 'sovereignty' in the first place, and how do platforms come to seem particularly well placed to funnel them regardless of the truth value of their promises? In their analyses of the masks and framings that sustain these platforms, Yates (2021: 11), Gillespie (2010: 352) and Stabrowski (2017: 341) mention in passing a link between platforms and a certain ordinariness – ordinary people, ordinary users. This chapter picks up this thread, reading platform literature in the light of Taylor's (2004) philosophical examination of how our intuitions of empowerment, freedom and sovereignty belong in a moral order based on the exaltation of ordinary lives.

Although this is *not* an ethnographic chapter and it does not follow the conventions of ethnographic writing, I put forward this argument as an exercise in anthropological theory. I do so for two reasons. First, because I would not have been able to develop these ideas had it not been for my ethnography of Uber's conflict with the taxi industry in Buenos Aires (del Nido, 2021). Second, and just as importantly, because the argument is, at heart, an anthropological examination of work carried out by other researchers. Some of this work is ethnographic or at least fieldwork-based, into Uber, Airbnb, Twitter, Wikipedia, Facebook and Craigslist; some of it is quantitative or relies on discourse or inductive analysis, but in all cases I approached it as an anthropologist seeking to understand what was to me, always, an ethnographic puzzle: the persistence of that universalism the editors mention, doubling as a perennial presentism, in spite of phenomenally varied local instantiations of platforms – or the ideas they sustain.

As the editors rightly point out in the introduction, this platform universalism often takes the form of Western universalism, transferring Western values and hierarchies to other contexts. Yet, the reader will notice this chapter does not follow the other exhortation of this volume, that is, to attend to regional or local practices, either in the cultural periphery within the West, as does Otto in this volume. This is a purposeful and deliberate decision. As a subject *from* the periphery who has made his career studying the periphery, I follow fellow anthropologist James Ferguson's reluctance to reify cultural difference when producing an argument one hopes will pertain to non-Western lives in a world as globalized as our own:

the question of cultural difference itself is ... tightly bound up with questions of inequality, aspiration, and rank in an imagined 'world'. While a relativizing anthropology has, out of a well intentioned but misplaced sense of 'respect', tried to treat different cultural traditions as 'equal', real cultural differences always take on meaning within contexts of sharp social and economic inequality. (Ferguson, 2006: 19)

I certainly do think attending to geographical variations *can* teach us something about the economic life of platforms beyond the West *other than* 'cultures are varied'. But Ferguson's point that interests me here is that, first, the point in which Western values end and our 'Other' values begin has always been contentious (Navaro Yashin, 2002); and second, that by now the moral economy of this ordinary life I posit here is enmeshed well beyond its birthplace in 1,600 capitalist northern Europe, animating prosaic discourses of equality in India (Medappa, 2022), the moral traction of popular freedom to choose in Argentina (del Nido, 2021) and the philosophical spine of humanitarian interventions in African and South American countries (Whyte, 2019). Its pregnancy is by now not something to prove but something to examine: why does it manage to persuade?

The social imaginary of an ordinary life

Although platforms as discussed in this volume are often elusive to define in any exhaustive way, this chapter will make the case that in one important way that works across definitions we can characterize them by capturing a feature that shapes how we understand their workings, and often, the idea of a platform. I will argue that what we call platforms are exceptionally good at evoking, and tapping into, a certain social imaginary common to the West and Westernized world. This is a social imaginary premised on the exaltation of an ordinary life.

I refer to this identification as a characterization, instead of a definition, because I do not mean platforms are the only entities doing this now or in previous times. In speaking of a 'social imaginary' and 'ordinary life' I am following philosopher Charles Taylor's understanding of what he called our modern condition (2004). A social imaginary is the broadly shared way in which we imagine our social existence, how we 'fit together with others' like us, and our normative intuitions, often unstructured and not explicitly laid out, concerning the right kind of relations we are to have with each other (pp 23–5). Social imaginaries in general, and ours in particular, may well derive from theories, like in our case doctrines of natural law and cosmologies of order in sixteenth-century Europe, and they may well be theorized, as Taylor himself is doing; but a *social imaginary* is different to a *theory* in that it is broadly shared and commonly understood in intuitive, affective terms. We participate in it not through technical or intellectual training but by growing into a moral imagination, a sense of legitimacy and a measure of justness. A social imaginary is not simply an opinion: it marks our understanding of moral order such that said order appears as not just virtuous but self-evident and no longer just one possibility among others.

Taylor's argument is that a particular social imaginary has hardened in the last few centuries around the idea of ordinary individual life. For most of human history, we used to make sense to ourselves and others within certain kinds of hierarchies and acceptable distributions of burdens that were not really up for grabs. We were only proper and actual agents when and if embedded in asymmetric yet complementary relations marked by ritual and permanence, such that the highest virtue lay in fulfilling our roles in terms of the whole: to best fulfil the role of a priest, a vassal, a *pater familias*, a servant, a lord, a hunter (2004: 13–19). In the last five centuries, a new conception of moral order gained traction and began to appear as self-evident: one premised on natural rights amongst individuals that pre-exist any political bond or hierarchy, any trade or destiny, rooted not in ritual or tradition but in a notion of freedom and mutual benefit guaranteed, ultimately, by individual consent. It is not so much that previous imaginaries pivoted on a lack of consent but that relations between people were not imagined in the key of consent or through notions such as choice, free will and popular legitimacy that now seem obvious to us. These notions are not just philosophical elaborations: they inform our sense of our own agency (in fact, the very fact of thinking of ourselves in terms of such a thing as agency) and our expectations of what our individual agency demands of others and of the world around us (p 21).

These were certainly not linear developments, and with time this imaginary borrowed from natural philosophy, theology, Christian practices and even what would later become physical sciences to place at the centre of our imagination the idea that we are individuals, that we owe it to others to recognize them as such and that the gauge of a good life is not how close we get to ritualized virtue but the extent to which we learn to tend amongst ourselves to our ordinary needs: security, sustenance, bare life. This is what Taylor means by a social imaginary premised on the exaltation of ordinary life, so self-evident to us that we struggle to imagine genuine alternatives: our institutions, our public debate, our Twitter feeds, our economic intuitions are steeped in and reproduce the idea that good politics is to be imagined through consent, that the self is something that must be empowered and realized, and so on.

That this social imaginary was, at one time, invented (for an overview see Morgan, 1989; Taylor, 2004; Sheehan and Wahrman, 2015) only emphasizes we sustain and reproduce it, and its demands on us, through the tools tending to its moral order. Here is where platforms come in: they are particularly good at reproducing and making sense of this social imaginary. I will make this case by examining how platforms reinforce three of the markers of this social imaginary: a premise of contingency, where we can all, in principle, be anything, and therefore should be allowed to be anything; a buffered, self-reflective self that learns to know herself and other ordinary lives with the right tools; and a mystical conception of legitimacy based on an organic link with such a thing as a consenting, wanting, willing people.

We tend to interpret the rise of a notion of individual like the one at the heart of this social imaginary as the result of an erosion of social, collective, public, communitarian or otherwise more-than-individual bonds. After all, Uber did promote its business in Argentina and elsewhere by encouraging people to be *their own* bosses (del Nido, 2021), and Airbnb did recast homes and entire neighbourhoods as underused capital (Stabrowski, 2017). This interpretation often comes with a denunciation of selfishness, when we study this individual in what we tend to refer as 'neoliberal' settings; an intellectual correction, arguing there is no such thing as an atomized individual, but individuals are always socially embedded, and so on; or a more militant, proactive exhortation to reimagine sociality in a key of communitarianism or some of the other things we allegedly lost. Callon refers to these approaches, on the whole, as re-socialization of what we take as an undersocialized individual (1998). We particularly worry when we believe such an artificially undersocialized individual is used to model behaviours and construct institutions and organizations such as platforms that effectively perform this undersocialized individual into life (see Daub, 2020).

As Taylor himself points out (2004: 17), this is not exactly all there is to it. This understanding of the individual as a site of ordinary life comes with an understanding of sociality, of how we belong *together* and of what we can rightfully expect of *each other* – its own moral economy of freedom and mutual benefit, where self-reliance is categorically different to self-sufficiency. As certain moral ties broke down, others took their place. Note that, by 'moral economy', I do not mean simply 'economic activities shaped by values', the current and most common usage of the term. As Hann (2016) and Carrier (2018) point out, this is, really, any exchange, since even the most 'capitalist' or 'neoliberal' exchanges are shaped by some sort of value or idea of the good. Drawing on Thompson (1971), Carrier speaks of 'moral economy' to think less of *values* and more of the *obligations* parties have to each other (2018: 23), or as Thompson says, 'what *ought* to be men's reciprocal *duties* (1971: 91, in Carrier, 2018: 25, emphasis mine).

What do these 'oughts' look like in real life? When Buenos Aires' residents tell those who are against Uber to not use it (del Nido, 2021: 89–112) or when Airbnb hosts demand of their elected government that it lets them rent out extra rooms through the platform (Stabrowski, 2017; van Doorn, 2020), they are putting forward a particular imagination of what they expect of those they share a polis with, of what they believe is rightful that they demand of each other – a particular ethics of freedom and mutual benefit, in Taylor's words. Letting someone go about their business is also a certain kind of obligation to that someone, even if we do not agree with them or their business.

Platforms, and the companies that develop and host them, did not invent this social imaginary or the moral order within it: they are simply unusually literal materializations of them in what I referred to in deliberately vague terms as 'Western and Westernised' space. There are surely places where this social imaginary does not hold and, precisely because of its unstructured, unsystematic and instinctive nature, it will probably always mix and compete with other social imaginaries: in fact, later in this chapter, I review an exception in the very centre of the same developed world where this imaginary was born, back then a theory of moral order. Still, the normative expectations of this social imaginary – an axiomatic morality of individual freedom, a self-reflection and self-knowledge in the key of choice and empowerment, a mystical sense of popular legitimacy and consent – still inform our instinct of what a good life can mean, from Twitter feeds to corporate PR, from developmental interventions in India (Chhotray, 2011) to post-neoliberal energy politics in Ecuador (Riofrancos, 2020). I invite the reader to reflect on the usefulness of thinking about this social imaginary not by examining how universally it holds but by testing how well it can give words to those intuitions I believe it has informed.

The instrumental contingency of ordinary life

One of the most salient and intuitive consequences of our social imaginary's concern with ordinary life is that differentiation among us is entirely contingent. This means we are, and *should* be, entirely equal and entirely equally able to undertake any activity in the pursuit of our ordinary needs. Differences are only to be judged *instrumentally*, on the basis of how well we manage to satisfy those needs for ourselves and others, rather than *morally*, that is, based on any shared hierarchy of virtue. In other words: there is no greater virtue in being a butcher rather than a teacher or a firefighter rather than a Lyft driver. In this instrumental contingency converged, historically, the practical relegation of one's relationship with God to a private sphere of earthly duty in many Christian denominations; the natural philosophies of order that made happiness an individual pursuit; and the theories of natural law of Grotius and Locke claiming that before being political, before entering any agreed upon hierarchy vis-à-vis each other, we are all equals (2004: 150).

This particular notion that I should be free to tend to my life however I see fit usually coexisted with competing imaginaries, such as the hierarchies of kin group, guilds, political parties, and by a public life that retained ritualistic and symbolic valence. It worked as an hermeneutic, a standard to think with and to steer by, and a teleological horizon, only realizing itself fully at the end of the rainbow. But as centuries advanced, our claims based on this moral order have gained in extension and intensity, demanding it be carried out more literally, and making more and more far reaching demands on our political life, on the expectations that this social imaginary must be fully realized here and now. This is in part due to the normalization of a seemingly self-evident subtraction logic: as the value of hierarchies and more-than-individual meanings is dislodged, 'what emerges is the underlying sense of ourselves as individuals' (2004: 64) and of what that individuality demands of the collective to fulfil itself.

To say that technological developments have accelerated this logic of subtraction is a truism, but platform economies have made it exceptionally persuasive in concrete, realpolitik terms. The entire premise of Airbnb's business, as Stabrowski argues, was that *anyone* with a spare room could rent it out, allowing *ordinary* (sic) people to make ends meet, by enabling them to generate supplemental income from their 'underutilized' domestic space' (2017: 341). It is because these were *ordinary* people, and not hoteliers, that Airbnb could actually present them as microentrepreneurs, 'conflat(ing) personhood, home and business' (p 340), then present this entrepreneurialism as a virtue (as opposed to, say, antisocial housing practices), and claim to be serving a 'higher *civic* purpose' (p 341). Similarly, in his study of Airbnb grassroots movements, Van Doorn shows how Airbnb hosts act in defence of *their* economic interests and liberties (2020: 1810) in a narrative of economic but also civic empowerment where they, the hosts, demand the *right* to rent out private homes (pp 1813–16).

That Airbnb benefits from this discourse and from its material implications is true and obvious but also misses a crucial point: these are also ethical claims about the rightful stakes of those who see themselves as the embodiment of ordinary lives in what is also, after all, a moral economy of rights and obligations – including the obligation others have to let them go about their business. Similarly, when Uber arrived in Argentina, a large segment of the middle classes protested for its right to choose how to use their car and how to move around the city: this was a civic language of contingency that demanded, and offered, recognition as such, regardless of how we feel about the moral universe it puts forward (del Nido, 2021).

The logic of subtraction also enhances contingency by delineating a specific *moral* opponent to those ordinary lives: those who are now, in light of the affordances of the platform technology, seen as *extra*-ordinary in ways that appear as hardened and non-contingent and thus should be disallowed, like the hotel lobby (van Doorn, 2020: 1816) or in the case of Uber and Lyft the taxi industry. This is, partly, because of what Gillespie calls the 'populist' rhetoric of platforms (2010). For example, from the outset Uber's business in Buenos Aires was open to absolutely anyone (including taxi drivers doubling as Uber drivers either for money or to ensnare Uber users and turn them in to the authorities, for Uber was strictly speaking illegal, and including me, an ethnographer who did not even own a car), and its barriers of entry were not too demanding. True, in a developing nation like Argentina, there are entire segments of the population without a car, or who may own one that is too old, or they may even be driving without permits. But the point here, as Taylor emphasizes, is that differences amongst us are now not moral, simply instrumental – there was nothing *inherent* to those people that would not have allowed them to belong in Uber's platform.

Certainly, most platforms need to act out this 'populism', to be viable, because of what Srnicek calls network effects (2017: 45): the premise that the more people already use a platform, the more new people will turn to it, which adds an extra incentive for the company to target that ordinary life *in its ordinariness*. But this 'populism' is also a concrete consequence of the materialization of the social imaginary of ordinary life in a different way. Contingency, to be operational in real life, demands a kind of openness so that individuals can take on a path if it suits them and leave it if it does not. We tend to logically associate this ability to leave with the 'empowering' workings of competition: mistreat me, and I will leave for something better. People must, ethically, pursue their individual call and be beholden to no hierarchy of value or meaning if they decide to 'fork out'. In his study of Wikipedia as an open platform, Tkacz shows how in this moral order, this leave-oriented sensibility fulfils a civic, or democratic, function (2015: 127–36): that anyone can come and leave is not only a business strategy but an ethical obligation that gives sense to this moral economy.

Ways of knowing in ordinary life

In this social imaginary where our individual lives follow personal calls and are, and should be, in principle free to 'fork out' and tend to our ordinary needs as we see fit, knowledge about ourselves and others does not come from institutions – a union, a ministry, a constitution – but from ordinary experience as we engage the world. The host to this ordinary experience is a sort of public sphere where 'people who never meet *understand themselves* to be engaged in discussion and capable of reaching a common mind' (Taylor, 2004: 85, emphasis mine). This is a reflective discussion: in this ethics of mutual benefit, our various, often contradictory, purposes and dispositions mesh as interlocking causes such that this public sphere constitutes a market, a linking of agents and their understandings of themselves and others (p 103). As these personal paths are contingent, choice is amoral: it results from how we know ourselves and others in this public sphere following that personal call.

The matter of how ordinary lives know, and the reasons for why this knowledge should matter, and eventually matter so much as to become industrial policy, remains at the core of the economic life of platforms, which Wikipedia illustrates in an unusually literal degree. As Tkacz (2014: 178) shows, Wikipedia founder Jimmy Wales imagined it as a platform for knowledge after reading Hayek's 'The Use of Knowledge in Society'. A neoliberal founding father, Hayek argued individual knowledge by any single entity, whether a centralized state agency or a man walking down a road, was always incomplete, wonky, fragmentary; only free and open information flows could aggregate all the relevant information about a particular subject, relation or fact, and views would coalesce, diverge, add up and build up to perfect, true knowledge (Beddeleem, 2020).

This is freedom imagined in the economic terms of ordinary life. Of course, this is also the ethical bedrock of the perfect neoliberal market, as consumption and production decisions are made by millions who bring their bits to the exchange. Neoliberal philosophy saw the market as a system of communication, not of allocation, and celebrated it for its epistemic virtue (Nik-Khah, 2020: 49). The key notion here is that neoliberal philosophy only developed the market as a critique and solution to the problem of knowledge by building on the *preexisting* logical history of ordinary life as natural site for a particular kind of truth (see also Tkacz, 20154: 18–20).

Platforms in general were designed to host, legitimize and magnify these ways of knowing of ordinary life and to concretize the promise that there are no limits as to what can be known by ordinary life in its terms: prices, amounts, qualities, details, intensities. Even when Wikipedians were pressed on the matter of gender imbalance among the platform's contributors, they did not see it as an issue of structural inequality but rather as a loss of potential information in the knowledge pool (Tkacz, 2014: 12). Contributions that are built upon count as good, ignored contributions count as poor, contributions get contested and editors bring their particular vantages to produce a forceful statement that is not necessarily an average but that reflects the forms of knowledge that went into building it (pp 42–7). Platforms like YouTube, Instagram, Reddit and Twitter also celebrate this marketplace cacophony, not just with low entry barriers, as mentioned above, but by providing the basic infrastructure – hashtags, likes, emojis, upvotes – to render choices and behaviours knowable to others. This also applies to platforms such as Taskrabbit, Mechanical Turk and Craigslist, where people can price their goods and services and see and recognize each other in those goods and services, reflecting on that personal call and on their place in this sphere.

This does not mean platforms do not moderate: all platforms do (Gillespie, 2018) or otherwise intervene in how we know what we can know through them. But these moderations and other platform interventions with respect to a particular statement or a particular kind of relation enter into the logics of circulation of knowledge about ourselves and others. Think about, for example, Uber. The company may argue its algorithms are not setting the price, but 'capturing' market prices out there. Meanwhile, research into its practices often suggests the company manipulates prices depending on data it collects[1]: from this perspective, and in important ways to policy, regulation and industrial oversight, this is a meaningful and consequential distinction.

But from the perspective centred on the world as ordinary lives know it, in this moral economy of knowledge Uber is *just another actor presenting its passengers with a particular kind of information that they can always decline*. In this sense, whether a price is 'actually' a market price or a manipulation is entirely beside the point: there and then, that is the price that particular person will know, and act accordingly (see del Nido, 2021: 147). Ironically, whether this is a 'real' market price is also irrelevant insofar as, when accepted, a market becomes the market price. The distance between the 'real' market price and whatever price is presented to an individual is what confirms the freedom to choose and the amoral condition of this contingency (see Sheehan and Wahrman, 2015: 76). The leave-oriented logics of contingency mentioned earlier also verify these statements as viable forms of knowledge regardless of their truth value or their virtue: one can always go somewhere else, and leaving is also a form of knowing.

This paradox also explains how and why rating mechanisms such as Uber's, Airbnb's and Amazon's work as knowledge of ordinary life. On the one hand, their presumed ability to capture virtually infinite and infinitely variable experiences and render them intelligible to others is a knowledge-enhancing virtue, the ultimate, most radical form of democratized knowledge: there are no barriers as to what can, or should, count as knowledge. On the other, strictly speaking, they can never really mean anything: consider an Uber driver whose 4.5 star rating reflects reckless driving, chattiness, sexism and bad odour in the car. If this knowledge mattered in literal, 'real' ways, we would have to confront the epistemological absurdity of trying to *literally* average out reckless driving, chattiness, sexism and bad odour (see del Nido, 2021: 153–6).

But because these ratings' very virtue is to *not* respond to any *actual* gradations or hierarchies of meaning, that is, they reproduce the openness of contingency where everything matters with equal intensity and interventions are allowed to aggregate, diverge, merge and flow, their inability to carry 'actual' knowledge and serve as such was never attached to their capacity to mean anything. Indeed, recent studies into Airbnb and Uber ratings have sought to flesh out the many biases that render this knowledge 'unreliable': a tendency to only leave positive feedback (Zervas, Proserpio and Byers, 2021), a game theory-like dynamics where knowing that each party is reviewing the other eschews 'real' feedback (Moriuchi, 2019) and so on. What matters from these interventions is that they aggregate to form what these companies, and often their users and regulators, understand as a self-regulating community (Stabrowski, 2017: 340) that learns to know itself. So it does not really matter that an Uber driver and her passenger rate each other upwards of what they would normally do out of a worry of being sanctioned, but that knowing themselves and others from their personal, contingent positions, they know how to inhabit real relations. After all, the entire point of game theory is precisely that individuals know they are not the only ones seeking to know things and intervene in the world, and acting accordingly (see Erickson, 2015).

As mentioned above, the ethics of contingency, that is, the disposition to fulfil ordinary needs freely, frowned upon forms of associative life that in any significant way prevented the forking out. An ethics adjusted to knowledge in and through ordinary life, in turn, delegitimizes knowledge organized around anything other than ordinary experience – values, abstractions and so on. As the ultimate jurisdiction over movement within its boundaries, the City of Buenos Aires regulates the taxi trade requiring, among other thing, certain vehicular check-ups, medical clearance for drivers and a whole set of demands that dictate how movements, and bodies in motion, are to be known: what mattered, when, how and to whom (del Nido, 2021: 67–71). Although usually studied as a kind of labour management (Rosenblat, 2018; Ravenelle, 2019), Uber's ratings also constituted a way of knowing movement and its relations in Buenos Aires that celebrated ordinary experience as a superior heuristic to that supported by any institution. In this sense, both the ethics of contingency and the ethics of ordinary experience as a way of knowing sustain this moral order against institutions. In the next and final section I will examine the kind of legitimacy that closes the circle.

The moral legitimacy of ordinary life

In this moral order, political society is instrumental and secondary to an ordinary life conceived in that ethics of freedom and mutual benefit among individuals. We imagine ourselves pre-existing, and standing outside of, our political associations and institutions, and we judge the latter on how well they fulfil their role: to protect and foster the freedom to take on any activity to satisfy our needs (Taylor, 2004: 87). Remember that along with contingency came the *moral* right to follow our call: *anyone* should be able to post, sell rides, rent out rooms and so on. That this right, in this social imaginary, is moral *and* pre-political is a crucial part of the problem: the only political society possible hinges on covenant, on mutual agreement, which implies we consent to government, and that it is in our power and among our prerogatives to at any point cease to consent, which renders obstacles to this covenant *immoral*.

Tracing this imagination to the writings of Hugo Grotius and John Locke in the 1600s (2004: 87), Taylor notes two accelerations. First, whereas this form of legitimacy always coexisted with forms of non-consensual rule or obligations such as those imposed by ritual, religion, kin duties and the like, as we get closer in history to our time the imagination of the political legitimacy of ordinary life gains exponentially in intensity and in extension of the claims its comes to frame: more and more varied aspects of life are subjected to the adjudication of popular will (however defined). Second, whereas consent as an imagination of political legitimacy tended to be located in a mythical time of foundational sagas (see also Morgan, 1989), and later on in the prosaic, metronomic time of democratic elections, increasingly we see constant, ongoing monitoring of consent by more or less reliable proxies, such as polls, focus groups, market research and other technologies to interpret what the people want (see also Frank, 2002).

What has emerged from these developments is a moral economy, an order of obligations, increasingly obsessed with a popular consent imagined in ever more intimate, instantaneous and unmediated ways. The litmus test for consent is popular legitimacy, which can be handled and framed in very different ways in real life but which demands of us increasing and increasingly absolute reverence, or in other words: who is going to stand in the way of what is presented as what the people want – and say so in as many words? This social imaginary brings with it an ethics of popular legitimacy, an injunction shaping our relation to what emerges as the popular will.

From the instant popular legitimacy was invented as a political illusion, the problem of representation haunted it (Morgan, 1989: 38): who should, effectively can, or must, speak for such a thing as a people? Here is where platforms seamlessly graft themselves, as businesses but also in other important ways, into a 400-year-old problem: partly for reasons explained earlier, and partly because of how they are managed, platforms readily tap the moral legitimacy of the people and activate this social imaginary. Wikipedia, for example, commits to gathering virtually all 'views', however cacophonic when together, and to manage them through forms of direct popular rule among its editors. Its aseptic distance from what emerges as popular concerns leads to what Mirowski calls 'radical populism' (2009, see also Tkacz, 20154). Similarly, Craigslist retains from the early web days the ideal of openness, minimal interference and inclusiveness (Lingel, 2020). Platforms like Uber, Amazon, Netflix, and Facebook are so enmeshed in such *ordinary* aspects of our lives that although businesses, especially those as powerful as these companies, tend to be seen as adversaries of consumers, 'these platforms live in a close and symbiotic alliance' with their consumers and the idea of a people at large (Culpepper and Thelen, 2019: 295).

When necessary, platform companies outright weaponize this alliance against 'politicians'. For example, when a judge ordered Uber to interrupt its activities in Buenos Aires and the city's minister for transportation warned the company its activities broke Argentine and city laws, the company retorted it was not leaving because the people had chosen it, encouraging its users via email to continue using its services (del Nido, 2021: 160–61). Similarly, as Pollman and Barry recall, when New York's attorney general deemed that gaming platform FanDuel was breaking the law, the company issued a statement referencing its 'popularity' and saying that 'this is a politician telling hundreds of thousands of New Yorkers they are not allowed to play a game they love and share with friends, family, coworkers and players across the country' (2016: 403).

In both these cases one notices something the Enlightenment added to this social imaginary and that would later fuel both demands for direct democracy and populist appeals: the notion that the farmers, ironmongers, tailors and other subjects of ordinary life knew better than their overlords what was good for them (Kazin, 2017). Yet a judge and a minister in Buenos Aires and an attorney general in New York are not overlords but public employees of representative and elective democracies, either put in those roles by democratically elected leaders or given those positions in the institutional distribution of power those democracies, founded on a covenant of consent, live by. Yet, in our contemporary social imaginary, 'the people' of Buenos Aires and 'hundreds of thousands of New Yorkers, their friends and family' *in their ordinariness* constitute a source of moral legitimacy whose raw immediacy overrides the original covenant there and then.

Culpepper and Thelen (2019: 290) argue that 'so long as platform users think of themselves as consumers rather than citizens' companies will still evoke, and draw on, this moral legitimacy; Thelen (2018) shows through the case study of Uber's arrival in Denmark how voters can be mobilized as taxpayers, that is to say, from a specific aspect of their condition as citizens, to resist the pull of this moral legitimacy (p 941). But the reality is that within this social imaginary the languages and identities of citizenship and consumption are often entwined: does not, in principle, the site of ordinary life have the moral right to tend to their business and associate with others as they see fit? As van Doorn shows in his study of Airbnb (2020), all the distances between these companies, as businesses and as platforms, and their users, as citizens and consumers, tend to collapse. To a degree, he argues, this is due to the company's strategic conflation of its users with itself: Airbnb fostered the creation of 'Home Sharing Clubs', associations of hosts, to piggyback on the moral legitimacy such associations of ordinary people would have on a political stage (pp 1812–15). Similarly, as Pollman and Barry (2016) show, when authorities in the US state of Virginia demanded Uber cease all operations in the state, the company sent the details of the state official involved in this decision to all its Virginian users, encouraging consumers, who in the very act of addressing their politicians act as citizens, to protest – a civic right.

In subtler ways, these distances collapse because in what van Doorn calls 'the cosmology of the "sharing economy"' (2020: 1815), broadly speaking analogous to what I refer to here as a social imaginary, 'it becomes trickier to discern what we are dealing with: Is Airbnb a business ... instrumentalizing its user base to fight for its cause, or is it a platform facilitating a grassroots movement that fights for *its own* cause, which happens to be structurally aligned with Airbnb's cause?' (2020, emphasis in original). We may think these companies are being cynical, but ultimately our entire political imagination is founded on the premise of the moral legitimacy of ordinary life and on the fact that we owe it a certain reverence. So, Uber may well send alerts to its users asking them to sign petitions (Pollman and Barry, 2016: 405), and Airbnb may well select which user narratives it puts forward to give the impression of the support of ordinary people and to sustain an imagination of what ordinary people look like – as Stabrowski (2017) and Yates (2021) show. Still, ultimately, are those people doing the signing, and arguing for home rentals not simply claiming the right to follow their call, described above, to tend to their needs as they see fit? Are they *not* sites of the ordinary life we have sacralized?

Companies developing platform economies did not invent popular legitimacy, and they are not the only ones able to tap into its moral mystique. Aside from their strategies to do so, or whether they simply converge with it by accident, in realpolitik terms they have turned the problem of representation inside out. They have dented our political imagination such that it becomes onerous, almost morally illegitimate, to argue that democratic institutions, and not an unmediated popular will conjured up strategically, are the rightful site of moral legitimacy. From this perspective, what Thelen (2018) presents as the Danish exception can in fact make sense as a particular case where those ordinary lives decided at a scale sufficiently large to pass for a people (de facto nullifying, by refusal to use, the company's attempts to build up its business there) rejecting an intrusion in a moral economy where paying taxes is integral to what Danes imagine as that ordinary life.

Conclusion

Platform economies have revolutionized our lives, but as Culpepper and Thelen argue, a similarly revolutionary case could be made for maritime trade, rail industries, pharmaceutical developments, electricity and dozens more (2019). In this chapter I have argued what is special about them is their ability to bring an unusually raw life to a moral intuition. The stuff of such an intuition did not just exist out there, but developed in time as a way to imagine such a thing as a secular, economic life with a telos that was no longer literally divine but mystical in what it awarded us, as individuals, and what it demanded of the kind of relations we entertain with each other as sites of bare, ordinary life.

The possible realization of a moral order that was never designed to be materialized so literally begs the question: what kind of polity could we produce, or end up stuck with, to accommodate such intensity? From a more utopian perspective, the workings of these platforms resemble, as Tkacz (2015: 14) notes, the never quite realized democracy of the multitude Hardt and Negri (2004) imagined: one that openly displaces the legitimacy of traditional forms of representation. In a manner ironically analogous to Grotius' displacement of the political to a secondary sphere, they argue following Negri (1999) that the people have a *constituent* power that pre-exists representation: the power of the multitude. Any *constituted* power that limits, mediates or tames this constituent power, roughly what we would call institutions, is in direct violation of a democracy that, by definition, can only reach its purest form, carnivalesque and non-hierarchical, in a sort of perpetually open, perpetually revolutionary state.

From a more realist perspective, in catalysing this moral order platforms seem to be further entrenching what Bickerton and Invernizzi Accetti label 'technopopulism' (2021). Contrary to the established notion that populism and technocracy cancel each other out, they argue both extol an unmediated conception of the common good. Increasingly, techniques of knowing the people – polling, surveying, referenda, and so on – interpellate people as sovereigns of ordinary life (p 63) whose voices add up to a 'collective intelligence' (p 75) to produce 'a straightforward implementation of the ideal of popular sovereignty, conceived as a direct translation of the popular will into policy' (p 43).

This chapter's discussion suggests the latter perspective has tapped into the possible future, increasingly present, polity for a moral order exalting ordinary life, authoritarian, majoritarian, unaccountable and maddeningly dystopian. The solution they propose? To repopulate and once again dignify institutions of representative democratic life, such as political parties and unions, whose role was always to mediate our differences, temper our impulses and protect us from the most strident, literal versions of ourselves; in the terms of this chapter, to shield us from what was conceived as a political fiction over the course of the centuries, never to come to life in such intractable and accomplished ways.

Note

[1] Alex Rosenblat, 'The algorithmic boss', public seminar [online], Available from: www.youtube.com/watch?v=B639VJ9rq9E&ab_channel=re%3Apublica [Accessed 6 September 2022].

4

Burdens of Legacy: Enumerative Accountability in Digital Markets

Vibodh Parthasarathi

In debates on media governance over the last 50 years, anxieties of enumerating readers and viewers of news have recurrently occupied centre stage. But platformization of the legacy news business has reconfigured past regimes of measuring and metrifying news audience. This chapter makes sense of the emergent regime by forwarding the idea of enumerative accountability. To do so, I posit the actors and forces involved in enumerating users in the platform economy in the longer history of those involved in newspapers and broadcast news in India. This helps me to distil the elements of continuity while also identifying heightened challenges of accountability posed by data brokers in digital news markets.

Introduction

This chapter is interested in the institutions and interests involved in seeking, gaining and normalizing the visibility of news audience. This commonly takes the institutional form of a business in audience measurement, be that pertaining to newspapers, broadcast news, online news outlets or across all the three. Typical actors in this business include industry or government-sanctioned enumerators, consortiums of news outlets and advertisers, third-party data-brokers and, in digital markets, intermediaries and platforms. The chapter thinks through the ideas, practices and stakes associated with audience measurement in legacy news markets and their reconfigurations amidst the platformization of the news media.

I view platforms as institutionalizing novel forms of market systems (Evans and Schmalensee, 2016), rather than simply creating new commodities.

This approximates what the editors of this volume consider a perspective rendered by 'the overall economic framing' of platforms (Gregersen et al, this volume). Elsewhere such a perspective has been termed as the 'markets approach' to platforms (Athique and Parthasarathi, 2020); this contrasts the 'affordances' (or 'operations') and the 'infrastructural' perspectives on platforms (Plantin et al, 2018), which the editors have well elaborated. My argument, in its essence, is about platformization of the media having reconfigured the key the dynamics and structures characterizing historical media markets in India (see Parthasarathi and Athique, 2020) This reformulation is achieved in at least three ways: creating overlaps and interdependencies between hitherto separate marketplaces; in offering multiple products in simultaneous transaction; and in mining, abstracting and marketizing the domain of the social (Athique and Parthasarathi, 2020). Additionally, these tendencies reconfigure the ways in which value is imputed and ascribed to media products, including to news (also see Bolin, 2011). As a corollary, I would claim platforms also reconfigure practices of gaining visibility over audiences and their behaviour – process wherein algorithms institutionalize the market for audience measures in novel ways. Methodologically, congenital to the 'markets approach' to platforms, as an economy of markets, is attending to the history of media markets, the trajectory of the business of audience measurement and specific contexts in which media platforms are studied.

The necessary precondition for any practice of measuring audience and consumers, much like enumerating subjects and citizens, is the ability to make visible the objects of measurement. The enterprise of colonial governmentality hinged around the ability to comprehend its subjects in an alien political, economic and cultural geography. This propelled creating and formalizing various administrative modalities of knowing the colonized subject and surroundings, such as through census and surveys (see Cohn, 1996). Over time, a body of measure and metrics got devised and deployed by the post-colonial state purposed at administering populations, allocating public investment, and everything in between.

Parallel to this was another trajectory, that of commercial actors evolving ways to gauge habits and preferences of the consumer. Some of their methods borrowed from those developed by the state, such as the survey. The desire to estimate consumer activity and comprehend their preferences was purposed to inform business strategy and refine commercial models. The long history of measuring media audience is part and parcel of these desires. In the formative years of radio in the US, market research commenced with aims that have since been normalized, that is, to gain visibility and quantify the acts and activities of media audiences (see Craig, 2010).

By the mid-twentieth century, enumerative practices by state and market actors alike got further institutionalized and incrementally infused by technology. The recent digital turn imparted a whole new qualitative and quantitative order in the mechanisms of gaining visibility. This is evident in pursuits of the state and market systems alike. The former is amplified in debates on biometrics and citizenship initiated from an array of disciplinary vantage points and across countries (for instance, Dagiral and Singh, 2020). The latter opens on to discussions on the role and ability of algorithms in bringing new forms of legibility over users of media platforms (Cohen, 2017). Cohen's emphasis is not only due to legibility being a decisive organizational feature of algorithms but the key 'institutionalized arbiter of the knowledge' relied upon by all participants in the platform economy (Cohen, 2017: 138). This is much the way the legibility afforded through biometrics provides a means for the state to reiterate itself as the ultimate bearer of knowledge about its citizens. At the heart of both these anxieties sit uncomfortable questions of enumeration, governance and accountability.

I begin the chapter by recalling the importance of enumerating audiences in debates on media policy. This provides the context to forward the proposition of enumerative accountability as a perennial challenge in media policy. To illustrate this, the second section reviews the practices of actors with stakes in measuring audience, namely publishers and data brokers, in the history of newspapers and broadcasting in India. While publishers adopted varied means to shield information vital for their publics and policy makers, data brokers created dependencies in the business of enumerating audiences. In their own ways, and often in conjunction, both actors undermined transparency and trust in enumerating news audiences in India. The third section explores the imprints of such a legacy in the wake of the platformization of news (Nieborg and Poell, 2018). The argument here is about the reformulation of the ways audiences are made visible, legible and measurable in the platform economy being part of the wider reconfiguration of legacy news markets by their platformization. This leads me to highlight elements of continuity and rupture that mark the behaviour of data brokers in digital markets and the stakes driving their behaviour. I find the competitive milieu spawned by data brokers, the opacity of their business practices and their disregard for audience rights impede trust, transparency and answerability in digital markets.

Audience measurement: appeals and challenges

Audience measurement and media policy

The measurement of audience is central to debates on media governance long before the platformization of the media. Audience measures can potentially contribute to address at least three longstanding policy challenges: nurturing diverse content, addressing (effects of) undesirable content, and the competitive milieu of media outlets (Webster, 1990: 59). Of these, challenges of diversity and competition are perhaps the most central to debates on the governance of the news media. Despite the early optimisms about the promise of the internet, these challenges did not wane in digital news markets; that the first is viewed to have enhanced and the second become acute are matters occupying ongoing research, as briefly captured below.

In hyper-commercial TV milieus, the original argument goes, competing news outlets could probe audience demand so as to largely 'give the people what they want' (Webster, 1990: 60). For this logic to work in addressing challenges of media diversity, TV ratings were long taken to be an index of audience preferences. This enduring consensus was displaced by expanding debates around the 'diversity principle' in media policy (see Valcke, 2011: 205; Karppinen, 2012; Duncan and Reid, 2013), especially the emphasis therein on 'exposure diversity' (see Napoli, 2011b; Helberger, 2012). To evoke a formidable scholar in these debates, it was via the diversity principle that the realms of audience measurement and media policy began to intersect more explicitly (Napoli, 2005: 352). This intersection is of heightened significance in the online media marked by the segmentation of audiences, separation of content from delivery, and convergence of delivery platforms (Helberger, 2005; Gibbons, 2015: 1384).

The second intersection between media policy and audience measurement pertains to the anxiety of media effects. In the development of newspapers and broadcast news in India, tussles over the undesirability of content, including their presumed impact, have found prominence in court judgements, policy documents and regulatory instruments (see Bhatia, 2016 *passim*). Elaborating, or questioning, the intellectual assumptions and other explanatory logics about media effects requires, inter alia, gathering an array of evidence on and about audiences. This includes data not only on audiences' immediate preference and behaviour but also about their related activities as citizens in a polity and as groups in society.

The third intersection between media policy and audience measurement pertains to discussions evaluating 'media health', especially that of news outlets. Here, the issue of temporality is crucial. Insights on investments and liabilities, revenues and costs, loans and profitability, of media outlets are derived in India from quarterly disclosures by listed news outlets and annual disclosures by the privately held ones, the latter comprising the vast majority. Thick data on audience preferences prove helpful in providing more immediate indicators, even if as proxies, of the health of a media outlet. No wonder journalists in newsrooms of digital start-ups in India are obsessed with audience metrics through the day (and night) and across cycles of specific news stories (see Aneez et al, 2017). Such practices, not coincidentally, brings us back to the first policy challenge, that of media diversity.

Accountability in audience measurement

Reviewing the expectations of audience measurement in addressing longstanding policy challenges, we stumble upon another challenge: that spawned by the institutional practices and commercial stakes constituting audience measurement itself. These could be subsumed in the anxieties among policy makers about the produce and process of audience measurement.

On the one hand, are discomforts about kinds of data generated, their usability and relevance in addressing core policy challenges, and the implications of associated metrics on the endeavour of evidence-based policymaking. Measures and metrics on audience are congenitally exposed to the specific logics and incentives of the institutional processes cradling them. This has driven scholars to be doubly sceptical about the trend to fetishize 'media metrics' (Freedman, 2014). First, while an 'objective' data-driven approach theoretically insulates policymaking from partisanship and bias, it does not necessarily mute the use of selective facts and subjective judgment to marginalize critical or countervailing propositions. Second, the 'objective' data (often masquerading as evidence) policy makers find ready and appealing is likely to be supplied by a narrow range of elite sources and commercial organizations, many of whom had originally harvested their data for totally different purposes.

On the other hand are concerns about the interests that gather and trade in such knowledge, the lack of transparency and public oversight over their enumerative operations, and the market structure of the business of audience measurement. Astute scholars point at audience measurement evoking policy anxieties similar to those spawned by social media: the absence of robust competition in their respective pursuits, their significant social repercussions, the risks to diversity imparted by their institutional norms and the proprietary opacity over their operations (Napoli and Napoli, 2019). This makes it easier to fathom why audience measurement systems, much like the more talked about social media algorithms, may also be considered as a 'black box'.

The proposition of '*enumerative accountability*' provides an umbrella to club a raft of anxieties instigated by the business of audience measurement in digital markets. Enumerative accountability seeks to hold actors providing knowledge about audiences and their behaviour, crucial to other actors in digital markets, answerable for the procedural opacity, organizational distrust and abuse of market power inherent in their commercial, industrial and strategic behaviours. My proposition joins hands with arguments about social and corporate accountability marking intense debates in public policy at large (see especially Bovens, 2007). Drawing on this, enumerative accountability deals with two broad obligations: the public obligations of business actors measuring audiences to demystify the scope and purpose of their practices; and the commercial obligations of these institutionally legitimized enumerators, and sundry data brokers, to other market actors who have infused their trust and/or hedged their bets on them to gain knowledge over and about media audience. Since these practices raise issues of transparency of and answerability to different interests around media platforms, my proposition is able to fruitfully locate audience measurement amidst earlier calls for algorithmic accountability in digital markets (see Ziewitz, 2016; Kemper and Kolkman, 2019). Lastly, the plea for enumerative accountability gains a particular methodological importance amidst the enthusiasm for 'evidence-based research' in media policy (for instance, Picard, 2011). In fact, questions of measures and metrics are central not only to the approaches embodying this intellectual turn in policy studies but equally to the scepticisms aroused by it (see particularly Freedman, 2014).

Positing enumerative accountability as a perennial policy challenge demands examining the business of audience measurement over a reasonable length of time – such as from the era when newspapers dominated public opinion to when online news is claimed to do so. A necessary element of this pursuit is identifying the various operational impediments to enumerative accountability in the news media; this, in turn, will help to evaluate the extent to which the deeper, structural impediments have persisted, or morphed, in the platformization of the news media. Pursuing such an evaluation across newspapers, broadcast news, and online news would also contribute to conceptually hone the appeal of the proposition.

Audience and measurement in a hybrid milieu

Conventional arguments about the news media view the Indian milieu indicating a shift from broadcast to online news; this is built on the earlier assumption of the era of broadcast news itself replacing that of newspapers. However, it is empirically prudent and methodologically productive to view the news landscape in India as a hybrid milieu. At the core of this hybridity is the overlapping, often synergizing, presence of newspapers, broadcast news and online news, as insisted elsewhere (see Chadwick, 2013). Although scholarship on India's hybrid milieu is in its infancy, it has brought to the fore a clutch of legacy and emergent traits of news governance peculiar to this setting (see Chadha, 2012; Parthasarathi and Agarwal, 2020).

Be it the conventional or hybrid reading of the milieu in India, three differences between print, broadcast and online sites of the news media must be foregrounded. Foremost, the constitution of 'news' itself, as an object of circulation and consumption, has morphed from print and TV to online. Second, while conceptions of audience in newspapers and broadcasting were that of an aggregate public, that in online news is moored around (additionally, or sometimes primarily) the individual. Third, and consequent to the first two, the purpose of enumerating audiences has undergone successive shifts from print to broadcast to online news – from approximating readership to measuring a sampled viewership, to explicitly curating users.

Notwithstanding the above, there are striking continuities in the institutional norms of audience measurement across print, broadcast and online news outlets in India.

To start with, measuring audience is a malleable endeavour. It provides tangibility to abstract ideas and thereby overcome the pervasive challenge in media policy of operationalizing normative concepts (Karppinen, 2012). Second, a sense of speculation resides in the business of audience measurement. For example, estimations of 'readership' in India are based on assumptions of one newspaper being read by four to six individuals, including those who are not the primary subscriber. Third, the primary incentive propelling commercial interests to enumerate audiences have remained the same across newspapers, broadcast news or online news. Building on arguments of the platformization of media reflecting the remaking of historical media markets (Bolin, 2011; Parthasarathi and Athique, 2020), I would claim enumerative practices remain integral to the stakes driving platforms as media markets, akin to that in legacy media markets. Fourth, measures by industry-accepted enumerators and third-party data brokers gain certain legitimacy when used by governments in policymaking exercises. For instance, the first Press Commission's observations on anti-competitive practices in newspaper distribution during the 1950s gained legitimacy partly because it was based on surveys by the Audit Bureau of Circulation (ABC), a consortium of newspapers-advertisers. Lastly, audience metrics invoke a sense of familiarity among stakeholders. Online users, and journalists, alike constantly encounter measurements about themselves – such as the popularity of the news fragments they produce, share or consume on Facebook.

Thus, despite differences in the purpose, conception and object of measurement across print, broadcast and online news, there exist significant commonalities in the institutional norms of audience measurement. Moreover, the regulatory history of the news media in India is marked by multiple path dependencies in harvesting comprehensive and reliable data on audiences, as my narrative will spotlight. These, in turn, indicate incremental impediments to enumerative accountability arising from both, the arena of media policy making and the business of audience measurement. Interestingly enough, these impediments relate to either unresolved debates in the governance of newspapers and broadcast news, or to questions of power and transparency in current discussions on online news. This is what makes me posit the problematic of enumerative accountability within larger concerns around the health, effects, and diversity of the news media.

Legacies of enumerative accountability

Experiences of newspapers and broadcast news in India suggest questions of enumerative accountability have long inhabited the institutional infrastructure of audience measurement.

In recalling the collection of relevant and necessary data on newspapers, I observe business actors shielding such information on the pretext of competitive intelligence. While this reminds us of the famous 'disclosure paradox' (Arrow, 2015), I see here a deeper problem: while information in public interest does not always get disclosed, what does get disclosed is not necessarily helpful in furthering public interest policymaking. The first Press Commission of 1954 discomfortingly noted newspapers' unwillingness to provide data it requested (GoI, 1954: 6). Following its recommendations, a Registrar of Newspapers for India (RNI) was created in 1956 'to remedy the chaotic condition of the statistics' (Jeffrey, 1994: 752).

Often news outlets took legal recourse to shield information. This confronted the Fact Finding Committee on Newspaper Economics (FFCN), constituted in 1971 to unravel prevalent business practices. Learning from the experience of newspapers not responding to questionnaires sent by the Press Commission of 1954, the FFCN was empowered to seek financial data from dailies. Refusing to comply, a leading and influential newspaper, *The Statesman*, went to Court arguing the economics of the newspaper business was 'not a matter of public importance' (AIR, 1975). Even after the Court made such disclosures binding, only 20 per cent of dailies responded to FFCN's questionnaire (GoI, 1975: 16).

There are further instances that testify the way dominant actors in the new media cock a snook at regulatory obligations and public accountability. Newspapers and TV news outlets have commonly resorted to uneven disclosures while ostensibly complying with their regulatory obligations. A sterling example are annual reports of companies laden with noticeable inconsistencies and omissions – such as not, or unevenly, presenting disaggregated data on distinct revenue streams (that is, advertising, subscriptions, rights-sales and so on). Although disclosures are relatively granular and consistent by listed companies, only a fraction of news outlets in India are on the bourses.

Whenever industry appointed bodies have sought to gather audience data, their efforts become contingent to the willingness of member companies. The Press Commission had noted a large number of newspapers were not members of the ABC – the first industry-driven, non-statutory attempt to gauge the consumers of newspapers in 1948. Instead, these newspapers chose to depend on their own, unsupported statements on circulation to secure advertisements (GoI, 1954: 85). Consequently, the ABC's initiative to assemble reliable circulation figures resulted in incomplete data sets on newspaper audiences. The unwillingness of members to adhere to the rules of industry bodies has raised larger questions on the efficacy of self-regulatory initiatives in India (see Ang and Pramanik, 2008). Since the jurisdiction of such bodies is limited to its members, individual media companies, when found violating or ignoring self-regulatory protocols, withdraw their membership to sidestep compliance.

Third, harvesting evidence about the news audience is victim to the state forfeiting its role in collecting public interest information on this crucial pillar of democracy. In the wake of neo-liberal economic reforms in India, the state rescinded its responsibility to thickly enumerate a host of service sectors, including the business of private cable and satellite (Das and Parthasarathi, 2011). This resulted in, inter alia, demand-side data on this business being loose, inaccurate, and opaque – be it the number of cable TV homes, the total audience or the viewership of specific news channels. Rampant under-declaration by cable operators prevented accurate counts of the most basic measure, such as subscriptions to TV news channels. A repeated defence of this was prevalent analogue cable distribution systems preventing the knowability of individual TV homes and their programme choices (see Parthasarathi et al, 2016). However, even after mandatory digitalization of cable networks technologically offered to overcome the knowability problem, audience data on broadcast news remains shallow and incomplete.

Since data on TV audiences was not gathered either by the state, as did the RNI for newspapers, or by an industry consortium, akin to the ABC for newspapers, a window of opportunity opened-up for third party data providers. This is how the business of TV ratings emerged in India. We are well aware that ratings do not merely introduce a palette of measures on the news economy; rather they introduce an apparatus of agreements, conventions, values and behaviours (see Balnaves and O'Regan, 2010).

The state choosing to sidestep a public function crucial to evidence-based policy research catalysed three different registers of enumerative accountability.

One, a 'market argument' got evoked to fulfil such a public function. This is manifest in a third-party data brokers assembling audience data, which marked the entry of Nielsen. Its efforts were directed at, not at a public function but, fulfilling the particular needs and purposes of various actors – that is, their clients – in the news business. Riddled with the discourse of 'choice', this market argument gained thrust when a rival audience measurement agency, aMAP, emerged. It deployed a mechanism to generate TV ratings overnight, thereby plugging the temporality challenges of Nielsen's weekly releases of audience data (see Taneja, 2013).

Two, in such a scenario, the business of audience measurement further gathered a speculative character. During the expansion of the press in the decades after the ABC and RNI were established, newspapers realized the difference between circulation and readership. The metric of 'readership' gained value since a newspaper was read by many more than those subscribing to it – although how many more, has remained a conjecture ever since the National Readership Survey was mooted in 1970.[1] On its part, the metric of 'viewership' in broadcast news has been derived from contentious samples of not only the number of audience but also the dispersion of sampled homes across India's numerous linguistic and cultural geographies.

Three, the state's withdrawal from this public interest obligation has shaped the picture of the news media refracted in official documents. Typically, annual reports from regulators and line ministries in India commonly quote audience data from Nielsen, third-party brokers and sundry trade publications – the phrase 'industry estimates' employed while citing these sources. While this legitimized the role of all such commercial actors, it also risks overlooking the omissions and commissions ingrained in their enumerations. These tendencies are witnessed in other jurisdictions as well. For instance, although the FCC is legally bound to combine in-house expertise with a transparent and complete collection of evidence (Frieden, 2008), policy makers are found to rely on the datasets developed by commercial providers, neglecting their own substantial data collection capabilities and responsibilities (Napoli and Karaganis, 2007: 56). To an extent media policy researchers become complicit in legitimizing such actors and their data by unreflectively adopting them – a practice that consequently gets normalized among students of media governance as well.

In such circumstances, public interest data risks becoming dependent on the commercial incentives driving data brokers to gain visibility on audience and their behaviour – that is to say, of satisfying the needs of their primary clients, viz. advertisers and managers of news outlets. This dependence also includes relying on the operational routines adopted by data brokers to assemble audience measurements. A case in point is the software deployed to generate overnight TV ratings, as aMAP was providing. The design of these automated systems tend to only perform routine tasks, as is also the case with systems to measure online users (see Taneja and Mamoria, 2012). Thus, certain types of audience data relevant to a particular policy issue become almost impossible to gather by existing systems, as also observed elsewhere (Webster, 1990: 69). In such circumstances, regulators and policy researchers get compelled to commission customized measurements from private enumerators – something which further legitimizes their roles and dependencies.

Such dependencies could be offset by the presence of multiple data-brokers and competing metrics. At the immediate operational level, this raises questions about the price of data provided by private companies. It seems price varies with the purchasing power of potential users, including that of policy researchers. In other words, the pricing of audience data appears to be based on, not the costs uncured to collect and process it but, the ability of prospective buyers to meet particular prices.[2]

Beyond operational concerns, the presence of competing data brokers and metrics have evoked matters of trust, central to policy debates on media governance. Here, I allude to two instances from the pre-digital era in India where the role of data brokers appeared dubious.

One, established actors tend to perceive changes in an existing systems of enumeration, including rivalling and/or additional measures, to adversely affect their entrenched interests. This was vividly demonstrated when the National Readership Survey (NRS) sought to enumerate the readership, as opposed to circulation, of newspapers. Some newspapers were uncertain about the actual extent of and nature of their readership; others saw 'readership' becoming a more valuable metric than circulation; still others suspected NRS data would end up directing advertisers to concentrate only on a few, large newspaper chains (Jeffrey, 1994: 757). This had led to the largest newspaper association in India unwilling to endorse the NRS, which in many ways mirrored the resistance of broadcasters in the US to Nielsen introducing local people meters (see Napoli, 2005).

Two, protocols of data collection in India by Nielsen and (until it lasted) aMAP are bereft of any public or third-party audit; this was unlike with RNI and ABC, however sloppy their efforts might have been. A different order of trust among stakeholders surfaced when Nielsen failed to protect the anonymity of sampled TV homes installed with audience meters. Over the last two decades, repeated scandals around TV ratings have dented the veracity and accountability of ratings data being generated and traded. Scandals instil apprehension among business actors about faith and accountability on the knowledge they paid for and relied on in designing their commercial and programming strategies. This prompted creating a consortium to enumerate audience, the Broadcast Audience Research Council (BARC), akin to the ABC for newspapers. But even here, the lack of public audits and oversight mechanisms exposed this initiative to opportunities and incentives for abuse (see Laghate, 2020). Revelations of BARC's motivated sample and other malpractices revived questions of trust in what is essentially public interest data generated by a private body.

Reconfigurations and continuities in digital markets

At the outset I had urged construing platforms as re-institutionalizing legacy media markets. As a corollary, I would further argue platforms also reconfigure practices of gaining visibility over audiences and their online activities. In other words, much as platforms indicate a new type of media markets, algorithms institutionalize the market for audience measures in novel ways (Fourcade and Healy, 2017; Zuboff, 2019). This reconfigured business of audience measurement reflects similarities, amplifications and ruptures to that in the heydays of newspapers and broadcast news.

Reconfigurations

The new order of enumeration orchestrated by algorithms is not about practices of enumerations alone but the institutional framework normalizing such practices. Heterodox conceptions of legacy media markets point at the three scales at which they are constituted: the micro-scale of product markets, the meso-scale of markets of operations and the meta-scale of markets of interest (see Parthasarathi and Athique, 2020). This ontological perspective can be easily extended to grasp the dynamics of digital markets (see Parthasarathi and Raghunath, 2022). In the platform economy, algorithms simultaneously cater to all three scales of markets. On the one hand, algorithms in news platforms 'metricify' emotions and tastes, utterances and relationships (van Dijck, 2014: 198); on the other hand, they offer new means to enumerate transactions, value and worth among competing entities (see Bolin, 2011; Mackenzie, 2018). At both scales, the effective and claimed capabilities of algorithms to enable legibility impart a radically new qualitative and quantitative order to legacies of audience measures and metrics.

In the early years of the internet, techniques of audience measurement were similar to those adopted in broadcasting. Software was embedded on computers to grasp internet usage, and surveys were carried out to probe attitudes and lifestyles of online audiences. In rudimentary techniques of automation adopted to census site activity (such as log file analysis), the problems faced were also similar to those when TV ratings were automated: be it their relevant universe and sample size, inability to enumerate all activity (due to local, proxy, ISP and regional caching), and limitations of tracking machines (like TV sets or mobile phones) and not their users and circumstance of usage (Coffrey, 2001; Taneja, 2013).

Metrics from newspapers and broadcast news, such as preference, got tuned to the incremental and/or specific purposes of enumerating online audiences. Resultantly, established measures, such as circulation in newspapers and viewership in television, got altered to 'page views' for online audiences but also led to fresh metrics manufactured, such as 'cost-per-click' (Bermejo, 2009). Akin to newspapers and TV news, the common measurement standard for online news privileges exposure based metrics, such as page views, over measures of audience behaviour falling under the broad notion of 'engagement', such as attentiveness (Thurman, 2014). But even in the TV business, actors had wondered whether engagement ought to replace exposure (that is, ratings) as the standard metric, while disagreeing on what might constitute engagement in uni-directional media (see Taneja, 2013).

As the figure of intermediaries grew, vendors of media products were compelled to, or wilfully rely upon them to sort, rank and filter information on audiences. This is akin to measuring audiences in print and broadcasting, being actively shaped by the inter-related decisions on what and how to measure audiences. It is here that legacy anxieties about 'knowability' of audience data got amplified; more so once the risks of algorithms as gatekeepers, often in the guise of enhancing the discoverability of news, got widely recognized (see Aneez et al, 2017; McKelvey and Hunt, 2019). These anxieties are justified by findings on algorithms influencing certain news flows based on estimations of what is relevant to particular users (Helberger, 2019); and furthermore, in them unduly amplifying and suppressing utterances, thereby emerging as instruments of cultural policy (see Just and Latzer, 2017; Hunt and McKelvey, 2019).

Giving due weight to the users of technology and the operations of technology, Bolin and Velkova insightfully differentiate between two types of metrics: 'representational' metrics, or those benefiting audience/users to craft and enhance their activities, and 'operational' metrics, fuelling the purpose of algorithms (2020: 1195–8). While the former, playing out at the micro scale, prompt and curate preferences of audiences as media consumers, the latter, playing out in the meso scale, offer competing suppliers of news content legibility over such consumption. The conception of operational metrics is particularly essential to our discussion. Compared to legacy media where audience (data) are provided to advertisers, the novelty of media platforms is that audience (and their data) are provided to, beyond media buyers and content curators, sundry commercial actors constituting the platform economy. This larger constituency for audience data is captured in arguments of platforms providing users to their algorithms (Gillespie, 2014). This unequivocally indicates algorithms, as actors, to additionally operate at the meta-scale of digital markets that is, in the markets of interests.

Continuities

The discourse of the 'unknowability of algorithms' is dangerous precisely because they are a consequential actor in platforms markets. Their role in digital news markets is far more central, and more insidious, than that of ratings agencies in legacy media markets. Nevertheless, numerous concerns about their role in enumerating audiences are similar to those we had observed in legacy media markets.

A large array of measurements and metrics provided by third party data brokers continue to be commissioned for the needs of their immediate clients (Napoli, 2011a: 3). These include advertisers, owners and investors interested in visibility on the business processes, and programme executives and content managers keen to gather metrics on the production process.

These actors, in turn, are at the helm of shaping questions of what and how to measure. These self and vested interests also resist new measurement systems and metrics, fearing the known and unknown implications of alternative measures.

Much like in legacy media markets, a fair part of audience data harvested on digital markets is dependent on the willingness and voluntary participation by digital news outlets to embed measurement tags. This voluntary nature, importantly, determines the universe and representativeness of the audience accessing online news outlets. If a publisher doesn't include Comscore tags on their pages, which can sometimes slowdown sites, they do not figure in measurements. Large news outlets appear keen to participate in these processes, which results in them gaining more attention from advertisers – which then, in turn, further distances the appeals of niche sites to advertisers. Examinations of media diversity from an audience centric perspective need to be particularly aware of such circumstances yielding relevant enumerations.

But here lies a larger element of continuity. Enumerations from intermediaries and third-party data brokers rather incidentally yield measures and metrics relevant to key challenges in media policy, be that of media diversity, health or effects. Moreover, measures/metrics from different data-brokers impede our ability of accurate and justifiable comparisons. Like with broadcast markets, we must be mindful about available audience measures surreptitiously propagating particular discourses about the platform media. For instance, while Netflix has neatly sidestepped disclosing audience data, what it made available is argued to be self-aggrandizing (Hunt and McKelvey, 2019: 317). More generally, wherever audience data is made available gratis, such as on websites of data brokers, it is reasonable to infer this serves at least two ideological ends: it propagates a certain perception of the state of platform media markets, and it reiterates the acceptance of certain measures and metrics.

All these concerns about the accuracy of measures collected and circulated about audiences in digital markets precipitate issues of the accountability of data-brokers. Impediments to accountability, much akin to those in legacy media markets, arise primarily because a fair array of data circulated about on platform audiences is devoid of external audits.

Impediments to enumerative accountability

Before moving ahead, let me recap my observations and learnings. In the expansion of news audience from daily newspapers, to 18-hour programming in TV news, to 24-hour online outlets, the aims and methods of measurement had expanded and mutated. These changes were not only formal but also substantive – that is, from comprehending the reader, to speculating the audience, to curating the user and more. In tandem, the purpose and practice of enumerating audiences also got reconfigured. Across these reconfigurations, impediments in collecting, availing and using data on audiences persisted. These raised questions of trust, transparency and answerability, in matters of producing and trading such knowledge – questions subsumed under the problematic of enumerative accountability.

I would claim these impediments reflect deeper, structural traits in the business of audience measurement – traits that have persisted and got amplified under platformization. In this section, I relate these constraints to four sets of dynamics: competition in enumerating audiences, opacity in the protocols involved, motivations of the constituent interests and abuse of user rights.

Competitiveness matters

The latest recommendations by the Telecommunications Regulatory Authority of India (TRA), the regulator of India's telecom, internet, and broadcast industries, on audience measurement in the broadcast business encouraged 'competition and multiple agencies for data collection', although it was silent on specific instruments to achieve this (TRAI, 2020). Nor did TRAI recognize the economies of scale and the convenience of one currency being primarily responsible for measurement business inhabiting a single provider (see Napoli, 2003).

In the business of enumerating audiences, data providers compete for limited resources of their primary clients, that is, publishers and advertisers. In recent years, additional clients have emerged, such as political parties and advocacy groups; but their needs are neither on a continuing basis nor entail, as yet, significant revenues for data providers. Historical trends in India and elsewhere suggest established data providers not only enjoy competitive superiority, but their dominance gets reiterated as additional clients of data emerge. This had led to a consensus on audience measurement being a natural monopoly (see Buzzard, 2002; Napoli, 2003), or at best a duopoly, as was the case one time with Alexa and Comscore in measuring web-traffic. However, there are two separate but interrelated issues here: the presence of multiple enumerators (that is, actors) and of multiple produce of enumeration (that is, metrics).

In broadcasting, we recall, that despite the incumbent monopolist of TV ratings in the US, Nielsen, repeatedly challenged by rivals in the ratings business, each time its monopoly got reinstated (Buzzard, 2002). Even outside the US, most markets for audience measurement have been characterized by a monopolist provider (Taneja and Mamoria, 2012). The immediate risk here is that of abuse of this monopoly-like position. For instance, the Indian news broadcaster NDTV took Nielsen to court alleging it had rigged ratings. This and other allegations led to Nielsen being replaced by the Broadcast

Audience Research Council (BARC) as the 'official' provider of TV ratings in India. However, in a few years BARC was accused for colluding with another news broadcaster, Republic TV, to fix viewership numbers. These instances suggest the risks of abuse by a data provider is irrespective of it being a for-profit and not-for profit body, as Nielsen and BARC respectively are; rather, it directly stems from the monopoly status enjoyed by them.

Arguments of a natural monopoly assume one purpose of audience measurement, that of producing a currency for advertising; this ignores why and how different actors in the media economy respectively need and utilize enumerations on media audiences. Studies on TV ratings in India argue a new enumerator finds buyers, even if their measures do not become the prime advertising currency, so long as they can service the demand for certain types of data (Taneja, 2013). These demands get determined by clients' satisfaction with the knowledge they are provided with about their audience, the effects of their commercial strategies and how such insights help to discursively represent themselves. Whereas data from Nielsen was used by advertisers and programme executives, that generated by a new and less popular provider, aMAP, was used for by actors who did not see the standard system aptly reflecting them (Taneja, 2013: 211). Thus, competition between data brokers seems contingent to their clients finding themselves 'properly' and productively represented in the enumerations produced. Precisely because different data brokers seek to gratify the particular desires of their clients, it becomes difficult for the enumeration business to generate standardized, comparable metrics.

Invisibility matters

The presence of competing data providers with competing measures (hypothetically) promises to tide over challenges of trust and answerability. But this still leaves out the all-important issue of the opacity of their enumerations. This immediately conjures imaginations of the proverbial 'invisible hand' in the orchestration of the media economy. The paradox here is about the invisibility of protocols that purportedly bring visibility to media audiences. There is therefore a compelling argument of impediments to enumerative accountability arising from the lack of transparency over enumerative practices.[3]

TRAI's latest recommendations are weak on this aspect, despite it noting anxieties of stakeholders on matters of transparency and accountability in BARC's protocols (TRAI, 2020: 5). Elsewhere, media policy was obliged to engage with practices of brokers of audience data. A landmark moment was the Congressional Harris Committee hearings in the US during the early 1960s, which involved systematic investigation into the purpose, practices and fidelity of audience research. Its immediate institutional outcome was an industry-funded organization to accredit, audit and review ratings agencies, the Broadcast Rating Council, subsequently rechristened the Media Ratings Council (MRC). Most significantly, the MRC accredited different third party data brokers and intermediaries for particular metrics. Thus Google, Facebook and Comscore, among others, are accredited to MRC for a particular set of metrics generated by them, rather than everything they generate.[4]

The MRC holds learnings for audits and other institutional oversight processes in India. In 2020, TRAI recommended changes to BARC's board structure, oversight committee, and the methodology adopted when concerns over neutrality and reliability were raised. Despite superficial changes, including diktats on government nominees on the oversight committee, there is a refusal to adopt statutory processes akin to those resulting from the Harris Committee. The risks imparted by the lack of oversight are compounded by existing audits being outside the purview of the Right to Information, to which only government bodies are subject to. We may only speculate whether this hurdle would have been adequately overcome if a public authority – say, the TRAI or the Ministry of Consumer Affairs – had played some role in co-producing ratings data. If oversight cannot be enforced with BARC, it is difficult to visualize oversight the enumerative practices of data brokers operating from outside Indian jurisdiction. Just as brokers of TV ratings have kept their protocols opaque, so have digital intermediaries and social media platforms. The lack of visibility into and oversight on such practices has impacted the state's own resource allocations. Government advertising and public service messaging on online news outlets, dogged by legacy issues of bias and accountability as they are, is based on measurements from ComScore India, one such trans-national data broker.

Power matters

The opacity of enumerations and lack of oversight have spawned a cacophony of claims, and counterclaims, about the behaviour of online news audiences. But impediments to enumerative accountability is not only about matters of accuracy and reliability; it is about the enterprise of evidence based policy research relying on enumerations generated by entities with significant stakes (that is, other than in the news business) in the online economy.

In the trajectory of the media economy the distance between those being measured and those performing the measurement – that is, respectively between publishers and enumerators, or between platforms and intermediaries – appears to get increasingly wilted. In fact, what augments the worrisome opacity of measurements is the overlap of enumerators of and participants in the media economy. With TV ratings we observed both pursuits involving an overlapping set of actors. That is to say, the interests coming together in producing TV ratings are the ones likely to benefit from it, as evident in the legal and managerial constitution of BARC. Similar is the case with digital intermediaries who are both enumerators and beneficiaries of the online media economy. Both pursuits hinge around the ability and power of gaining legibility of the audience. Nielsen collects data supplied by Facebook, YouTube and Hulu in compiling its online viewership statistics. That organizations selling advertising are the ones measuring their own viewership is what precisely precipitates concerns of enumerative accountability. These concerns vary from over-reporting as with Facebook (Jackson, 2016) to misleading audience metrics by YouTube (Keller, 2018). From such a vantage point enumerative accountability gets posited as a normative matter, that of public oversight on the knowledge informing the design of public interest regulation.

The ability to generate a bouquet of currencies, offering actors to leverage knowledge for different strategic ends, stands as a key competitive strength in the enumeration business. Possessing such a capability in complex regimes of legibility, that is, through the use of algorithms, imparts commercial power to providers of data. Thus, the question of monopoly in the enumeration business raises different challenges when measures and metrics are produced not by third parties, but by actors central to the online media economy, such as intermediaries. Intermediaries are consequent actors in the business of enumerating audiences while also possessing high stakes in the production and business processes of the online economy. In fact, their role and efficacy as enumerators of the news market relies upon them being agents of discovery and distribution in the news business. Since Google brings 32 per cent traffic to online news outlets in India (Aneez et al, 2019), it plays a pivotal role in marketing certain types of audience measures. That this could call for impediments to mobilize usable evidence being posited in the wider field of competition regulation, is something worthwhile to at least theoretically pursue.

Rights matter

Audience labour offers a productive vantage point to further thresh out aspects of enumerative accountability in the online media economy. The emergence of advertising driven television had triggered extensive debate in media studies on the audience commodity (see Smythe, 1977). Not only do audiences expend labour, to recall this argument, in consuming media products, but such content is the surplus generated by audiences after labouring to consume advertisements. The audience commodity debate spiralled into a different orbit with online interactive media, irrespective of whether scholars reiterate or question the original proposition (see respectively Fuchs, 2012 and Caraway, 2011). Discussions on users' rights and ownership of their data are but one dimension of this. A deeper proposition would be about the contribution of users in building the edifice of the entire information economy (see Manzerolle, 2010). This contention talks to subsequent conceptions of the role of users' labour in producing what we identified as representational and operational metrics (see Bolin and Velkova, 2020: 1198). Although enumerative accountability in the former is most immediate to this chapter, aspects of the latter are no less relevant. In both, the efficacy of algorithms generating metrics depend on the labour produced by online users. This provides a pathway to frame ongoing contests on privacy and transparency around online data within older debates on media labour. This includes the rights of audience vis-à-vis those of enumerators and media companies, both of whom harvest surplus by the labour of audience.

Efforts to develop 'independent' enumeration and sources of data face the challenge of potentially violating the platforms' terms of service or privacy agreements with users, and, furthermore, require developing complex methods to investigate highly unstable objects of research (Hunt and McKelvey, 2019: 317). The point is not only about the desire for this but also about such decisions being a matter of public deliberation and record. Connected to this are techniques of online audience measurement that are aimed at surveillance. At one level, arguments about the efficacy of these techniques end up valorizing surveillance (see Caraway, 2011). The tension between gathering evidence about audiences and the risks of surveillance is visible in recent debates on data protection in India. The revised data protection Bill empowers the government to direct, in consultation with the Data Protection Authority, data fiduciaries to hand over anonymized personal data or other non-personal data for the purpose of 'evidence-based policy making', without any clarity on such an avowedly empirical approach (Sinha and Basu, 2019). This offers further thrust to protocols of measurement in the online economy being a crucial object of public scrutiny and deliberation, thereby reiterating my claim of considering enumerative accountability as a public value.

Conclusion

Ongoing debates on digital markets have largely responded to economic, political and regulatory anxieties catalysed by platformization (Van Dijck et al 2018). However, a thick examination of the economic lives of platforms, as this volume endeavours, would also require historically contextualizing the platform phenomenon. One avenue to pursue this, as attempted in this chapter, is to locate the dynamics of and relationships between dominant actors in digital news markets in the historical development of legacy news markets. This provides a sense of the ways in which the platform economy has reconfigured the dynamics of the traditional media economy.

Over the preceding pages I have delved into this matter by taking up the case of the enumeration of news audiences in India. What makes India particularly significant is it inhabits one of the largest markets for newspapers and linear broadcasting while also proving to be one of the fastest growing online news markets. No doubt the business of enumerating audiences in digital markets embodies practices, strategies and intent that are vastly different from that in legacy markets. Yet, a prominent continuity is the persistence of enumerative accountability, propelled by heightening concerns over transparency, trust, and market power in the 'measurement business'. These concerns echo and intersect a wider set of anxieties in ongoing debates on platform regulation.

The question commonly raised in debates on media regulation is whether platforms ought to gain thick insights into users' behaviour and lives — be it to provide them better recommendations, or provide advertisers deeper competitive intelligence. This, in turn, evokes questions about the knowability of such enumerations. However, in this essay I have been interested in another question of equal urgency in media policy studies: the kinds of accountability entailing, and constraining, practices of knowability. I see this rather fundamental to those arguing over the first set of questions.

This chapter has provided an array of empirical, normative and ideological reasons to think about the latter question — what I posed as the problem of enumerative accountability. Our overview of audience measurement practices in segments of the news business, especially their continuities across comprehending readers, speculating viewers and curating audiences, provide a compelling ground to think about enumerative accountability. Since the functional and structural impediments to such accountability are located in the political economy of the media business, it is time to explicitly confront this longstanding knot in policymaking. That matters of enumerative accountability are intertwined with other knots on the high table of policymaking in the era of algorithms brings added urgency to such efforts.

Notes

[1] National Readership Survey Council in India consists of members from the INS (Indian Newspaper Society), AAAI (Advertising Associations of India) and ABC (Audit Bureau of Circulation).

[2] Beyond rudimentary metrics on TV Ratings available on BARC's website, researchers are obliged to purchase (select) granular/vertical information such as, 'Television Viewership in Thousands' or TVT and 'Average Minute Audience' or AMA for viewership, and 'Insertions' for advertisers.

[3] Here one is reminded of frameworks developed for algorithmic transparency in journalism, that is, the disclosure of information about algorithms to enable interested parties, including audience, to monitor, check, criticize or intervene (Diakopoulos and Koliska, 2017: 81).

[4] See www.mediaratingcouncil.org/Accredited%20Services.htm

5

Voice Intelligence and the Future of Engagement Metrics on Commercial Platforms

Joseph Turow

The rise of smart speakers as digital platforms marks a new era in the relationship between marketers and their audiences.[1] From the beginning of the commercial internet around 1994, marketers have used audio and audiovisual technologies predominantly in one-way commercial messages. In the years after the introduction of Siri on Apple phones in 2010 (with other phone manufacturers following with their own voice-driven assistants), marketers and academics encouraged people to speak rather than type when online and on apps (see, for example, Spector, 2013; Stanford University, 2016; Philips, 2022). The emphasis on speaking has accelerated during the past several years, as smart speakers that encourage a 'voice first' mindset have made their way into tens of millions of homes. The rise of voice-driven platforms and the marketing intelligence they provide points to a future of personalized biometric engagement that will reshape the ways marketers consider and interact with individuals. Voice comprises only one form of this sort of engagement, and smart speakers comprise only one form of platform. The companies that centre on marketing and voice are part of a complex of organizations I call the voice intelligence industry – a business built by marketers to collect information from the ways individuals talk and sound. The industry raises profound concerns about media, audience metrics and democracy that will inevitably apply to other types of personalized biometric engagement.

The aim of this chapter is to use the emergence of voice intelligence marketing in the US to present concepts that help explore these concerns and their implications for the individual and society. As this volume's editors point out in their introduction platform processes are not universal and need to be 'provincialized' – that is, explored with an eye to the history and current context of the societies in which they are studied. So, for example, Vibodh Parthasarathi's chapter in this volume presents an analysis of the history of the anxiety surrounding India's news industry's construction and counting of audiences. He speaks of continuities and changes of enumeration approaches and justifications of audience enumeration from the broadcast era to the era of digital platforms. In this chapter, I explore the approaches and justifications driving the understanding and enumeration of audiences in a new platform, smart speakers, within the US context. My work is based on systematically searching for and reviewing thousands of articles about voice technologies, smart speakers and the firms involved with them. Using Factiva and LexisNexis, I searched for those articles in trade magazines such as *Advertising Age*, *AdWeek*, *Variety* and *Mediapost* as well as general publications such as the *New York Times*, *Washington Post*, *Wall Street Journal*, *Wired*, *The Verge*, *Quartz* and *Business Insider*. I also searched online for blog posts regarding voice technologies on Amazon, Apple and Google sites, specialty sites such as Voice.ai and commentaries on activist sites such as the Electronic Frontier Foundation, Center for Digital Democracy and the Electronic Privacy Information Center. I reviewed dozens of patents regarding voice technologies through the US Patent Office website. I attended an important voice industry conference where developers showed off their newest voice apps and discussed emerging trends. In addition, I interviewed 44 marketing executives and technology experts whose names I learned through my readings and conference attendance. They kindly spent from half an hour to over an hour and a quarter answering my questions about the complex technologies, business policies and government policies that are guiding the voice intelligence industry's approaches to audiences.

I organized and analysed all this information in accordance with key themes that I noted. Based on this research, I will describe the new metrics of engagement and explore how these developments affect not just marketers but the media system and society at large. Although my US findings may not map onto the voice-intelligence worlds of other societies, they may point to questions and dynamics that researchers could valuably ask across various social and industrial contexts. I especially want to present seven theoretical constructs that might be malleable to exploring other societal environments: *voice-first platform*, *the industrial construction of audiences*, *unending spiral of personalization*, *seductive surveillance*, *habituation*, *resignation*, and *the hidden curriculum* reflect ideas about the development and audience acceptance of new metrics that should have legs beyond the US situation. The *industrial construction of audiences* is a process I have been calling attention to for over a decade (see Turow, 2005 and Turow, 2011). Digital resignation is a social phenomenon that colleagues and I introduced in 2015 and has been adopted by others (Turow, Draper, and Hennessy, 2015). *Voice-first platform* is a term used within the voice intelligence (see Dasika, 2018), and the *unending spiral of personalization* is a concept that developed with this project. Seductive surveillance, habituation and the hidden curriculum are ideas others I will note have put forward that fit well with the industrial dynamics I have observed. A theme of this chapter is that taken together these terms can become part of a vocabulary that researchers who study biometric interrogations on platforms around the world can use to compare and contrast findings.

The emerging voice intelligence industry

Marketers' increasing interest in the consumer's voice during the first two decades of the twenty-first century relates to its alleged uniqueness. What people say is important, but who they *are* through their voice is biometric – a part of their body that can be used to identify them instantly and permanently. And because a person's voice belongs to no one else, it's extraordinarily valuable, not only to its owner but also to a new sector of society that is designed to exploit it: the voice intelligence industry. Led by companies the public knows well, such as Amazon and Google, and firms most people do not know, such as NICE and Cognito, this industry is deploying immense resources and breakthrough technologies in order to analyse your speech patterns and vocal-cord sounds for information about your emotions, sentiments, and personality characteristics, all so that companies can better persuade individuals, often in in real time. Soon marketers may be able to draw conclusions about an individual's weight, height, age, ethnicity and more – all characteristics that scientists believe are revealed by that person's voice. Companies will be able to score individuals as more or less valuable, show them different products based on that valuation, give them discounts that are better or worse than the ones they give other people and treat them better or worse than others when they want help. In other words, marketers will be able to voice data to model ways to discriminate between them and others in unprecedented, powerful ways.

The emerging voice intelligence industry involves such tools as smart speakers, car information systems, customer service calls and 'connected-home' devices like thermostats and alarms. When you talk, their 'intelligent assistants' can draw inferences about you using analytical formulas generated by artificial intelligence. In the United States and the European Union, the best-known vehicles for such activities are Amazon's Alexa, Google Assistant and Apple's Siri. In China, Baidu is doing it with its DuerOS voice assistant, and Tencent with Xiaowei. Each carries out its work through tens of millions of smart speakers (WiFi linked audio devices), smartphones and car audio systems. Google Assistant, accessed mostly through smartphones and Google Home cylinders, is now available in more than a billion devices (Bohn, 2019). Amazon claims that its Alexa personal assistant is present in 'hundreds of millions' of devices (Bhattacharya, 2017). A different, though related, ecosystem of firms is creating voice initiatives propelled by artificial intelligence in customer contact centres (Rubin, 2020).

Public attention to the voice industry has centred primarily on smart speakers such as the Echo and Google Home. These are cylinders (or more recently other shapes) that sometimes come with screens. Ask a question or make a request, and the devices can access a wealth of information sources through app-like add-ons contributed by thousands of companies, nonprofits and even individuals. The industry representatives I interviewed noted that owners most typically use the voice apps to check the weather, set timers, learn recipes, listen to music, play games, ask facts and buy things. In the United States the explosion of smart-speaker sales began around 2014 with the introduction of Amazon's Echo and its assistant, Alexa. The Google Home came out about a year and a half later, and then smart speakers from other firms came tumbling out. Apple and Samsung used preexisting assistants (Siri for Apple, Bixby for Samsung), and companies like Sonos built speakers that link to Alexa or Google Assistant, or both. Press attention during this period has see-sawed between the latest capabilities built into these devices and the new social dangers they represent. Many stories centre on Alexa or Google Assistant's ability to 'listen' and then answer. The gizmo starts recording whenever it hears the wake word ('Alexa', 'Hey Google', 'Siri'), and it tracks sound for up to 60 seconds each time. Ask 'Alexa, what's the temperature in Chicago?' and a woman's voice (which you can change to male) will provide a direct response. Try 'Hey Google, how many plays did Shakespeare write?' and a female voice (which you can also change to male) will give a concise (and correct) answer (37) along with two sentences that elaborate.

Amazon and Google, the highest-profile forces in voice today, are not yet using the maximum marketing potential of these tools, including voice-profiling patents they own, evidently because they are worried about inflaming social fears around the collection of people's voices. But contact centres, which are out of the public eye and thus more audacious about profiling people based on how they talk, may represent the future. As people get used to giving up their voice virtually everywhere, stores, banks and other sellers that develop their own voice assistants will have fewer qualms about exploiting what their customers say and how they say it. Google and Amazon may ultimately feel compelled to join them.

Rise of the voice-first platform

To understand the allure that marketers see in biometric engagement through voice, it is useful to begin with the term *voice-first platform*. A fairly common term within the voice intelligence industry, a voice-first platform denotes a combination of hardware and software that its creators – marketing firms – use primarily to engage audiences via voice. Increasingly, smart speakers come with video displays. The industry refers to these as voice-*first* platforms because the main form of interaction, and the main driver of video presentations, takes place through the voice. A signal characteristic of platforms that Tarleton Gillespie (2018: 24) points out is they typically present themselves (falsely, he notes) as open to all comers – 'a neutral piece of scaffolding for user agency', as this book's editors describe it (p 6). Think of popular internet properties that scholars and industry practitioners call platforms – for example, Facebook, Google Search, Twitter, YouTube, TikTok, WhatsApp – and it becomes clear that the firms that own them allege that everyone is welcome. This approach is the opposite of non-platform media firms in analogue or digital form – for example, the *New York Times*, the CBS Television Network, the Warner Bros film company. They perform complex filtering activities to accept very few of those who want to be part of their products. As it turns out, while platforms present a rhetoric of being open to everyone, they do treat different comers differently. The most discussed example is 'moderation', where a platform removes certain posts, and even contributors, in response to various social controversies. Nevertheless, the rhetoric of platforms, as opposed to non-platform media, is that anyone can enter, contribute and interact with the material. This swarm of engagements provide the fodder for the overwhelming way platforms make money. Drawing huge audiences to participate in activities without explicitly charging them, the platforms use computerized exchanges to help advertisers target individuals based on multiple datapoints about them, including what they do on the sites. The platforms also offer 'attribution' technologies that are supposed to allow the advertisers to learn whether the ads were successful. These dual sets of metrics lie at the heart of the platforms' business models (Turow, 2011; Crain, 2021).

But it is at this juncture of engagement and proof of the engagement's worth that the Achilles' heel of contemporary platform metrics become evident. On the surface, the ability to target audiences and attribute success to the target message surpasses any advertising medium that preceded the internet. The accomplishment typically involves specialists in data mining, logistical regression, and cloud computing to track people's everyday activities via 'the little data breadcrumbs that you leave behind you as you move around the world', in the words of MIT computer science professor Alex Pentland (Edge, 2014). This puts to commercial use former CEO of Google Eric Schmidt's comment that the information Google collects on individuals enables it to know 'roughly who you are, roughly what you care about, roughly who your friends are' – to the extent that it knows its customers better than they know themselves (Jenkins, 2018).

The glitch in this personalized nirvana is revealed by Schmidt's use of the word 'roughly'. Put bluntly, the data about people and their behaviour that companies bring together are sometimes wildly inaccurate. The secret worry of internet marketing – a view that burst into the open during the 2010s – is that tracking, profiling and targeting are fraught with challenges for the entire digital ecosystem. Data may not be up to date, profiles may be created based on multiple users of a computer or phone, names may be confused and people may lie about their age, income or even gender to confuse digital marketers.

Advertisers are also uneasy with the well-known problems of click fraud and ad blocking. 'Click fraud' takes place in pay-per-click advertising when the owners of digital locales that post ads on a domain are paid according to the number of visitors to those domains who click on the ads. The fraud happens when a site or app owner pays people, or create an automated script, to click on ads to accumulate money deceptively. 'Ad blocking' is using software (less commonly, computer hardware) to remove advertising content from a webpage or app. While industry players debate the specific reasons for these activities and have tried a variety of solutions, they agree that they cause substantial economic losses. A 2018 study by Adobe found that as much as 28 per cent of all website ad traffic was click fraud (Bruell, 2018). A 2017 report by the Juniper consultancy projected just 9 per cent for 2018, but even that lower proportion would cost the industry about $19 billion despite major attempts to combat it. Juniper estimated that by 2022, ad fraud would cost the industry $44 billion annually (Juniper, 2017). As for ad blocking, eMarketer found in 2018 that one quarter of all US internet users – 71 million people – block ads on at least one device a regular basis. The firm added that this 'share will continue to rise as consumers express frustration with their digital advertising experiences' (Perrin, 2018).

The hope for a new chance at audience knowledge is what leads to the *unending spiral of personalization*. Marketers believe that to remain competitive, they must gather as much data as possible about current and prospective customers and send them individualized messages and product offerings. Yet because of the very nature of this work, marketers never feel they are doing enough to know their targets and reach them efficiently. They will always be looking ahead to technologies like voice intelligence that promise new forms of information made possible by greater intrusions into people's lives. That is, today's new technology will soon also fail to satisfy the drive to uncover deeper knowledge of the customer, leading to the next innovation – for instance, linking voice intelligence to even more intrusive technologies. In view of this perspective, the unending spiral of personalization is the guiding spirit behind the new marketing order.

Currently, using voice to infer emotions is the centrepiece of this process. 'Reading human emotions and then adapting consumer experiences to these emotions in real time' will 'help to transform the face of marketing', says an executive from Affectiva, a consultancy spun off from MIT (Shapiro, 2016). Executives in the call services business also see voice-driven personalization as marking a new era, with emotions analytics at its heart. The CEO of Clarabridge, a provider of phone response technology, foresees that new voice technologies will help identify 'key indicators' of a particular caller's loyalty 'such as effort, emotion, sentiment and intent'. The head of another firm asserts that 'this drive to personalization is already benefitting from using artificial intelligence to learn deeper meanings in what people say' (Business Wire, 2018).

The development reflects what Vibodh Parthasarathi in this volume notes is 'a whole new qualitative and quantitative order in the trajectories of visibility and knowability'. He points out that the new forms of 'enumerative accountability' include biometric identification systems used by media platforms as well as government entities. He underscores that the work – and interplay – of both marketers and state actors (government officials) of interrogating their populations biometrically raises 'uncomfortable questions of accountability and transparency'. The focus here is on the corporate activities surrounding voice intelligence, though, as Parthasarathi suggests, the enumerative activities in the one societal sphere will inevitably the other when it comes to understanding and controlling large populations.

Voice, AI and the industrial construction of audiences

In the US, companies large and small are rushing to shape the voice-intelligence frontier of personalization. To do it they are creating a new metrics agenda: mining customers' voices using computer-driven artificial intelligence processes with the customer having only the dimmest understanding of what is taking place. The hallmark of this new world is what we might call the *industrial construction of audiences*. Our ideas of who we are will come from the efforts of many organizations working together, often for platforms such as smart speakers. Some firms will provide software, others hardware, others data about individuals – all to create personalized profiling that will predict our commercial value in any given situation. The guiding principle among the executives I interviewed in the voice intelligence industry – and reflected in the technologies they are developing – is that the new gold in people's speech is not in what they say but how they say it, and how they sound when they say it. A common way of getting to the metrics involves artificial intelligence – specifically machine learning based on samples called training sets. Take two labelled training sets – say, one of people who are nervous and one of people who aren't – and feed the data to an algorithm, a dynamic formula that is designed to detect patterns among a large number of data points about speech: tones, speed, emphases, pauses and much more. Some of these speech characteristics are so complex that only a computer with particular instructions could detect them. Say the algorithm learns to pick up the subtle signs that indicate (at a certain level of statistical confidence) whether a speaker is part of the nervous or non-nervous group, and that it can do the same with new samples in the future. A next step might be to determine whether the nervous-sounding group is more likely to buy certain products, default on loans, or do other things that marketers would find important. Still further steps might involve linking those findings to other knowledge about the individuals. It is possible that adding information about gender, geography and jobs, for example, could add to the ability to predict whether a nervous person is more likely to buy certain foods, take certain vacations, or return products often.

There are other, more complex versions of this approach to metrics. One family of methods, deep learning, uses algorithms in multiple layers that try to find patterns in different aspects of the phenomenon; say one layer concentrates on the waveband frequencies of the voice and another on the ways syllables are used. These patterns are then analysed together to draw conclusions about the whole. Optimists about voice profiling point to attempts by healthcare providers to detect diseases such as Parkinson's or post-traumatic stress disorder (NYU Langone Health, 2018; Dao et al, 2022). Characteristics of a person's voice may even indicate suicide risk, according to a team led by Louis-Philippe Morency, a computer scientist at Carnegie Mellon University. Morency's group tentatively concluded that if people who have attempted suicide have 'a soft, breathy voice', they are more likely to reattempt than those 'with tense or angry voices' (Chen, 2019). Such efforts are intriguing, but scientists are at the beginning of a long road, with many questions ahead about the accuracy of their results and whether factors like the instruments they are using or other circumstances of testing, rather than the voice itself, could be influencing their findings. Another concern is the confidence level: how statistically significant should the findings be before they activate social programmes – for example, to check the voices of people who have attempted suicide? Should 90 per cent confidence be enough for getting a voiceprint and potentially disrupting someone's life, or should 99 per cent be required? And lurking behind all the results is a worry about algorithmic bias: that if the training sets are not large or diverse enough, the conclusions reached might not reflect the entire population and may even lead to discrimination (Kearns and Roth, 2019; Kordzadeh and Ghasemaghaei, 2021). Consider, for example, if the training set of suicide attempters did not include people whose voices have always been breathy, regardless of their mental state. If a social policy based on voice tagged them as suicide repeaters, it might cause unnecessary trauma for them and their loved ones. These sorts of discrimination often relate indirectly to race and gender. Kate Crawford and Ryan Calo are two of many observers who argue that machine learning inevitably introduces race and gender biases (Crawford and Calo, 2016).

Despite these cautions, businesses have been moving into voice intelligence. For example, Amazon and Google smart speakers can identify the voices of individuals in a household. Spotify holds a patent that asserts its ability to profile a person based on age, ethnicity, and other characteristics when the person asks for songs. Beginning in 2020 Amazon distributed a Halo health and wellness band that would be able to analyse the tone of its owner's voice, 'qualities ... like energy and positivity' to tell the owner how they sound to the owner's boss, spouse, friends and others. The company asserted that the Halo's security features made its analysis off-limits to anyone but the person speaking; the voice profile, too, was explicitly not for use by third parties (Amazon, nd). Yet it is hard not to understand the Halo's professed capability as a proof of concept. Even though the fitness product does appear to have sold well – distribution stopped in 2023 (Welch, 2023) – the entire voice profiling idea of the Halo can easily be ported to the marketing realm and beyond, as Amazon's and Google's voice-profiling patents explicitly assert.

Moreover, voice profiling already goes beyond what Amazon and Google do. The customer phone service (or 'contact centre') business was first out of the gate in profiting from individuals' unique voices. Contact centre firms such as Callminer, Neuraswitch, and Verint already evaluate a caller's sounds and linguistic patterns for emotion, sentiment and personality (Callminer, nd; Verint, nd). Executives from contact centre firms noted in interviews with the author as well as in firm publicity that linking those biometrics with the caller's name, the firms regularly tell reps how to respond to customers who supposedly reflect certain emotions or personality characteristics in their voice (see Turow, 2021: 90–96). For example, contact centre software routinely shunts customers pegged as 'talkative' to reps with a track record of getting along with such people and of getting them to spend extra money ('upselling' them). 'Today we're able to generate a complete personality profile', said the CEO of Voicesense, which claims to be able to use people's voiceprints to accurately predict loan defaults, people's likelihood of filing insurance claims and customers' investment styles, among other key indicators (Chen, 2019). The head of the CallMiner call analytics firm was just as bold. 'Our vision is to empower organizations to extract meaningful and actionable intelligence from their customer conversations', he stated. 'AI has become a cornerstone of providing those capabilities with efficiency and scale' (Bernard, 2018). The CEO of voice-emotion detection start-up Beyond Verbal summed up the claim and implied the ambition. 'Nearly two decades of research', he asserted, 'tells us that it's not what someone says, but how they say it, that tells the full story' (Vrankulj, 2013).

The corporate uses of seductive surveillance, habituation, and resignation

This overview may suggest that such discriminatory personalization by marketers would make many people nervous. In the US heightened concerns about privacy and data losses speckle the news and pepper the talk of lawmakers (for an overview of public issues centring on privacy, surveillance, and choice, see Turow, Lelkes, Draper, and Waldman, 2023). Wouldn't an effort to push the voice intelligence on American society cause a furore, even if the industry doesn't show all its cards? Few people currently know that when they call customer service there is a decent chance that how they are treated will be partly based on a computer analysis of their voice. But eventually the industry's cover will be blown. So it makes sense that the voice intelligence executives at Amazon, Google, Apple, Samsung, Bank of America and other companies should already be thinking about this nervous environment. They surely know, for example, about Gartner's 2018 finding, reported in the *Wall Street Journal*, that 63 per cent of four thousand people surveyed in the United Kingdom and United States 'didn't want AI to be constantly listening to get to know them' (McCormick, 2019).

That's where *seductive surveillance* enters the picture. Pinelopi Troullinou (2017) coined the term in her 2017 doctoral dissertation to explain why people 'willingly' participate in activities that allow organizations such as cell phone companies to keep tabs on them. The phrase describes an effort to present target audiences with packages of devices, prices and possibilities that are attractive enough to overcome any concern they might feel about the marketing surveillance carried out through those devices. And since surveillance drives personalization, it follows that marketing-oriented firms with an interest in personalized inferences based on voice want to create an environment that keeps people buying and operating the devices despite any gnawing surveillance concerns.

Amazon and Google both reportedly sell their smart speakers at a loss, with the hope that in the future marketing and advertising through them will more than make up the difference. The prices can be attractive. During sales periods in the early 2020s, Amazon sold its Echo device for substantially less than $30. Moreover, it appears voice executives understand that the best way to do this is to turn people's use of voice assistant devices into a widely accepted habit. To academics this is a familiar tack. The twentieth-century French sociologist Pierre Bourdieu famously used the term *habitus* to describe a person's mindset regarding the carrying out of routine activities – that is, habits (Maton, 2008). He asked, 'How can behavior be regulated without being the product of obedience to rules?' His answer was that regularized behaviour results from a person's interactions with social position ('capital') and the goings on in society ('the field'). These forces are not static; changes in a person's social position and in what governments or companies do can affect the person's mindset in particular ways. Bourdieu's key point (quoted by Maton, 2008) is that a person's mindset is both shaped by outside forces ('the field structures the habitus'), and once internalized, helps a person understand and accept the logic of the institutional forces that created it ('habitus contributes to constituting the field as a meaningful world').

The sociologists Tony Bennett and Francis Dodsworth (2013) believe that Bourdieu's concept of habitus is useful in understanding how people become socialized into acting predictably in the world, but that a major limitation in his writings is that he focuses on the individual's habitus – what and how people think systematically about the world – while paying little attention to the ways companies, governments, and other 'material agencies' shape the mindset and the habits that flow from it. Bennett and Dodsworth argue that an understanding of 'the processes through which habits are formed and reformed' must take into account their relation to a wide range of material things in society, from the effect of schoolroom desks on young students' routines to the ways that specific logistical models in a company influence how employees handle shipping. They use the term *habituation* to refer to the process by which forces in society cultivate the creation of habits.

It's not hard to see how habituation and seductive surveillance are linked. Seductive surveillance is a dual strategy – a balancing act – by which companies get people in the habit of using voice across a range of devices. Troullinou (2017: 48) suggests how this seduction works in ways that allow organizations to keep tabs on individuals. With phones, she writes, 'the user is seduced by discourses of convenience, efficiency and entertainment into handing over personal data, and thus being transformed into a subject of surveillance'. She quotes two researchers who say that designing a seductive product 'involves a promise and a connection with the audience or users' goals and emotions' and suggests that 'seduction operates at multiple levels, from technology to marketing discourses and governance (p 54). Though she doesn't specifically mention the phone's voice assistants, the generalization would presumably apply to them, too.

This focus on seduction provides a useful beginning for exploring how companies persuade people to regularly speak to devices even as they are uneasy about the implications. The academic and trade literature says much less about how firms play down surveillance in order to reduce users' concerns. Communication professor James Katz (quoted in Trillinou, 2017: 13) suggests that 'over time people get inured' to being tracked and profiled. It's an important insight, but it doesn't explain why people didn't resist actively before they became inured. One answer is that from the start, companies try to stop people from learning what's taking place. This is a refrain that shows up often when researchers explore how companies with other types of technology relate to the public. For example, Sarah Roberts

(2018), writing about social media firms, suggests that the platforms cultivate an 'operating logic of opacity' that discourages users from trying to engage with these systems. Nora Draper and I (2019) have written about the features of language that internet firms use to cover up the surveillance they are enabling. One common approach is placation, where a firm appeases customers by assuring them it cares about their privacy – often in ways that bear no relation to what is described in the privacy policy. Another approach is diversion or trying to get customers not to pay attention to disclosures about information use. You know about this approach if you've ever tried to find a website or app's privacy policy; it's in tiny letters at the bottom of the page or way down in choices on the app. If you actually attempt to read the policy, you'll find that it's often full of jargon, as if it were deliberately written to confuse and discourage the reader.

Draper and I (2019) argue that these routine corporate practices not only obscure what the companies are doing; over time, and as habituation develops, they encourage a sense of *resignation* – a feeling among users that even though they would like profiling not to happen, they can't do anything about it. Such feelings of resignation showed up in research by a team from the Annenberg School for Communication in 2017 and 2018. From a representative telephone (cell and wireline) survey of the US population, we characterized 58 per cent of respondents in 2017 and 63 per cent in 2018 as resigned based on their agreement with two statements: 'I want control over what marketers can learn about me online' and 'I've come to accept that I have little control over what marketers can learn about me online.' We also explored Americans' sense of resignation – as opposed to whether they believe in trading data for benefits in a calculated way – through questions about supermarket shopping and loyalty programmes. We found, for example, that a large proportion of Americans – 43 per cent – say they would let supermarkets collect data about them despite indications elsewhere in the survey that they disagree with consumer surveillance. We also found that the more they know about the laws and practices of digital marketing, the more likely Americans are to be resigned.

Following our report, a few other studies (for example, Hargittai and Marwick, 2016; Hoffman et al, 2016; Marwick and Hargittai, 2018) identified related sentiments, reinforcing our finding that many people are resigned to companies' use of individual data. The voice intelligence industry appears to cultivate resignation as a way to play down press concerns about surveillance. The industry's recurring theme is that giving up your voice for activities in and out of the home is inexpensive, convenient, fun, emotionally satisfying and natural – even if it can make you feel nervous and unable to control information about yourself. Voice technologies are also touted as offering increased choice and personal efficiency – the very definition of individual sovereignty in modern times.

Voice-assistant platforms, marketers and personal freedom

My interviews with marketers in major advertising agencies revealed that advertisers, clearly intent on playing a central role in this marketplace that is still developing, are creating new personalization strategies, tied to new ways for gaining consumer consent, for the voice era. The MediaPost trade bulletin reflected this sense of urgency. 'Relax, it's still early days', said a columnist, who then warned 'but the voice revolution is moving quickly!' (Kounine, 2019). If they get what they want, the power of marketers to redefine key metrics as centring on voice – responding successfully to people through both what they say and how they say it – will transform what it means to say anything in public – and some seemingly private – spaces. The public policy questions that emerge from these developments are substantial.

For example, the voice assistant's central purpose as a marketing tool complicates the idea of personal freedom in alarming ways. By design, buying into voice-intelligence technologies seduces you to relinquish the sovereignty of this part of your body to provide a new type of metric to marketers. The aim is that companies can use it to audit you, assess your value, and perhaps discriminate against you in ways you may never learn of or understand. But it's not just the opportunities for discrimination that should worry us about these new platform metrics. Smart-speaker platforms have become the epicentre of 'conversational' interactions between individuals and thermostats, lights, as well as other smart-home devices in the most private space coveted by marketers, the home. Beyond any specific persuasive message people may receive, the habituation that Amazon, Google, and Apple are encouraging together with voice-driven firms such as Samsung (general appliances), Phillips (lighting), Lutron (smart light switches) and LG (for voice-activated television programming) are beginning to create a new *hidden curriculum* for American society – teaching people that giving up your voice is part of what it means to get along in the twenty-first century. Educational sociologist Philip Jackson coined hidden curriculum during the 1960s to describe how schools implicitly lay out norms and values that are crucial for navigating the outside world (see Martin, 1976). Communication scholar George Gerbner convincingly generalized this sort of implicit education to the media. He argues that 'culture powers' from business, government, education, medicine, the military, and other areas of society deeply influence widely shared media views of reality. Their power to affect this hidden curriculum, he points out, 'is the ability to define the rules of the game of life that most members of a society take for granted' (Gerbner, 1973: 71).

It's no great stretch to see how the idea of a hidden curriculum can apply to the voice marketing relationships people learn to consider normal, even if they are resigned to them. It also makes sense that once people accede that *giving up your voice is part of what it means to get along in the twenty-first century* when it comes to marketing, they will accept the idea when it's applied to other key areas of contemporary life – for example, political campaigns, asylum seekers and prisons. Here we see examples of the interpenetrations of commercial marketing and government spheres that Parthasarathi suggests via his historical analysis. Consider that in New York, Texas, Florida and other states officials are paying Securus Technologies and Global Tel Link to extract and digitize the voices of incarcerated individuals and the people they speak with over the phone. The technology was created for the US Department of Defense 'to identify terrorist calls out the millions of calls made to and from the United States every day' (Joseph and Nathan, 2019). Hiring those firms, prison authorities ushered hundreds of thousands of incarcerated people's voice prints into large-scale biometric databases. Securus and Global Tel Link algorithms then analyse the databases to identify the individuals taking part in a call, and to understand the networks of calls the individuals made. In some jurisdictions – New York is one – the software analyses the voices of people receiving the calls 'to track which outsiders speak to multiple prisoners regularly' (Joseph and Nathan, 2019). Wardens see the biometric identifications as ways to be sure that prisoners won't make calls using other prisoners' PINS and that and that they are not speaking to formerly incarcerated prisoners in patterns that suggest illegal activities. Prisoners' rights advocates worry that people who were never incarcerated (for example, family members) are having their voice prints ensnared, and they point out that state corrections agencies seldom mention the voice print databases to inmates and their families. Jerome Greco, a forensics attorney at New York's Legal Aid Society told journalists 'Once the data exists, and it becomes part of what's happening, it's very hard to protect it or limit its use in the future' (Joseph and Nathan, 2019).

Unlike addresses, driving licence numbers and app activities that comprise just a few of the 'demographic' metrics that signal contemporary individuals to marketers, biometric markers such as voice are enduring and typically unchangeable. In that respect, the voice intelligence industry represents a new form of market-driven individuation, one guided by elements of people's bodies of which they have little control except – perhaps – to give permission for their use as data. This chapter argued how in the US *the industrial construction of audiences, unending spiral of personalization, seductive surveillance, habituation, resignation* and *the hidden curriculum* form an interrelated web of marketing activities that continually identify new ways to think about individuals, get permission from individuals to do that, and then discriminate among them based on the findings. At present, voice-first biometric platforms are emerging for marketing, partly because of advertisers' concern that traditional audience-personalization categories are no longer adequate. Next, marketers may accelerate their use of facial recognition, with increasingly sophisticated use of generative artificial intelligence, in home and car platforms as markers of engagement and profiling metrics. People's gaits and their head movements during conversation may be other areas of marketing/AI interest. Can the solicitation of personal urine or blood swatches encouraged through seductive payments of cash, internet subscriptions or product discounts on 'free' platforms be that far behind?

Note

[1] This chapter contains excerpts from various chapters of the author's book *The Voice Catchers* (New Haven, CT: Yale University Press, 2021). Yale University Press has kindly consented to the use of this material here.

6

Brokering Data Markets: The Agentive Power of App Builders at the Edge of Platforms

Eva Iris Otto

The mobile app economy is premised on the work of intermediaries like the Danish app agency Monocle, which build apps for and upon the frameworks of Big Tech platform companies while selling apps to local markets. Recently, the integration of advertising and user data into apps has further integrated Big Tech platform companies into the app economy. Analyses touching upon the relationship between intermediaries and platform companies tend to posit this relation as either symbiotic or exploitative, in both instances neglecting the agentive power of local app developers. This, however, glosses over the crucial work of brokerage that such intermediaries perform in liaising with and translating between different markets. This chapter shifts the perspective to the intermediaries and their role as triadic brokers as they navigate spaces of opaqueness, and highlights how companies such as Monocle give shape to software materialities and user-data entities when brokering between local markets and transnational economies dominated by multinational platform companies.

App developers and Big Tech platform companies

Platform companies are closely intertwined with the rise of data collection and transnational user-data economies. At the same time the production of mobile applications (apps) is both premised on and closely intertwined with the world's largest platform companies, multinationals such as Alphabet[1] and Apple. Platform companies have, since the beginnings of mobile app development, regulated key aspects of the production of apps. Recently, with the rapid expansion of the collection of user data, a number of platform companies, among these Alphabet and Meta,[2] have become integrated even further into the app economy through providing services for user data collection, 'helping', as they like to present it, app developers to 'maximize the surplus value they can extract from apps, while simultaneously expanding their own service infrastructure' (Blanke and Pybus, 2020: 2). As the preoccupation with user data grows – within the world of app development as much as anywhere else – so does the power of platform companies grow with it.

This chapter concerns the tripartite relation between Big Tech platforms,[3] local app-developing companies and their customer companies catering for local markets. By focusing on the mundane app development work of a Danish agency in the context Danish markets, I demonstrate how such local app developers become the intermediaries between multinational platforms facilitating the tools, frameworks and publishing stores for building the app (and data) infrastructures at the one end, and local companies buying apps at the other end.[4] This chapter thereby contributes an empirically derived perspective on platforms from what can be considered the edges or provinces of platforms and the way they integrate and expand in a specific situated regional contexts. Current literature variously posits app developers and developing companies as either exploited labour, under the thumb of Big Tech platform companies who control the important tools of production, or as part of a symbiotic relationship with platforms, all feasting on the value of personal user data. While these two perspectives contribute important insights into the political economic context of app development and app economies, they tend to overlook the important agential work that app developers conduct in brokering between local markets and transnational economies, in the process translating local market concerns and the business models and technical frameworks of platforms.

To nuance these more overall political economic – and often quite theoretical and abstract – perspectives, I therefore bring an empirically derived argument, based on long-term ethnographic fieldwork within the Danish app agency Monocle,[5] which develops apps for private companies and public organizations in Denmark and northern Europe. Few empirical studies have attended to the everyday work of making apps within app and data markets. The present study, by focusing on the local app developers as brokers, brings complexity and nuance to established perspectives on platforms and user data economies. According to anthropologist Johan Lindquest, 'the metaphor of transnational flow needs to be specified empirically and brokers are critical in this process' (2015: 872). Indeed, I argue, the figure and the concept of the broker offers a privileged point from which to analyse contemporary platform economies. By disaggregating and attending closely to the multiple markets (geographically and typographically) that an app company such as Monocle brokers, this chapter contributes to current perspectives on platform and data economies by showing how local app developers simultaneously expand and curb the reach of platforms in local user data markets and profit while doing so. To understand the type of brokerage that Monocle – as representative of its peers in the field – engages in, I introduce the notion of a *triadic brokerage*.

Thus, as indicated my answer to the call of this volume to 'provincialize' the platform is to shift attention to the work that happens at the boundaries of platforms, while also highlighting practices in a specific regional province: Denmark and northern Europe. This perspective enables me to nuance both the power and reach of platforms, as well as offer fresh insight into how – in concrete practice – the business models of platforms become embedded into daily app development practice by a crucial group of brokers working to align ideals about data and software materialities between markets.

Brokerage: bringing the intermediary into focus

As noted, existing work on app and data economies tend to present the relation between intermediaries such as Monocle and Big Tech platform companies as either symbiotic or exploitative. According to media scholars Michael Daubs and Vincent Manzerolle (2016), for example, the global app economy is dominated by the duopoly of Apple and Alphabet, which together own most of the operating systems, facilitate the 'tools' of production (such as the coding frameworks in which to produce apps) and, importantly, control the market places in which apps are published. This setup of the app economy as a market model echoes the sixteenth-century mercantile 'putting out' system:

> In this system, 'a merchant "puts out" work: he provides the artisan with the raw materials and a part wage, the remainder paid on delivery of the finished product' (Braudel, 1979, p. 316). The historical expression of this system, Braudel (1979, p. 321) notes, provides the 'first hard evidence of a merchant capitalism which was intended to dominate though not transform craft production'. (Daubs and Manzerolle, 2016: 56)

According to this line of argument the cognitive and creative labour of app development is subsumed by large platform companies playing the merchants in a model resembling mercantile-era logics. By facilitating the tools for production, but outsourcing the cost for materials, infrastructure, skills development and social security structures, platform companies optimize their own revenue while minimizing risk and leaving developers with limited rewards, in effect exploiting developers' work

(Dyer-Whiteford, 2014; Daubs and Manzerolle, 2016). Such an analysis echoes wider analyses of platform companies and their engagement in modes of organization that entail the exploitation of labour of others (that is, described under terms such as cognitive capitalism [that is, Parikka, 2014], platform capitalism [that is, Srnicek, 2016; Langley and Leyson, 2017; Kenney and Zysman, 2020] and surveillance capitalism [that is, Zuboff, 2019]). While platform companies try to outsource risks, this is also requires constant adaption, as illustrated by the analysis of Gregersen and Ørmen (this volume), who demonstrate how YouTube try to control which users and producers they ideally want, to avoid crises of legitimacy. In the case of app development, we might note that Apple and Alphabet thereby also control the relationships with producers such as app developers differently. Such perspectives on outsourcing and control contribute important insights into the larger political economic power dependencies between smaller actors such as local app developers and large multinational platform companies. However, how these smaller actors navigate such dependencies in their everyday work is still underexplored, leading to the need for empirical studies such as this chapter.

While one (Marxist inspired) strand of literature posits app developers as subsumed under the platform duopoly of Alphabet and Apple, another strand of work, oriented more towards data economies, sees the app developers themselves as part of an exploitative ecosystem that profits from extracting data from users. This gathering of user data has for instance been described an 'accumulation by dispossession' (Fourcade and Kluttz, 2020) highlighting the extractive logic of the system. Many have argued that user data has become a new form of capital restructuring economic power balances in the twenty-first century (for example, Van Dijk, 2014; Zuboff, 2019; Birch et al, 2021). User data is, for many of the platform companies, integral to their rapid growth and expanding influence. Apart from a few significant exceptions (such as Fourcade and Kluttz, 2020), in these existing studies smaller entrepreneurs and app makers are reduced to two (stereo)-typical roles. One is as the powerless part in processes of user-data extraction, akin to the type of analysis of centring on platforms further up. The other considers app developers and smaller entrepreneurs more as a (frictionless) part of the system of user data extraction, dominated by the larger platform companies. For instance Tobias Blanke and Jennifer Pybus (2020) demonstrate how large digital advertising platform companies – Alphabet and Meta especially – integrate themselves into the mobile app market by a logic of decentralization of 'distributed services' such as software development kits that help app developers implement functions such as user data tracking or ads. According to them platform companies manage to present this as a way to increase the value of apps for their developers, while at the same time expanding their own reach (Blanke and Pybus, 2020).

To summarize, the general takeaway point that is shared across these different critical studies of data and platform economies, local app developers like Monocle are posited as either exploited by or symbiotically part of platform ecologies and the processes by which they extract user data, depending on whether the analysis focuses on developers' labour, or on the technical code processes by which user data is created and extracted. While both of these takes carry important insights into the market mechanisms of platforms and their relation to intermediaries, they fail to recognize the spaces for manoeuvre that intermediaries in situated app economies navigate, and the power they have to shape the concrete software materiality of user data economies. While important, then, the agency of actors such as Monocle is not recognized through these current approaches. Putting these political economic and critical data perspectives in dialogue with a long anthropological tradition of engagement with the *broker*, however, will allow to me to attend to the significant work that intermediaries such as Monocle do between transnational and local contexts. Indeed, as I show, much creativity occurs in the gaps between transnational user-data economies and local user data markets.

To do this, I draw on a long anthropological engagement with brokers. Anthropologists such as Eric Wolf (1956) and Clifford Geertz (1960) first highlighted the particular position of the broker as a person able to navigate and connect local and transnational relations and thereby make a profit. Wolf, for instance, describes the broker as able to 'stand guard over the crucial junctures or synapses of relationships which connect the local system to the larger whole' (Wolf, 1956: 1075–6 in Lindquist, 2015). While recent approaches to brokerage have gone in many directions (Lindquist, 2015), one line of more recent work on the broker, from an actor-network theory perspective, has refined the conceptual work of brokers as not only engaged in human mediation but also linking and translating non-human relations (Hobbis and Hobbis, 2020). In this perspective brokers are considered part of infrastructural junctions. Following this line of conceptualization, I attend closely to the work of Monocle when building software materialities at the interstices of multinational platform companies and local markets. Introducing the earlier anthropological concept of the broker therefore fundamentally contributes to denaturalize the place of platforms in local markets. The perspective of the broker is well situated to attend to the generative work of intermediaries such as Monocle in building particular kinds of software entities and shaping valuations of user data in turn shape the different socio-material markets in which they work. It calls for attention to empirical studies of local contexts that can recast perspectives on the reach and power of platforms and data economies while relating it to the work done by actors such as Monocle to variously realign, further or curb this reach in the interstices of markets. Below, to contextualize my analysis of Monocle's brokerage work, I briefly outline the position they occupy in the Danish digital landscape.

Situating Monocle: the middlemen

As mentioned, Monocle is highly dependent on the frameworks and marketplaces of multinational platform companies for their production of native apps in the app economy, while also being embedded in local markets, constrained by local legal structures and imbued by local valuations. Denmark's advanced degree of digitization and dependence on digital infrastructure, for both private and public markets, shapes the general work of Monocle as an app developer. In Denmark, digitization is often described as a 'growth motor' of the future (Petersen, 2018) and the Danish government likes to present Denmark as a digitized and digitally literate country (Erhvervsministeriet, 2021). This digitization agenda is generally met with optimism (Digitaliseringspartnerskabet, 2021) and both state actors, such as the Danish digitization agency, and private sector actors such as the Danish industry association, push for increased digitization (for example, Dansk Industri, 2021; Digitaliseringspartnerskabet, 2021). This drive for digitization has furthered the market for digital services – from websites and apps to AI solutions. At the same time, as part of the European Union, Denmark is regulated by the newly implemented general data protection regulation, which has raised concern with the collection and use of user data by private citizens, companies and institutions. In short, the Danish context is shaped by an optimistic approach to digitization and a well-supported digital infrastructure, on the one hand, and a growing preoccupation with personal user data as something that should be managed correctly and carefully, on the other hand.

Within this context, a range of agencies, bureaus and software companies operate to design and develop apps for a local app market of private companies and public organizations in Denmark, influenced by the values and restraints of the above context. Providers for this localized app market range from multinational software corporations with hundreds of employees, through medium-size companies with employee counts in the tens to the smallest one-person companies. What they have in common is that they cater to organizations (which I refer to as customers within this chapter) whose primary product or service is usually non-digital, but which are becoming increasingly digitized as part of a larger transformation within the public and private sector, including turning to custom-built apps.

Monocle is situated among the agencies and software companies facilitating this digitization. I conducted long-term in-depth fieldwork within Monocle from June 2020 to October 2021, focusing on the daily practices by which such companies build apps for the Danish market.

For this chapter I build on observations of everyday work in offline and online settings concerning sales, design and coding, many informal talks with employees next to the computer and over ubiquitous coffee breaks, observations of sales meetings, webinars and a series of formal interviews with the CEO during the 14 months in which I followed their work. To contextualize, I draw on participation in sector events and conferences in the period 2020–21, as well as national reports and sector publications. Monocle mainly sells apps to a market of Danish customers, with expansions into Scandinavia and Germany.

While the work of Monocle as a digital agency in Denmark caters to a transformation strongly supported by national interests, Denmark is also a relatively peripheral market for the digital developments of Big Tech related to smartphones. The population is not large enough to command a serious outlay from Apple or Alphabet, coupled with language barriers for the uptake of English software. This is a source of frustration for Monocle, which is fully premised on the frameworks, tools and marketplaces of Big Tech actors. Notably, developer features such as speech recognition for use within apps, announced at the white shiny events of Apple, are not applicable to Danish consumers. Such frictions created by the integration and dependence of this regional context on what are at heart American Big tech platform companies, highlights how specific geographical elements such as language barriers also in quite mundane ways form what platforms are to people in the transnational economic 'provinces' of platforms. The reach of platforms, as I will expand below, is shaped by very specific technological, (for instance language recognition) and economic and cultural conditions (see Yuan and Zhang, this volume).

Local data-brokering, a triadic relation

While Monocle has to deal with the unavailability of services geared for its specific local context, it still subscribes to many of the idealizations about data that align with the services offered by multinationals that are available in a Danish context. In fact the employees at Monocle contribute to the valuation of user data, and in the process Monocle also fashions itself as a particular type of expert. As the CEO of Monocle described it to me animatedly: 'currently we are the hands and feet, but we need to get the head in there also' (*Lige nu leverer vi hænder og fødder men vi skal have hovedet med*). By this he explained to me that more value lies with being able to facilitate user data to their customers – what he called facilitate 'the head' – rather than the software production of the app, or the 'hands and feet'. While a lonely swallow does not a summer make, this, was by no means a single occurrence. In fact, the idea that the future of app development lies in user data permeates Monocle's explicit value proposition to customers, its webinars and sales pitches and the strategic decisions it made. In webinars, Monocle would highlight how user data – for instance, based on previous purchase history – would help personalize the app experience, while also facilitating customer loyalty. In presentations the sales consultant would point out that with an app – as opposed to a website – 'you (the customer) have full control over your data'. Throughout the year in which I did fieldwork, Monocle successfully worked on getting an agreement with a data analytics company for which they would develop the mobile software developer kits that would enable Monocle to make the packages that other app-developing companies could use to collect user data. This strategic collaboration allowed Monocle, as the CTO phrased it, 'to be the expert' on facilitating that service to potential customers. As an extra bonus, it made Monocle partners with a data-collection company, which would refer new customers. In short, being able to collect and visualize user data for its customers is seen as the way towards creating value and selling successful apps that customers would want by the people at Monocle. Collecting and using user data is considered the future of developing app solutions by Monocle as well as the customers it builds them for.

This expertise is practised on a discursive level, but it is also a more implicit part of the work practices of Monocle. To illustrate, let me turn to the process of building an app for the company SkinBeauty, which I will use as a case to illustrate my argument around brokerage in the rest of this chapter. Each second Monday, project leader Christian and the head of the digital project at SkinBeauty, Anne, meet up to discuss any current tasks and questions of new features and developments related to the app and back-office system that Monocle is making for the beauty clinic:

> Meeting online today, they take off at the current meeting based on a longer conversation that has been running through previous meetings and emails. SkinBeauty wants 'some statistics for the app'. At the last meeting, Christian asked Anne to detail exactly which statistics they would like. Because as the back-end developer of Monocle, Jonathan, explained to both her and me: ' I can definitely make up some statistics, but those are not necessarily the ones you want.' Then he continued 'Statistics can be a small or huge task, depending on what you want'. Anne promised to return with an email describing exactly what they wanted after her own meeting with the CEO of SkinBeauty.
>
> Now Christian is making sure that they are in alignment, before taking the tasks to the developers. SkinBeauty had not specified statistics as part of the original project. It is therefore a new wish – from the perspective of Monocle – to have user-statistics with the app.
>
> Christian goes directly to comment on the latest email that Anne has sent him with their wish-list of the statistics they would prefer.

'I have looked at your list. Some of the things you would be able to see in [your own backend] system, others are part of Firebase, which is already part of the project. So it doesn't seem too bad.'

When Anne indicates that she doesn't know what Firebase is, Christian elaborates, 'Firebase is like Google Analytics, just with apps. It is part of setting up the app project – so you have statistics in there.

'Things like daily, weekly and monthly active users will be part of what you can see there,' he elaborates, adding 'which pages the users visit, and how they move through the app' will be included too.

App development is like a patchwork quilt of packages of code that app developers build into apps. These packages typically ensure particular functions. Some packages come from open source. However, increasingly packages within apps are bought or built by platform companies, such as Alphabet and Meta (see Blanke and Pybus, 2020; Lai and Flensborg, 2020). Among these is Firebase, owned by Alphabet since 2014 and mentioned in the short interchange above. Firebase is now a 'backend-as-a-service' for mobile development that facilitates a host of functions such as data synchronization, app notifications and authentications. In the example above, the user data analytics of app use that Firebase facilitates are the most relevant. In practice, including a package like Firebase is a bit like following a complicated cake recipe (see Figure 6.1). It is standard for developers to include packages in their app project and involves writing specific lines of code that sets up a user at Firebase and creates a unique ID which then connects the app to the Firebase framework.

Firebase has become a routine element within Monocle's apps. The attraction of Firebase to developers at Monocle comes partly from the type of entity that Firebase is. It entails a host of services, not just user-data collection but also crash detection, and thereby integrates functions that developers consider elemental for building good apps. The overlapping of user data gathering with more general data-gathering of app-functionality, relates user data statistics to basic understandings by developers of how to build well-crafted apps. However the inclusion of Firebase as a standard – unless customers want otherwise – by Monocle also facilitates statistics of useful user data for Monocle. Such statistics are not only considered valuable by the customer – in this instance SkinBeauty – but by Monocle as well, since it uses them in performance statistics illustrating the success of their apps to sell new apps. Being able to show a high download statistic for their previous app, for instance, or that they build apps for a large number of weekly users, is a selling point they use actively to generate trust in meetings with new clients. In effect, Monocle thereby brokers a connection between (a) the customer's desires for user data, for instance in order to sell

Figure 6.1: Screenshot of the way Firebase provides information for developers on how to integrate Firebase into their code projects

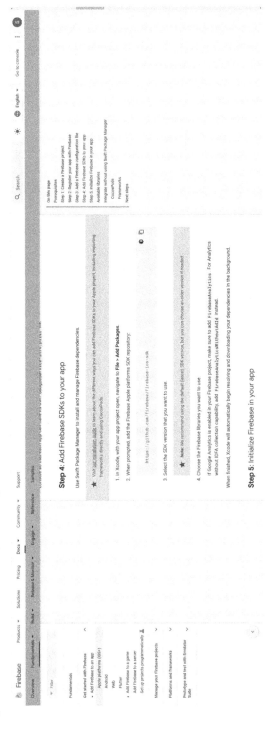

Source: https://firebase.google.com/docs/ios/setup?authuser=0#analytics-enabled (Accessed 31 January 2023)

more beauty products; (b) their own interests in and uses of the same user data for selling more apps; and (c) the transnational user-data economies of multinational platform companies, which also benefit from this development. They thereby connect three different markets by the relatively simple act of building Firebase into the app project. For Monocle it is a double bonus since it is both paid for the act of building it, and benefits from the user data statistics Firebase generates.

While materially expanding the reach of platforms services into local markets, Monocle does this while framing itself as an expert in a particular fashion. As I showed above, it positions itself as the 'facilitator' of statistics. As Jonathan says, statistics can be many things depending on what 'the customer wants'. In a sense they distribute the responsibilities of 'wanting data', a practice they harbour some suspicions about. Instead, Monocle likes to position itself outwardly as the technical expert that can deliver 'whatever the customer wants', frequently pointing out that of course it can build x, y and z, the only factor being how much the customer is willing to pay. Through repeating phrases of this nature, it creates and maintains the impression that the technology is completely malleable to the market interests of customers, on the one hand. On the other hand, Monocle constantly puts forth suggestions for how a customer such as SkinBeauty could build and expand its use of user statistics. While deferring to a customer's specific concerns or needs, Monocle will put forth suggestions and templates, based on its interpretation of both 'what the customer wants' but also what it perceives as good app-building practice, thereby more subtly trying to direct how customers expand their collection of user data.

In these templates, services such as Firebase tend to fall within the standard model, subtly being positioned as part of the technical expertise Monocle possesses rather than as statistics that can 'be made up'. To understand such a categorization we need to have a precise understanding of the field of app makers to which Monocle turns for making its own assessments of good app-making practices, as and what are accepted measures of success for app development. As CEO Morten put it to me while illustrating the way particular measures act as standardized measures of app success: "First, the only metric of interest was downloads, but that doesn't tell you much about how many people actually *use* the app. It is only recently that this [daily, weekly, monthly users] became the established standard – the mobile market is moving so swiftly." Monocle looks to other app makers, both in Denmark and abroad, to find 'the established standard' and adjusts its understanding of what good app development is, as well as what kind of measures can credibly measure app success.

As such, the interconnected position in which Monocle refers to others 'like us' for its evaluations of what good app development entails, creates in a sense a brokerage field of app-developing companies. Commonly, brokerage is described as either a binary relation, where the broker is the middle person between local levels and everything beyond that, whether national or transnational – or, in newer brokerage literature, as a figure linking infrastructures or networks (for example, Hobbis and Hobbis, 2020). However, to fully capture the kind of brokerage in which Monocle engages, it must instead be envisioned as a tripartite relation, with each direction different in kind from the others. Between customers and multinational platforms Monocle brokers the implementation of service packages through their skills and expertise. As such, it brokers between local data markets and transnational user-data economies. However, it shapes its expertise in relation to a (local) app market – which, in turn, shapes the valuations and ideals that Monocle employs in its daily brokerage work. To fully grasp this relation, I suggest we think of the kind of brokerage relation Monocle engages in as triadic.

The nature of triadic data-brokering: navigating opaque spaces

Brokering data is a practice of continuous adjustment in Monocle's daily work. On the one hand, the policy environment in Denmark and Europe is continuously developing, and on the other hand the technical platforms that Monocle builds onto are subject to frequent changes. While brokers in anthropological literature have been conceptualized as Janus-faced characters – mainly because their knowledge base and position can be *opaque* from the outside – here I want to stress that the brokerage work that Monocle engages in is itself characterized by constantly negotiating spaces of opaqueness, as opposed to opacity.[6] Let me first turn to two situations to illustrate the role opaqueness plays in the workings of Monocle. These situations centre on two types of activities, one concerning the concrete considerations of coding platform services into the app project and the second concerning compliance with the General Data Protection Regulation (GDPR).

Technical integration of different packages, platforms and services is a continual challenge within software development because it is difficult to foresee the effects of merging systems and the time it will take to integrate third parties. Therefore developers tend to prefer adding packages which they know are easy to integrate with the packages they already use. They know this is the tactic that platform companies also capitalize on. One Android developer at Monocle described the effects of Firebase's sales strategy like this: "It is free for the first number of servers or apps, and then when you reach a certain number it costs a bit. And then it is clever to get some of their other products, because they integrate well. And in this way you slowly get more and more."

Developers are usually unable to access the base code of services from platforms and thereby see exactly how the packages work; instead they must work through interfaces commonly described as Application Programming Interfaces (APIs). This is in effect what Firebase in the above example offers. Developers routinely have to work around this by testing the effects of what they implement and making sure that the system does 'what it is supposed to'. Part of this happens by literally clicking through apps, trying out settings and relying on the log code that shows what is happening in the app while running the app. Other tactics involve testing whether data points arrive in the tracking services, or using existing third-party frameworks to analyse the systems. Such packages thereby become opaque spaces, or black boxes (Seaver, 2019), within the app. Developers can see their effects but have no access to how they work internally. Opaqueness also relates to the level of control that Monocle has over the user data it procures for its customers. Data services allow Monocle to access user data in specific ways. These specific ways have effects on the future possibilities for getting user data with an app. Let me turn to an example in which Jonathan is scoping the integration of using Firebase to get user data for SkinBeauty.

One week after the meeting with Anne, Christian has arranged a meeting with the back-end developer Jonathan to estimate the time it would take to implement the statistics Anne and SkinBeauty want, so that she can assess whether offering the statistics is worth the extra cost in developer hours. In addition to the daily, weekly, monthly statistics mentioned before, Anne and SkinBeauty want two other measurables: the number of app users using a so-called 'surgical operation track' and the number using the loyalty-system of rewards the app facilitates. The following is from the last part of the meeting between Jonathan and Christian:

> Jonathan reiterates what he has already mentioned once, describing the way he envisions procuring the different statistics: 'I'll get the bottom ones [daily, monthly, weekly users and downloads] from BigQuery, which will get the data from Firebase, and the top ones [other statistics] we will get from the database.' Christian asks if instead it would be possible to get all statistics directly from the database. According to Jonathan, this is not possible, due to the way the database is set up and the system is built. But when Jonathan suggests he could change things in the system to get that data, Christian quickly shuts down the possibility of changing the system. 'No, that is what Firebase is for.'
>
> Jonathan interjects: 'The only thing with Firebase is that it is anonymous data. It gives a nice overview, but doesn't let you know who it is.'
>
> Christian, imagining the range of future use for the system, follows with: 'One could imagine that if you pressed on the Operations or

Loyalty, [envisioning these numbers as pressable buttons] then you would get to a list of which users it contained.' Jonathan, agreeing from a technical point of view, adds: 'You could definitely envision that in time.'

He continues, 'But daily, weekly, monthly active users – there I think the number is from the ones using the app continuously, but for example don't use the rewards they get in the app. That is data we don't have. That is something we must get from Firebase.'

Jonathan continues, 'those [the operations and loyalty statistics] are not graphs, just numbers. Interface wise it is quite simple. So [it wouldn't take] more than 5 hours to make it.' A pause, thinking, then: 'The other thing – daily, weekly etc. That would need to be set up. It is funny that I have never worked with BigQuery [API from which to get data], but I imagine we can steal from the other project. It isn't the same but it is similar. And then there is quite some design [making the graphs]. I am thinking I will use this specific program to make the graph' ... The crucial point is that I don't know how long it will take me to get a hold of the data.'

Within this situation, first opaqueness lies in scoping the size of the task. In discussing the specific data construction, the reliance on Firebase for certain tasks becomes clear, and also shapes the specific types of data entities that can be created (or tracked). The routine inclusion of Firebase in the project leaves Jonathan with the ability to get daily, weekly, monthly users – but only in anonymous form, a second form of opaqueness. While it might be technically feasible to get the measures in a different way and create a different data entity – as Jonathan alludes to by describing how he could restructure the database – it is not feasible according to Christian, whose role it is to keep the project on track in terms of cost and time. Project and market logics lead to a technological 'lock-in' of the ways that Monocle builds data-tracking (for statistics), which has implications for what it can do later in terms of building user-data collection. In this particular situation, for instance, they discuss the way they can use the data configuration through which they get statistics of loyalty and surgical operations, which correlates directly with a user, to later target specific users. The statistics based on the data configuration that Firebase offers does not allow for a direct reference between a statistic and an individual user – ironically, in this situation Google protects the privacy of the individual from the perspective of Monocle and SkinBeauty. In effect, the process by which user data is collected by the service Monocle uses has black-boxed the data for it.

While the code packages or service packages that platform companies as material infrastructure provide are black boxes to the developers at Monocle, platform companies also act as opaque entities from the perspective of

Monocle in a legal sense. With the implementation of GDPR in a European context, all companies that store or process user data must comply with a host of regulations meant to protect users from companies aimlessly collecting and storing data. Effectively, this means that either Monocle or its customers – depending on who is the data owner – must have data agreements with all the subcontractors it uses for storing or handling user data, including data-tracking services like Firebase. Further, the data owner is responsible for following up on the data-processor companies it uses. Through the legal requirements of GDPR, Monocle, and consequently its customers, are forced to consider the service providers as companies that they choose to make – or not make – contracts with.

In such processes, customers express varying feelings of responsibility concerning data processing. Turning to SkinBeauty, they expressed more concern than other customers about data practices and their responsibilities. When Monocle initially made a list of the companies that provided services for the app, Anne pointed out that these were many. She took them to the data officer at SkinBeauty, and over the course of some meetings and talks with the CTO at Monocle, SkinBeauty ended up shortening the list by using services from the same company instead of using more specialized services. Thereby they engaged in a trade-off where they spent more resources on developer time to set up the storage and user-data handling systems for the perceived safety of using fewer companies for data processing. However, it was not only the *number* of companies potentially acting as data-processors that facilitated this reduction. Rather, as Anne expressed to Jonathan and Anders about the company they ended up choosing, Amazon: it was a *large* platform company, which was *well-known*, had *many other customers* (like themselves) and would *therefore probably be more likely* to have their data practices in order.

From the perspective of Monocle and its customer, the data practices of potential services providers are legal spaces of opaqueness that potentially affect their own legal responsibilities to their customers. With the evaluation of service providers forced by GDPR, breadth in terms of services gives an advantage, as well as being a company that is big and well known. The imperative to trust the data processor prods customers to look at what their peers do. In practice, these tendencies favour large, well-known platforms that can deliver hosts of services over smaller fry that rely more heavily on open source, which developers had tended to favour.

To understand the types of opaque spaces Monocle and its customers navigate, it is necessary to conceptualize platforms and their services as both companies and software-material relations, at least in the way that they present in Monocle's everyday work. As the introduction of this volume describes (Gregersen et al this volume) academic literature has considered platforms as variously a material structure, a type of company and as an overarching economic framework. To understand the nature of brokerage in which Monocle engages, we need to consider how platforms appear both as companies and as material structures of software, separately and together. While the types of opaqueness might be different, the fundamental type of navigation – in relation to both platform companies and their software materialities – entails navigating opaque spaces. This, as we saw in the examples above, does not stop Monocle from using them and building on top of them. It does, however, shape the way coding works and the way legal considerations take place.

Lastly and notably, opaqueness leaves ample space for suspicions concerning user-data practices of platforms among Monocle and its customers. While the suspicions of Anne and SkinBeauty are clearly exemplified by them choosing not to trust the smaller vendors, suspicions about data practices among Monocle's developers are often expressed on a discursive level. Either by categorizing Google as the more morally suspicious company, because 'they live off of your data', as one developer put it, or by ascribing such suspicions to customers, such as when one developer explained to me about Firebase services: 'It is just a really good service, but sometimes customers don't want to use it because of the data part.' In spite of the ambiguity and lingering suspicions ascribed to 'the data part', generally these services are seen as part of the game when developing apps forming part of the foundation or technical infrastructure. However, while suspicions concerning the ability or desire to stick to 'good data practices' can affect changes in the way that platform services are brokered by Monocle, such as in the case of SkinBeauty, more commonly other market concerns are the limiting factor for the expansion of platform services. To illustrate this, let me turn to one more closeup of the process by which SkinBeauty developed user statistics.

Brokers limiting the pervasiveness of platform services

The collective valuing of user data that Monocle reinforces through its webinars and sales pitches means that at times the types of user statistics that customers want fall entirely outside the services that platform companies deliver. This could be due to the specific functions of an app, because greater control over the data is desired, or to secure specific affordances of the data, or simply because it is easier to get the data directly from the database. The preoccupation with user data among Danish market role-players, and the linking of user data with avenues for future value by both its customers and Monocle, fosters interest in measurables that go beyond the standard daily, weekly and monthly user statistics. As Bruno Latour describes, brokers do not merely 'carry meaning' (Latour, 2005); they reshape and reform meaning, and are 'also producers of the kind of society in which they re-emerge' (James, 2011: 319 in Hobbis and Hobbis, 2020).

Going back to Anne and Christian's discussion about the types of statistics that SkinBeauty wants for the app, the importance of ease and specificity of the app is clearly present when they discuss the measures of loyalty and operations that Jonathan and Christian were scoping above.

> Christian moves on with the list in the email, elaborating on the other statistics SkinBeauty would like. 'It's not so much ... amount of users of the operations track and loyalty programs and such things. Those are specific things that would be easier to make in the app, than to make Firebase do it.' Anne points out that between the different types of statistics, these last ones are the interesting ones to them. 'These relate to our KPIs' [Key Performance Indicators]. 'We know that many who get an operation go and get filler or Botox somewhere else. The idea with the app is to get people into the loyalty program. So I want to be able to see who from the surgical operation track goes over to use the loyalty track.'

Part of the push for user data is based on more localized market concerns and constraints, such as the interest in keeping people from getting filler somewhere else or the concerns with GDPR, which together make local user data markets, geographically and typographically (type of customers) distinct. The services by multinational platform companies only partly align with the interests in local data markets, and in the gap between the two, Monocle navigates and builds user data flows in different ways. The brokerage from Monocle here changes from a triadic relation to a more classic dyadic relation, by brokering in such instances between the local data and the local app markets that Monocle is embedded in. Local data markets thereby also curb the expansion of platform services. Such practices point to the fact that local data markets not only occupy a space distinct from platforms, but can and do proliferate beyond their reach – in this case through the work of the app company Monocle.

Anne Mette Thorhauge (this volume) introduces the useful concept of tangled markets in relation to platforms. In her chapter, she describes the way value translates across both formal and informal markets made possible through particular software configurations and business choices of the gaming platform Steam. In comparison with her case, the local and global data and app markets that Monocle connects through the practices of integrating packages for collecting user statistics are separate markets that can exist without each other; however, the brokerage work of Monocle can be considered a form of entanglement of these markets. In their work they build routes for value translations. With strongly entangled markets the power and reach of platform companies over time might become bigger, but as should be clear from this chapter, whether such entanglement work can be successful depends both on continuous work of brokerage and developments in local values and legal frameworks.

Conclusion

In this chapter, I have considered how intermediaries such as Monocle broker the ideas and software that enable user-data flows from apps made for local, non-digitally premised companies to multinational platform companies. As mentioned, anthropologists studying global-local relations have pointed to the significance of brokers for understanding these relations, nuancing our understanding of transnational flows. While Blanke and Pybus (2020) show the expansion of the integration of platforms into apps, and thereby the growing level of dependency, my study considers the processes in app development and local markets that prompt developers to use, or not use, such platform services. As code has not – yet – found a way to autonomously make code, these actors are crucial for understanding the overall market dynamics through which a process like platform monopolization occurs.

To fully understand the workings of Monocle, I argue we must consider them part of a brokerage triad, instead of the common dyadic conception of brokerage work. In this triad, they engage with a market of other app makers that function as their competitors, prompting the use of user data as an evaluative measure of an app's success but which also embody a professional feedback field, giving direction as to what good app development is. Further, they engage with a fast-growing local data market, and increasingly engage in gathering and using user data specifically for Danish companies. And lastly, they engage with multinational platform companies that facilitate services through which user data can be collected, aggregated and visualized. These platform companies form part of transnational data economies in which data is increasingly valorized and linked to processes of assetization (see Birch et al, 2021). As such there is a connection between my argument and Manzerolle's chapter (this volume), in which he points out how 'media materialities … support particular modes of connectivity and related habits of thought' (p 21). Implementing software packages and linking up to platform companies can be seen as creating a particular mode of connectivity essential to platform practices. Complimenting a focus on abstractions and logics, I here turn to more messy everyday practices in the work of brokers such as Monocle, but I echo the overall point of attending to the configuration of the connection between (software) materiality and markets as a way to consider current platforms. Through the work of Monocle, platform companies gain reach through the alignment of their services with local user concerns and valuations. However, in the end, the reason for using or not using platforms is fundamentally the same from the perspective of Monocle and their customers: a high valuation of user data.

Finally what might we contribute to platform studies from this vantage point? One aspect of platforms we can highlight from this vantage point is their perceived dual nature at the edges of their ecologies. Approaching them as material software that is somehow aligned to an uncanny degree with local market concerns and ideals reveals how platforms, when seen as material software structures, become opaque entities. Instead, they need to be approached as black boxes in coding that should be integrated into the app project as seamlessly as possible, through testing and trying. In this instance the platform service piece of code is allowed to exist as a black box – exactly how it executes its commands and what happens downstream in time in the platform-service piece of code, integrated into the app project, is not of concern for linking it into the project at that instance. However, when discussing data agreements, the platform – not as material service and code but as company, and 'responsible' entity – is being considered. It is precisely the multiplicity of platforms, and their successful alignment (in many cases) with local markets, that ensures their entry into a Danish app and data market. It is therefore also no wonder that platforms leave ample space for different analytical approaches (Gregersen et al, this volume).

However, what is also clear from looking at the work of Monocle and their colleagues is the amount of work – still – needed to include platforms for data-gathering purposes into apps. This is not a simple tale of whether platform software services are 'the best' or of developers either blindly believing in the benevolence of platform companies or closing their eyes. However, there is a general sense of distributed responsibility, with it 'being the customer's choice' or 'something the user can choose to react to' and, crucially, a suspicion does not amount to actual harm, and therefore a moral need to 'act' from their perspective. Only some arguments hold weight enough to change practices within local Danish markets.

The practices at the provinces of platforms are thereby more messy than the neat characteristics underlying descriptions of platform capitalism or logics. While this analysis builds on local market concerns in a Danish and Scandinavian context, the premise that localized concerns influence the way multinational entities can and do enter into local processes is a universal one (see Yuan and Zhang, this volume). If we take this point to its furthest conclusion, we should heed how platforms are always provincialized as both situated and variously aligned with local markets. Taking this point to its furthest conclusion, we might in turn ask what an analysis of the situated alignment with local markets would look like in Silicon Valley?

Notes
[1] Alphabet is the parent company of Google.
[2] Meta is the parent company of Facebook.

[3] Big Tech, commonly refers to the dominant information technology companies, based in the US. These include Alphabet (Google), Amazon, Apple, Meta (Facebook) and Microsoft. Most of these are also considered platforms.
[4] Local companies and public institutions in DK increasingly buy apps via app agencies.
[5] In an effort to protect employees, this is a pseudonym, as are all names of employees of Monocle.
[6] "Opacity" is usually used in technical contexts, and invokes a nuance of it being a measurable quantity. "Opaqueness" is normally used when speaking colloquially, and can also be used metaphorically to mean "incomprehensibility resulting from obscurity of meaning" (Merriam-Webster).

7

The Political Economic Process of 'Platformization': The Historical Trajectory of Alibaba

Elaine J. Yuan and Lin Zhang

Introduction

In September 2014, Alibaba Group Holding Limited (Alibaba hereafter) debuted on the New York Stock Exchange with at the time the world's largest ever initial public offering (IPO). The event not only cast the spotlight on the company but also brought attention to China's rising internet industry, as an integral part of the global digital economy (Shen, 2021). In the past two decades since its inception in 1999, Alibaba grew from an e-commerce start-up to a tech Titan permeating many aspects of China's digital economy, from retailing, logistics, finance, cloud computing, to media and entertainment, pharmaceuticals, even smartphone and automobile manufacturing. Indeed, Alibaba has played a crucial role in China's post-2008 economy restructuring that revolves around high-tech and innovation (Hong, 2017; Zhang, 2020a; Shen, 2021). Yet, contrary to the conventional perception that China's digital borders are completely sealed off by the 'Great Firewall', global financial networks, with the acquiescence of the Chinese state, have been playing a significant role in the development of Alibaba throughout the trajectory of its domestic and overseas expansion in the past decades (Hong, 2017; Zhang, 2020a; Shen, 2021).

In November 2020, another much-anticipated IPO of a historic size on both the Hong Kong and Shanghai Stock Exchanges for Ant Group, a FinTech firm growing out of Alibaba' digital payment arm, Alipay, was suddenly halted by the Chinese financial regulators a few days before its schedule. Despite similar recent anti-trust regulations in the US and EU, the sudden turn of the event was widely perceived by the global business community as another sign of Beijing's relentless and widespread crackdown on its private tech sector since late 2020 (for example, Bloomberg, 2021; The Economist, 2021). Popular media had since then been filled with speculation on the fate of Alibaba and its legendary entrepreneur founder, Jack Ma, as a result of the latter's confrontation with the party state (Shen, 2021).

The latest headline news came in late March 2023, when Alibaba announced its largest corporate restructuring in the company's history (Banerjee, 2023; Greeven, 2023). The plan was to adopt a holding company structure while breaking the company's businesses into six independent units,[1] each with their own management structure and potential to pursuit external fundings and future IPO. Although these businesses had been operating separately for several years, and the stated goal of the restructuring was to further realize their market values (McMorrow, 2023), the news was taken as a signal that China was loosening up its regulatory pressure on the tech sector at the crucial conjecture of economic recovery in the aftermath of the COVID-19 pandemic. At the same time, the media speculated that the move paved the way for other Chinese tech giants to undergo similar reorganization to meet Beijing's demand for 'common prosperity' (Banerjee, 2023).

The digital platform as a disruptive innovation seems to have ushered us into a new era of global capitalism (Spencer and Kirchhoff, 2006). In the mainstream discourse, platformization, led by information and communication technology (ICT) driven firms and entrepreneurs, is often conceptualized as a result of a universal process of technologically coordinated market practices. Platforms create new markets by harvest user data through digital technologies such as algorithms and data mining organized by exclusive interfaces and infrastructures (Nieborg and Helmond, 2019). At the same time, platforms decrease barriers of entry for all parties of multiple markets with the strategies of network externality and cross subsidization (Gawer, 2014). In doing so, platforms provide a new way to distribute social economic resources such as capital, labour, and data. Under this framework, platforms such as Alibaba are a result of consistent economic change revolves around innovation, entrepreneurial activities and market power. The growth of platforms as monopolies or oligopolies is an endogenous process of replacing old ways of doing things by new ones.

Through an account of Alibaba's trajectory of development in the past two decades, this chapter argues that platformization, the process in which a company expands into a monopoly or oligopoly in multiple interconnected markets with significant implications for the existing socioeconomic institutions, is not simply a result of applications of digital technology or the reorganization of the corporate structure. Technological features such as network externalities and economic calculations of transaction costs, though they may be necessary, are not the sufficient conditions for platforms to take shape. Digital platforms, as well as the technological and economic discourses associated with them, have emerged from the long-term tendencies of global capitalism at the critical conjunctures of the post-war economic booms and busts (Srnicek, 2016). Their development is premised on widespread and multi-faceted transformations of broad social economic structures, institutions and norms (Athique and Parthasarathi, 2020). Set in this broad framework, this chapter argues that 'the platformization of Chinese society' (De Kloet et al, 2019), exemplified by Alibaba, has taken place as a set of historically and culturally specific processes and relations constituted by constantly shifting and interacting forces in China in responding to the global convergence of technological and economic development (for example, Zhang, 2020a).

A framework for the political economic process of platformization in China

There have been two main perspectives in explaining the rapid growth of China's ICT sector. A market-oriented perspective, mostly propagated by the business community, links the country's ICT leap forward to the application of the Silicon Valley model of entrepreneurship (for example, Wadhwa, 2011 and 2013). This perspective deems market forces a key to the burgeoning internet industry since China's telecoms and related sectors became integrated into the global digital capitalism in the 1990s. In this light, the growth of the private ICT sector was tied to the rise of rational actors, represented by tech entrepreneurs, such as Jack Ma, responding to the changing needs and incentives of the market (for example, Tse, 2016; Anwar, 2017). This view often evaluates China against a yardstick constructed upon liberal market ideals that favour the autonomous individual in the free market and consider the state an impediment to entrepreneurial creativity (Zhang and Yuan, 2022).

A state-centric perspective, in contrast, emphasizes the highly persistent and cohesive role of state governance in China's post-socialist economic development. The fast development of the tech sector has been contingent on the state's drive to transform its economy. Indeed, research on the political economy of China's ICT industry has highlighted the state's active support through favourable and targeted policies, significant investments in public goods (for example, digital infrastructures, basic research and education) and market-oriented institutional reforms (for example, property rights, labour markets, and capital markets and so on). The post-2008 boom has been especially shaped by the state's push for mass entrepreneurship and innovation as part of its effort to restructure the export-heavy economy (Hong, 2017; Li, 2017; Zhang and Yuan, 2022). Meanwhile, the state not only resists the pressures for further liberalization but constitutes viable alternative growth dynamics by continuing its control over foundational economic institutions such as those of labour and finance. Consequently, state-manipulated institutions compel actors to react to challenges in ways that reinforce the state power instead of looking for alternative strategies.

This chapter takes a critical look at Alibaba's historical development in the context of China's accelerated market-oriented reforms and integration in global capitalism since the 1990s. Drawing on the literature on the state/market relation in the Chinese economy (for example, Ang, 2016; Zheng and Huang, 2018), we conceive Alibaba as embedded in a complex constellation of social economic actors including the Chinese state leadership, industrial and local bureaucracies, and public and private economic actors. The main function of Chinese state and its various agencies is to set objectives and mobilize the bureaucracy and economic actors into action (Naughton, 2021). Economic actors, while responding to state policy initiatives and calls, follow predominantly commercial considerations in making decisions (Zheng and Huang, 2018; Shi and Ye, 2021). Moreover, instead of a highly cohesive and strategic actor, the state system driving China's globalized economic development is significantly fragmented in terms of functions and incentives. With different state actors playing differentiated roles, the complex interplay between the leadership, central and local bureaucracies, and public and private firms shapes the domestic institutions, which in turn affect the economic rules, norms, and relations of their interaction (Shi and Ye, 2021).

In line with this conception, we chart a course of Alibaba's growth that is different from either the liberal free market or state-centric accounts. Instead of the rational actors reacting to constraints and incentives of state policies as their external environment, we follow the lead of Herrigel (2010) to posit, economic actors actively create their goals, adjust their interests and define the context in which they act. We show that the evolving interests and goals of Alibaba are not pre-given but emerge out of interactions with other economic actors including the state and bureaucratic agencies about how to understand, define and resolve challenges posed by political and economic developments both home and abroad. While under the common pressures of global capitalism, platforms often employ similar strategies (such as datafication and financialization, more on the topics later) regardless of their localities, they continue to take on considerably different forms that are deeply rooted in their political economic relations (for example, Athique, 2019; Zhang, 2020a). These differences among platforms across the globe, however, are not 'reproduced because institutions (or underlying political economic power relations) constrain actors to respond to challenges in particular ways. Instead, differences are reproduced because actors in very different contexts are creatively responding to challenges in ways that recompose their identities, relations, interests and, ultimately, institutional forms of governance' (Herrigel, 2010: 6).

Through a historical review of Alibaba's development path in the past two decades, we depict how the organizational forms and goals of Alibaba are expressed through its interaction with state policies and actors on the various levels. We begin with Alibaba's early efforts to build its online marketplaces then move to discuss its domestic and overseas expansion in its specific socio-economic context. In doing so, it challenges the narratives of platform economy as mainly a process promoted by entrepreneurs through technological innovations.

The historical trajectory of Alibaba

The trajectory of Alibaba is one telling story of how Chinese platforms developed in the dynamics of China's increasingly globalized digital economy in the past decades. Expanding from an online marketplace for small and medium-sized enterprises (SMEs), Alibaba has nowadays grown into one of the world's largest digital platforms consisting of diverse groups of market actors across multiple economic sectors and industries. Far from a hapless victim susceptible to the whimsical political will of an authoritarian Chinese state, however, the history of Alibaba in the past two decades clearly indicates that China's economic and industrial policies have played a critical part in the genesis and development of the country's internet industry, of which Alibaba is but one example. Alibaba's contour of growth corresponded to the developments of such important government projects and initiatives as the country's accelerated economic reforms and integration to the global market, its post-2008 tech-driven economy restructuring, its rural revitalization and poverty reduction projects, its digital governance and urban development programmes, the 'Belt and Road' Initiatives (BRI), and the recent all-round shift toward concentration on 'dual circulation'.

In the following section, we divide the history of Alibaba into three chronologically intersecting yet thematically distinct phases. In each phase, we highlight the main goals and interests of the company and trace their relation to the state's policy drives and local developmental programmes in the period. We demonstrate that these policies are not taken-for-granted contexts but result of actions of relevant actors responding to the overall institutional, technological, and market demands and crises during the period.

Phase one: the establishment of the e-commerce businesses (1999–2007)

The early years of Alibaba as an e-commerce start-up was demarcated by the establishment of Alibaba.com, its business-to-business (B2B) online portal, in 1999, and the market domination achieved with Taobao.com, its consumer-to-consumer (C2C) online retail portal, in 2007. During this period, China's fast-growing export-driven economy, relevant state policies, and the deficient infrastructure in the fragmented and inefficient market of cross-border trade, created the structural opportunity for Alibaba's e-commerce businesses. The company took off by tapping into the entrepreneurial energy of SMEs and individuals as emerging players finding new markets.

The Chinese state's 'open door' policy in the late 1970s shifted the direction of China's economy from self-reliance in the Mao era toward its reintegration into the global market. The subsequent market reforms in the 1990s, and its official entry into the World Trade Organization WTO in 2001, led to the rapid growth of an export-driven economy – at a rate of more than 30 per cent per year from 2004 to 2007 (Naughton, 2021). Concurrently, SMEs emerged as a major category of non-state economic actor in the following two decades since 1990s. This period saw a series of policies, issued by the state and its various agencies, with regards to the economic transition, the development of SMEs, and the application of ICT for economic growth.

SMEs first cropped up in the development of enterprises in rural towns and villages in the 1980s, further expanded during the restructuring and privatization of the state-owned enterprises in the 1990s, and thrived during the export boom in the 2000s. They accounted for 99 per cent of all registered corporations in China around the early 2000s (Zheng and Huang, 2018; Shen, 2021). Seeing the importance of SMEs, the government promulgated regulations such as the SMEs Promotion Law in 2002 to improve their business environment and protect their rights (Shen, 2021). Although the relevant policies had helped unleashed the energy of SMEs, the existing state bureaucracy still stood as an impediment to the further liberalization of the market (Nee, 2010). While motived by the potential of overseas markets, SMEs often had limited means to secure export deals and expand production because they often lacked access to state-controlled infrastructures and resources that at the time often prioritized large state-owned enterprises. It was in this context that, Jack Ma, a persevering entrepreneur with 'raw determination', launched alibaba.com in March 1999, seeking opportunities in helping connect SME exporters with overseas buyers in the growing market (Forbes, 2000). Impressed by its growth potential, the global business community soon took notice of Alibaba's '*B2B for the Little Guys*' approach, ranking it one of the best B2B websites in the world (Forbes, 2000). By the end of 2001, Alibaba became the world's first business website to exceed one million members (Liu and Avery, 2021). To further secure its financial needs and achieve its ambition as a global player, alibaba.com went public on the Hong Kong Stock Exchange in 2007, achieving at the time the largest Internet IPO in Asia and second largest worldwide, after Google (Liu and Avery, 2021). Alibaba's B2B branch remained the company's most valuable asset up to 2008 when it was overtaken by the fast-growing C2C sector. Until then, its steady profit firmly established the parent company as an alternative infrastructure for SMEs to overcome the deficiency of the existing state institutions to directly seek overseas outlets for their products (Shen, 2021).

While it was the entrepreneurial effort that founded Alibaba, its germination, and that of the fast-growing e-commerce sector in general, benefited from many of the state policies to promote the role of ICTs in the e-commerce development (Lin, 2017; Yue, 2017). As early as 2001, the state launched an 'Enterprise Online' initiative, aiming to help connect domestic producers with the global market through the internet, with a special emphasis on the SMEs (Shen, 2021). In January 2005, the State Council issued 'Several Opinions on Accelerating the Development of e-Commerce (关于加快电子商务发展的若干意见)', a top-level government document defining the important role of e-commerce in information-driven industrialization as the new mode of economic growth (State Council, 2005). In 2007, the State Development and Reform Commission together with the State Council Information Office jointly issued the first of a series of five-year guidelines to address specifically the development of e-commerce. Among the many guidelines in 2007, for instance, was one that urged government agencies at the various levels to make full use of third-party e-commerce platforms (such as alibaba.com) to help establish stable and large-scale demands for their services. The guidelines also emphasized the importance of greater involvement of SMEs, advocating for their use of e-commerce platforms to strengthen their management and profitability (Jiang, Zhang, and Jin, 2021). Three more five-year national guidelines were issued in 2012, 2016 and 2021 respectively, laying out principles that were intended to guide subsequent action and form the keystone of the structured policy process in promoting the e-commerce sector.

Alibaba's C2C branch, Taobao.com, was launched in the spring of 2003. Taobao expanded the company's business scope by appealing to a younger generation of e-commerce entrepreneurs who did not necessarily have connections to China's export manufacturing sector (Zhang, 2020a). Taobao continued with the strategy to serve small businesses and branded itself with an image of an efficient, accessible, privately owned alternative to the state infrastructure. In line with the strategy, it offered free transaction services for the first years of its inception, which was crucial for expanding its user base and eventually winning out in the market.

Taobao couldn't have done this without the funding of overseas capital. Because the state-sponsored financing institutions continued to favour state-owned enterprises over private businesses in their lending structure, access to global venture capital was critical to Taobao's survival at the early stage when the company followed a 'growth-before-profit' strategy similar to those of many prominent US counterparts (Srnicek, 2017; Zhang, 2020a). Indeed, the dynamism of China's fledgling internet sector soon attracted the interest of post-dot-com-bubble global venture capital as a new and exciting site of investment. This translated into a constant flow of funds into Chinese tech companies like Alibaba (Zhao, 2010; Clark, 2016; Jia and Winseck, 2018). Among Alibaba's investors, the Japanese investor Softbank, for instance, injected several rounds of capital into Taobao during its prolonged competition with eBay to sustain Taobao's operation when the portal was unable to generate profit. This stable inflow of venture capital money allowed Taobao to prioritize the expansion of the platform's user base. Consequently, Taobao defeated eBay China in 2005 with an overwhelming lead in market share. By 2006, Taobao became a monopoly over China's e-commerce market, driving eBay out of China almost entirely (Zhang, 2020b). As of 2020, Cainiao.com commanded the largest share in the e-commerce market both at home and abroad (Alibaba Group, 2021).

Meanwhile, the Chinese government showed a largely laissez-faire attitude toward Alibaba's development in those early years, including its entanglement with overseas capital, as it often does with fledging private sectors (Zhang, 2020a). The reason was not least because of its increasingly important role in digitalizing China's manufacturing base, driving domestic consumption, and providing alternative self-employment opportunities and encouraging entrepreneurial endeavours, all of which aligned with the Chinese state's post-WTO ambition to boost domestic consumption and expand digital and cultural industries (Hong, 2017; Zhang, 2020a).

Alibaba's early development seems to confirm the analysis of sociologist Barry Naughton, an expert in China's economic and technological policy. He pointed out that the main goals of China's policy package from 1978 through the first decade of the twenty-first century (until about 2006–07) were to promote marketization and investment in human and physical capital. These policies released the tremendous energies of a slew of new economic actors. This, according to him, was one primary reason that China emerged as an economic and technological super-power today (Naughton, 2021).

Phase two: 'platformization' and 'infrastructuralization' (2008–mid-2010s)

The structural opportunity for Alibaba was further opened up during China's accelerated economic restructuring since the 2008 global financial crisis. The sudden contraction in exports during the financial downturn forced China's manufacturers to look inward toward the country's growing domestic consumer market. At the same time, the Chinese state ramped up its efforts to overhaul the export-oriented low-value-added manufacture-based economy. Technological innovation, creativity and entrepreneurship became the new visions through which the nation reimagined itself in the post-2008 global world (Hong, 2017; Zhang, 2020a).

During this period, Alibaba increasingly took on the characteristics of a 'platform' comprising a growing number of multi-sided markets, from finance, cloud computing, logistics, to media and entertainment, with its data-driven technological interfaces (Gawer, 2014; Nieborg and Helmond, 2019). In 2004, Alipay, the third-party online and mobile payment service previously attached to Taobao, became an independent company. In 2008, Alibaba launched Tmall, a business-to-consumer (B2C) e-commerce channel, complementary to its C2C businesses. A year later, the company founded Alibaba Cloud (aka Aliyun) based on its former in-house cloud computer arm. The year of 2013 saw the founding of Cainiao Smart Logistics Network company. The list goes on. The growth of Alibaba as a platform company, however, was not simply a result of its increasing computational capacities and programmable interfaces, nor was it defined by its role as a cost reduction intermediary for mutually beneficial relationships between a group of independent market actors. Its trajectory continued to follow the contour of China's broader economic development.

Despite the efforts of the Chinese state during this period, China found it hard to overcome the inertia of an old economic model. As the pressure of unemployment and underemployment ran high, it become an urgent priority to generate employment opportunities to absorb surplus labour from the shrinking manufacturing industries. A dismal job market, meanwhile, had led many people to seek alternative or supplemental employment or self-employment opportunities in the rapidly expanding e-commerce industry. As a response, government policies during this period further granted the e-commerce sector a central role in the transition of China's economy from export-heavy to domestic consumption-driven. In addition to the five-year guidelines mentioned previously, the State Council, for instance, announced the 'Opinion Regarding the Active Promotion of E-commerce Development and Accelerate Nurturing of a New Drive of Economic Development (关于大力发展电子商务加快培育经济 新动力的意见)' in May 2015. The opinion highlighted the importance of e-commerce in facilitate two new economic engines for industrial upgrading – entrepreneurship and innovation, and the provision of public goods and services by the government (Li, 2017). On the basis of the groundwork laid by the State Council, numerous other policies and regulations provided policy and legal frameworks for growing and regulating the e-commerce market (see Lin, 2017; Yue, 2017; Jiang et al, 2021).

The convergence of these factors led to an e-commerce boom – the total transaction value of e-commerce rising from RMB3.14 trillion in 2008 to RMB21.8 trillion in 2015 (Kong, 2019). Companies such as Alibaba became increasingly indispensable to the Chinese state's economic restructuring efforts. Alibaba's growing importance contributed to the consolidation of its dominating status in the e-commerce market. Between 2007 and 2014, the company's annual revenue skyrocketed from USD$0.29 billion to USD$8.05 billion, leading to its high-profile IPO in 2014 at the New York Stock Exchange (Zhang, 2020a).

In the context of the post-2008 economic restructuring, the State Council initiated the 'Internet +' and the 'Mass Entrepreneurship and Innovation' (大众创业万众创新) policy drives in September 2015 to further promote industry upgrade through digital and network technology and nationwide entrepreneurial and innovation efforts. The fast-growing ICT industries were seen as a key to solve China's long-term growth problem and to ease the tensions between sustained development and social equity in China. All at the same time, Alibaba, seeking to tapping into the growing capacities of its cloud computing platform, increasingly relied on data-driven strategies to pursue expansion beyond the e-commerce market (Alibaba.com, 2016). During this period, the company sought actively to assume a role in digitalizing China's existing manufacturing base with its data and computing infrastructure, and driving domestic consumption and entrepreneurial endeavours (Hong, 2017; Zhang, 2020a). Its positioning as a privately owned but in many ways public-serving infrastructure allowed the company to assert many quasi-governmental ambitions, such as poverty reduction, economic redistribution, job creation, public infrastructure and values building (Shen, 2021). Since Alibaba achieved monopoly in the e-commerce markets, the company had shifted from its earlier positioning as a private alternative to failing governmental infrastructures, to a monopoly power keen in cultivating government ties to further its market expansion (Zhang, 2020a). Deepening collaborations between Alibaba and the various levels of government in China helped expand Alibaba's reach further into both urban and rural markets. 'Taobao Village' and 'City Brain' are two exemplary cases.

Taobao Village

As the urban market increasingly saturated, Alibaba made its priority to tap into in China's vast and underserved rural areas. It started to lobby the Chinese state to spearhead the rural e-commerce development. Consistent with the state's long-term efforts to development rural economy, calls from the industry were met with a series of state documents to encourage rural e-commerce between 2010 and 2015 (Zhang, 2020a). The State Council, for instance, issued 'Instruction Regarding How to Facilitate the Acceleration of Rural E-commerce Development' (关于促进农村电子商务加快发展的指导意见) in November 2015. At the same time, funds were allocated to support the development of rural e-commerce in remote and underdeveloped central and Western regions (Zhao, 2015). In line with the greater importance placed on rural e-commerce by the central government, policies that actively promoted the development of rural e-commerce were crafted and implemented at the subnational level in the following years (Kong, 2019). Rural e-commerce became central in the state's strategic 'new approach to urbanization', 'targeted poverty alleviation', and 'rural revitalization' (Li, 2017; Kong, 2019; Zhang, 2020a).

The 'Taobao Village' initiative, Alibaba's flagship e-commerce programme, was a result of a close collaboration between Alibaba and local governments at all levels to harness local resources and generate employment opportunities in rural villages. First appeared in 2009, Taobao villages refer to those significantly engaged in e-commerce with a total annual online revenue of at least RMB10 million and at least 100 active online shops (Luo, 2018). According to Alibaba's in-house research institute, the number of Taobao Villages across China grew to 7,023 in 2021 (Aliresearch.com, 2021).

Handicapped by the lack of funding, technology and practical knowledge in the rural regions, the development of rural e-commerce depended on first of all investments in basic services such as infrastructure construction and personnel training. Alibaba started its rural e-commerce infrastructure projects in 2014 to establish retailing service centres at both the county and village levels in order to connect rural areas, as both potential consumption markets and production sites, with its online platform. As of 2020, through its strategic partnership agreements with various levels of government in different provinces, Alibaba's logistic service stations were expanded to cover about 1,000 counties and 30,000 villages in 29 provinces (Aliresearch.com, 2020). Technical aspects such as reliable network access, trustworthy online transaction methods and convenient logistics services were only necessary but not sufficient conditions for success. Taobao villages were the result of combined efforts of grassroots entrepreneurs and supportive government policies and measures (Kong, 2019). Local governments support came in many forms, from the construction of basic infrastructure and e-commerce industrial parks, and service centres, to the provision of low-interests loans, tax concessions, administrative assistance, connection with experts and research institutes for training and planning (Li, 2017; Kong, 2019; Wei, Lin, and Zhang, 2020).

While its ultimate goal is to expand its market, Alibaba's rural e-commerce programmes have significant social economic effects on rural areas. Many Taobao villages increased local incomes by selling local agricultural products, traditional handicrafts and goods obtained from nearby wholesale markets through the e-commerce platform (Li, 2017). As clusters of e-commerce business grew, a primitive ecology of e-commerce came into being with emerging ancillary sectors such as delivery and marketing services to provide new job opportunities (Kong, 2019; Wei, Lin, and Zhang, 2020). While the sustainability and exact benefits of these programmes are subject to closer examination and debate, Alibaba's rural Taobao projects helped the state advance its development goals and mobilize local officials to participate in these efforts, thereby emerging as a private subcontractor for the state (Zhang, 2020b).

City Brain

The Chinese state has long made the adoption of ICTs a priority for its ambitious government modernization project. Under the auspice of 'the Internet+ Government Service' policy since the mid-2010s, platform companies, with their powerful digital infrastructures and technical know-hows, became increasingly valuable to government agencies that seek to apply data-driven approaches to urban governance. During the rapid urbanization over the past 30 years, the Chinese state strategically promote various models to promote urban development. Since the early 2010s, smart city development gradually occupied a central part of government agendas (Caprotti and Liu, 2022). According to the data in 2018, all sub-provincial cities, 89 per cent of prefecture-level cities (a total of 241 cities), and 47 per cent of county-level cities (51 cities) in China were having smart city programmes (Wu et al, 2018).

'City Brain' was a smart city programme launched by the Hangzhou municipal government in collaboration with Alibaba Group in 2016. The ongoing programme utilizes a comprehensive suite of voice, image, and video recognition technologies enabled by the AI programme run on Alibaba Cloud to enable real-time analysis and modelling of urban data. The goal is to allow the city to automatically deploy public resources, improve urban operations such as optimizing traffic flows and eventually anticipate intelligent responses to unfolding events such as natural disasters and public health crises (Curran and Smart, 2021).

Given its experimental nature, due to constant software and hardware upgrades to the city's system, the programme requires not only collaboration between Alibaba and the city government, but also 'the assemblage of a technological development network' including other firms (Caprotti and Liu, 2022: 1562). As many as seven city departments (such as traffic departments at the various levels) were involved in the development of the programme. In addition to Alibaba Cloud, several other tech companies, some of which have significant state shares, are also part of the tech solutions. During the process, the city had to make changes to its existing administrative structure to adapt to the interface with the tech companies and other stakeholders active in the flow and interchange of data. A Bureau of Data Resource, for instance, was established in 2017 to standardize and coordinate the use of data in urban services, and to maximize the utility of data gathered through the City Brain programme (Caprotti and Liu, 2022). Alibaba produced and marketed its smart city products as both city-specific and flexible to be modified and applied to other Chinese cities. By the end of 2018, City Brain had been exported to, and implemented in 15 other Chinese cities, and in Kuala Lumpur, the capital city of Malaysia (Shen, 2021; Naughton, 2020).

Caprotti and Liu (2022) commented that Hangzhou's City Brain programme was a result of coproduction by multiple actors, ranging from state, provincial government officials, and the Hangzhou city administration, to corporate executives in the private sector as well as actors in categories that don't neatly fit into either state or private sector, such as state-owned enterprises (SOEs). Within the broad state policy landscape to stimulate a new data-intensive tech-driven urban economy with experimental developmental programmes, local municipal administrations initiated development programs by translating policy directives into contextualized local priorities while co-designing and co-implementing the local programme in collaboration with corporate actors such as Alibaba, which needed to develop their own niches in the competition with other tech companies in the smart city market (Caprotti and Liu, 2022).

Critics pointed out that China's data-driven urban governance may be 'more likely to effective in improving bureaucratic administrative operations than in fostering participatory-democratic developments or progress towards civil society' (Hartford, 2005). Instead of providing user-friendly, transparent, and responsible public services, governments may use the system and big data analytics such as those of City Brian to strengthen their political and social control through digital surveillance and censorship (Ma et al, 2023). At the same time, tech companies such as Alibaba are mostly motivated by the goal to optimize their AI models and mine the data needed to grow profitable platform services (Curran and Smart, 2021). Nevertheless, empirical studies of China's Smart City programmes showed that the digitalization of public administrative system led to significant government restructuring, including cross-departmental and -regional information sharing, the reorganization of administrative processes, and power reallocation (Gao, 2020). For instance, Big Data Bureaus, the kind founded in Hangzhou, have appeared at the province, prefecture, and county levels across China since 2016 (Gao, 2020).

Phase three: globalization and financialization (the mid-2010s and onwards)

Riding the high tides of the Chinese state's geopolitical ambition, tech companies such as Alibaba made China's global economic policies, such as the BRI and associated 'digital silk road', springboards to speed up their global expansion. During this period, Alibaba's dominance in domestic digital markets and entanglement in global financial and technological networks seemed to reach a peak. The swelling importance of China's Big Tech firms forced China's policy makers and regulators to recognize their common interest in coordinating with the former in development and governance. Nonetheless, this alliance was precarious teeming with tensions and conflicts in context of the ever-evolving digital economic landscapes both home and abroad. Big Tech's growing influence over data security, labour relations, entrepreneurial innovation, capital flow, and public discourse posed unforeseen risks and challenges (Zhang and Chen, 2022). The recent round of government regulations reflected the challenges posed by monopolizing digital platforms to state governance as well as platform mechanisms' crucial role in reshaping state–corporate–capital–labour relations in contemporary China (Zhang, 2020a).

Globalization

In a sense, globalization has been one of Alibaba's main goals and strategies since its inception rooted in cross-border e-commerce. Over the years, its overseas expansion has taken place along three cross-cutting and mutually beneficial dimensions: its core e-commerce businesses, its digital infrastructures, and capital investments to diversify its profit structure and risks (see Shen, 2021). Some of Alibaba's moves to expand its e-commerce businesses overseas included establishing AliExpress, a B2C portal in 2010; purchasing Lazada, a Southeast Asian e-commerce company in 2016 (alibabagroup.com); Daraz, a Pakistan platform, and Trendyol, a Turkish platform in 2018 (Reuters, 2018; 2021). Its e-commerce infrastructures have kept abreast with its growing online markets. Nowadays Alipay serves over 1.3 billion users and 80 million merchants (Hong Kong Exchange News, 2020); and Cainiao Smart Logistic Network reaches 224 countries and areas across the world (Taobao.com, 2023). Much of Alibaba's global expansion has been achieved through merger and acquisition (M&A). Since 2009, Alibaba has made over 85 M&As across the globe. Nearly one-third of these deals took place in the US market. India and Israel were also among Alibaba's major international markets (Li and Li, 2022). Additionally, Alibaba has purchased numerous stakes in businesses outside the e-commerce sector – software, digital mapping, robotics, mobile gaming, transportation, cell phone manufacturing, and media and entertainment.

While the business world deemed the company's overseas expansion 'a classic example in the area of international entrepreneurship' adapting agilely to 'changing markets, competition, and consumer demand' through 'its unique business model' (Anwar, 2017: 368), many observers linked its accelerated globalization since its 2014 IPO to the Chinese state's increasingly assertive 'going out' policy, especially the BRI global initiative. Proposed by President Xi Jinping in 2013, BRI was considered a major policy defining China's relationship with the global political economy. With the reference to the ancient trade routes across Eurasia, BRI has a grand aim to build land and maritime links between China and major Eurasian and African countries through infrastructure building, trade, and capital investment (Shen, 2018: 2683).

While international relations scholars deem BRI China's response to the US's 'pivot to Asia' (Ferdinand, 2016; Keane and Yu, 2019), political economists believe it is driven mainly by pressing domestic economic challenges such as industrial overcapacity and the rise of China's financial capital interests (Shen, 2018; Shi and Ye, 2021). In this infrastructure-heavy initiative, the Chinese government, through its call for a 'digital Silk Road', accorded digital infrastructures equal importance as that to the traditional ones (Naughton, 2020). The state granted its tech companies a key role in enabling 'corporate China's global expansion' and constructing a 'China-centered transnational network infrastructure' (Shen, 2018: 2685; Shi and Ye, 2021).

Rallying around this massive government endeavour, Chinese IT enterprises actively sought relevant financial opportunities as well as political and diplomatic support for their own overseas economic advancement. Alibaba's project to develop an Electronic World Trade Platform (eWTP) in line with the official digital Silk Road framework exemplified how the commercial objectives of Internet enterprises may dovetail with the state's geopolitical goals. The notion of eWTP was proposed by Jack Ma in 2016 when chairing the Taskforce for SME Development at the G20's Hangzhou Summit. In contrast with the existing global trade regime that privileges big corporations, eWTP is branded to serve the interests of SMEs in developing countries through digital payments, logistics and financing services – some of the core businesses of the Alibaba Group (Alibaba Group, 2016, para. 7 quoted in Shen, 2018). Some exemplary cases of eWTP included Alibaba's first global digital free trade zone established in Malaysia in March 2017 (Shen, 2018; Naughton, 2020) and planned new data centres in India, Indonesia and Malaysia, all of which are BRI priorities. Consequently, Alibaba Cloud reported a growth of over 400 per cent in overseas markets in the 2017 fiscal year (Shen, 2018).

Financialization

China's post-2008 economic transition opened up new space for private FinTech companies to break into the previously state-monopolized financial industry. Alibaba's financial enterprise started with Alipay, its answer to PayPal, in October 2003. Over the years, Alipay quickly grew into the leading third-party mobile payment system beyond e-commerce, consolidating its role in China's emerging cashless society (Wang and Doan, 2019; Zhang, 2020b). Alipay has since come to account for roughly half of all online payment transactions in China. On the basis of Alipay's success, Alibaba established Ant Financial Services Group in 2014. Currently, Ant Group includes Yu'ebao (Surplus Treasure in Chinese), an investment service established in June 2013 that allows users to turn their Alipay account balances into money market funds; Huabei (Just Spend) in 2014, a consumer virtual credit service; and Jiebei (Just Borrow) in 2015, a micro-loan service. A data-driven strategy has been central to Ant Group's quick expansion in the finance sector. The company utilized its enormous user data collected from the e-commerce portals and the online payment system to develop and customize new financial services and investment products, for example, by turning detailed shopping behaviour data into credit scores. After 2015, Ant Group also branched out via a slew of venture capital investments and acquisition deals domestically and abroad (Zhang and Chen, 2022).

The company's post-2008 growth in the financial sector played well along the state-led financialization process. Beginning as an immediate response to offset economic slowdown in the aftermath of the 2008 crisis and accelerating during the new Xi-Li administration (2012–), the financialization process has seen the Chinese state refashion itself as a shareholder and institutional investor in the economy and resorted to a set of financial means (as opposed to fiscal means) to manage its ownership, assets, and public investments (Wang, 2015: 1). Concurrently, the government took a supportive stance towards a growing 'internet finance' sector, encouraging internet companies, in collaboration with traditional players such as state-owned banks and insurance companies, to provide financial products and services such as investment brokerage, microloans, P2P (peer-to-peer) lending and insurance (Wang, 2017). In parallel with Internet finance, 'inclusive finance' (普惠金融) has also been part of the government policy. It aimed to widen the access to financial services in rural, marginalized and traditionally underserved regions by the big banks with the broader goal to drive economic growth through bottom-up market-led development by providing much-needed credits to broader groups of actors (Loubere, 2017). In growing an increasingly financialized economy, government policies also emphasized the role of the internet and digital technology (Wang, 2017). Encouraged by the favourable policies and resource allocation, internet companies such as Baidu and Tencent were quick to seize the opportunity, adopting the discourse of financial inclusion and technological innovation into their market-expansion strategies. It was during this period that Ant Finance became the world's largest investment fund, managing over US$165 billion from more than 260 million investors and making up 60 per cent of market share (Loubere, 2017).

The consolidation of multiple sectors by Fintech firms transformed financial industries, challenged policy and regulatory regimes, and reshaped the cultures of finance in China (Wang and Doan, 2019). Blurring lines between traditional banking and financial sectors and digital tech industries as well as the murky role of the state as both a stakeholder and a regulator posed significant challenges to existing legal and regulatory regimes of platform economy (Zhang, 2020b). There was at the time no grand regulatory framework given FinTech's cross-sectional nature. Existing regulations treat different businesses sectors separately. China's central bank, for instance, deals with Ant Financial with a 'distributive' approach – each of Ant Finance's sectors (online payment services, investment, consumer and business loans, crowdfunding and so on) had to apply for a sector-specific licence (Wang and Doan, 2019).

Meanwhile, Alibaba was very sensitive to regulatory changes and often adapted swiftly. For instance, Alipay made an effort to convert its shareholder structure from a foreign joint venture to a purely domestic company before its Third-Party Payment licence application in 2010 because foreign ownership had to be approved by the State Council in addition to the Central Bank, therefore may entail much uncertainty in the process. Later when the Central Bank started to crack down on internet finance frauds in 2016, Alipay swiftly altered its company registration in the National Enterprise Credit Information Publicity System from 'financial service company' to 'network technology company' to avoid further implication. Following this path, the company has obtained licences in securities, banks, funds, payment and clearance, and insurance (Wang and Doan, 2019).

The interaction between Alibaba and regulatory agencies has been an on-going process in which both the state and market agents respond to evolving situations and crises. The direction for the co-evolving is not linear but an organic component of the co-evolution so that it can effectively adapt to the constantly changing situation. In this light, the FinTech market may have currently reached a critical moment. As Alibaba's role in the finance sector grew government regulators became more cautious and interventionist. The relationship took a turn after Yu'ebao's encroaching on the wealth management turf of state banking institutions. Furthermore, the state embarked on a nationwide campaign to contain financial risks after the burst of the equity bubble in July 2015 and the fall of the P2P lending sector due to widespread fraud and ruthless capital extraction and leverage after 2016. Ant, particularly its profitable consumer credit and company loan services, came in for mounting regulatory scrutiny. Soon after the sudden halt of Ant's IPO, the Chinese government announced two new draft documents that would regulate the microloan industry and platform economy, respectively (Zhang, 2020b). However, researchers have pointed out that the new regulatory regime is still largely supportive and has left plenty of room for the continued development of the industry (Loubere, 2017; Wang and Doan, 2019).

Conclusion

The rise of digital platforms has caused great concerns about the 'platformization' of society whereby the platforms extend their influences into many social realms through technological means for private profit goals (Van Dijck, Poell, and De Waal, 2018), especially their functioning as critical infrastructures (Plantin et al, 2018). Along a similar vein, the discourse of platformization in China emphasizes technical features such as digital interfaces, data streams and algorithms, not only as distinguishable features of platforms but also the main force driving their functional metamorphosis into infrastructures (de Kloet et al, 2019; Plantin and De Seta, 2019). The 'infrastructuralization' of platforms is a result of merging of platform properties such as participation, modularity and programmability with those associated with infrastructure such as scale, ubiquity and criticality of use. These hybrid entities rely on these technical configurations to maintain and extend their social and market power (Plantin and De Seta, 2019).

In contrast, this chapter conceptualizes platformization as a broad political economic process, influenced by historical circumstances, situational imperatives, intuitional relations and state ideologies. It traced the trajectory of Alibaba's growth from an e-commerce start-up to a multi-market platform in relation to the Chinese state's broad economic goals according to the country's structural position in the evolving global digital economy. In doing so, it demonstrates that Alibaba's platformization process has taken place in a set of historically and culturally specific processes and relations constituted by shifting and interacting forces both home and abroad. Consequently, the organizations and technologies, governance mechanisms and market strategies of Alibaba are subject to constant adjustment. The structure and new rules of China's digital economy is configured according to the relative power of actors to define the forms of economic activity and accompanying social arrangements.

At the same time, as many empirical studies quoted in this chapter have shown, the role of digital platforms as infrastructures is not necessarily a unidirectionally corporate-or state-led development. Neither are platform-enabled infrastructures one-fit-all structures with little regard for geographical specificity, and local technological capacities, economic and development priorities. Rather, as Taobao Village and City Brain programmes show, they are economic, geopolitical and cultural processes that are relationally co-constituted by networks of actors including platform corporates, the state actors and municipal authorities at multiple scales (Kong, 2019; Caprotti and Liu, 2022).

There has been a persistent tendency in both economic theorization and popular discourses to draw binary distinctions between liberal-market capitalism and its often statist 'others' (Peck, 2021). The dichotomy of the state as the embodiment of inert economic institutional structures vs liberal free-market West is perpetuated by opponents of the Chinese state to justify the recent China-targeting trade war and technological sanctions as necessary measures to contain the 'China threat' (Alami and Dixon, 2020).

The underlying assumptions of such discourses is that the two parties are distinct actors acting in their interests in their respectively self-contained spheres. Alibaba's historical development demonstrates that the two are inextricably intertwined. The rational and strategic actions of platforms need to be articulated to specific socio-historical dynamics as constituting a broader shift in contemporary capitalism (Zhang, 2020a). Instead of an antagonistic relation, markets and state agencies interacted and adapted to each other in China. This coevolutionary process manifested itself in diverse forms, over the course of different periods of development (Ang, 2016).

Note

[1] The six units are: Cloud Intelligence Group, Taobao & Tmall E-commerce Group, Local Services Group, Cainiao Smart Logistics Group, Global Digital Commerce Group and Digital Media and Entertainment Group.

8

Efficient and Illegitimate: Legitimacy Problems in the Platform Model

Andreas Gregersen and Jacob Ørmen

This chapter outlines an approach to the analysis of platforms built on the basic insight that platforms are owned and operated by companies. The approach conceptualizes platform companies as organizations, since this allows for leveraging insights from the considerable body of existing scholarship which focuses on the relationships between organizations and their environment, a key component of which are other organizations.

Our aim is not to replace the existing structural-formal analyses of platforms as a particular type of hardware-software-infrastructure coupled to a set of operations embedded in a larger economical system – all of this is clearly important for understanding platforms, and much of the infrastructural perspective is directly compatible with the present approach. Rather, we seek to synthesize existing and well-established perspectives focusing on platform structures and internal operations with a less established organization-environment perspective from organizational theory – in effect introducing a different perspective on the relationship between internal operations of platforms and their environment. The result should be a framework that allows for understanding how platform companies strategically relate to and organize their environments and how the resulting relations may lead to serious problems of legitimacy.

Our argument, in a nutshell, is that one of the entrenched perspectives on internal platform operations ostensibly delivers a blueprint for the near-perfect organization in terms of input–output relations and profitability. This blueprint can be found in its essence in the popular business paperback *Platform Revolution* (Parker, Van Alstyne and Choudary, 2016), where a platform is defined as 'a business based on enabling value-creating interactions between external producers and consumers' (p 5). The operative keyword here is 'external producers' signifying that production facilities are kept outside the organization, and platforms are thus said to 'invert the firm' by shifting the production to the environment. This is one of the dominant business models for platform companies, where the company operates a so-called lean platform (Srnicek, 2017: 76), which follows a 'hyper-outsourced' model where everything except critical infrastructure is kept outside the firm. This lean platform structure is often tied to a multi-sided market structure, and the key motive for the lean structure is for the platform to serve as a matchmaker, a centralized conduit for making and monetizing connections. The key value creation mechanism lies in this process of matchmaking.

Several of the largest digital media platforms, such as Facebook, Instagram, YouTube and TikTok, base their operations on acquiring massive amounts of user-generated content, which is then funnelled into the multi-sided marketplace structure without immediate remuneration to the content producers. When seen in traditional terms of input–output, these platforms acquire enormous amounts of textual and audiovisual products at near zero cost. Moreover, these products are typically served forward to end users with little if any refinement or processing. Acquiring a key resource ready for distribution at zero cost should make for an ideal arrangement in terms of input–output efficiency, but major problems arise once we turn to the assessment of the resulting output in the eyes of the other sides of the multi-sided market. For several of these stakeholders, platform output has been deemed highly problematic to the point of being unacceptable, which has led to serious *problems of legitimacy* for the platform company in charge of the platform. As we argue here, these problems of legitimacy are far from incidental: rather, they arise directly from the platform matchmaking model and its efficiency.

To scaffold this argument, we propose to resuscitate some fundamental insights from some of the classics of organizational theory. In the following, we will quickly outline resource dependence theory and institutional theory before proceeding to show how this brings added value to our understanding of the present platform economy and its future. Then, we very briefly outline the operational perspective of platforms as multi-sided markets and move on to describing three legitimacy problems for platforms, using YouTube as an illustrative case. We show how these problems can be formalized as arising from specific combinations of marketplace sides and their respective concerns regarding the legitimacy of the matchmaking and market-making operations involved. In our discussion, we touch upon a strong trend in the business model of digital media platforms, namely the move from an advertising platform towards an integrated system of carefully cultivated and curated brand-safe content and creator-driven e-commerce.

We formalize this trend as a response to the legitimacy concerns bound up with multisided markets, and we end with a view towards the competition between platforms and their battle for supremacy.

Organizations and their environment

A major shift occurred within organizational theory in the 1970s, where the field started shifting its attention from internal to external aspects of organizations. Key ideas in this shift were those of open systems and loose coupling and the focus changed from internal operations and management to the manifold relationships through which organizations relate to their environment. Resource dependence theory (RDT) was one of the early theories driving this shift of attention. RDT in its classic incarnation (Pfeffer and Salancik, 1978) is built upon a simple proposition, namely that access to certain key resources is a basic problem for any organization, since such resources represent a fundamental need for procuring the necessary input to a desired output. A baker needs to procure a steady supply of flour, a producer of semiconductor chips needs to acquire silicon, a media company needs to acquire content to distribute and so on. Applied to platforms as matchmakers, a matchmaker needs whatever product or service it wants to feed from one side of the market to the other(s). All organizations need to keep track of resources essential for their survival, and the general assumption in RDT is that organizations will act strategically to ensure that such resources are not controlled fully by other organizations, since that would make the focal organization highly vulnerable. The notion of input–output flow is another important foundation for RDT, and it is connected to a fundamental distinction within the theory's conceptual framework, namely that of *efficiency* and *effectiveness*. In Pfeffer and Salancik's operationalization, efficiency is 'an internal standard of performance', which can be measured via 'the ratio of resources utilized to output produced' (Pfeffer and Salancik, 1978: 11). In other words, efficiency is a way to evaluate the economic fitness of a given organization by measuring the cost efficiency of the input–output flow. Pfeffer and Salancik emphasize that efficiency thus defined can be estimated solely from an internal perspective – 'the records of the organization's own activities are all that are needed' (Pfeffer and Salancik, 1978: 33). To the outside observer, this may sound very much like the blueprint for a highly effective organization – after all, being cost-efficient is a major component of organizational survival. However, *effectiveness* in the context of RDT is to be understood differently and with a much wider reach than mere internal accounting: Effectiveness is described as 'a sociopolitical question' in that 'organizational effectiveness is an external standard of how well an organization is meeting the demands of the various groups and organizations that are concerned with its activities' (p 11). Effectiveness is thus ultimately a question of *legitimacy* in the eyes of the environment, and this is also the terminology deployed by Pfeffer and Salancik. The main idea is that organizations live or die not just by access to resources but by acquiring and maintaining legitimacy.

For reasons that go way beyond this chapter, RDT has arguably been partly supplanted by the institutional approach to organizations within organization theory. One could make the argument, however, that many insights from RDT have been incorporated into institutional theory. We follow this line of thinking and orient ourselves to the synthesis proposed by Oliver (1991), which took some of the initial steps necessary for integrating RDT and the institutional perspective. Oliver argues that both approaches are undergirded by a set of shared assumptions, the primary ones being related to issues of autonomy and legitimacy. The overall motives for most organizations are thus to ensure *autonomy* through acquisition of key resources and at the same time maintain *legitimacy* through socio-political relationships with key stakeholders in the environment. While both motives are present in RDT, one of the major insights of the institutional approach to organizations was and remains the elaboration of the latter idea, namely that organizations seek and gain legitimacy from their environment. In Meyer and Rowan's (1977) classic formulation of the institutional approach, the main pathway to social legitimacy for an organization is through an orientation to the major social institutions of the organizational environment. An additional insight of Meyer and Rowan, however, was that organizations may orient themselves to such institutions through ritualized enactment of organizational forms considered legitimate by the environment, *regardless of the efficiency of the resulting internal operations*: instead of doing something because it is highly profitable or otherwise rational, organizations may do something because it is deemed 'the right way to do things'. This meant that internal operations might become *decoupled* to varying degrees from activities performed ritually in accordance with prevailing social institutions. This was in some respects a novel idea – a company could be successful not because it was economically efficient but because it was seen as legitimate by the outside. But this decoupling runs both ways: organizations might thus merely *perform legitimacy* – they could be virtuous on the outside and rotten to the core, as it were.

At this point, it should be easier to see how this chapter problematizes existing notions of platforms and their operations by drawing upon organizational theory. Our argument is a 'pivot to the past' in two ways. First, it seems that platform scholarship has lacked an interest in the early insights of organization theory. Although an institutional approach to platforms exists, it has thus far made little contact with institutional organizational theory and almost zero contact with the strand of institutional theory which takes on board insights from RDT. This may be because parts of RDT have become part of the tacit backdrop of business and organization theory, but we believe the approach is directly applicable and productive because it allows for understanding a fundamental problem for the platform model, namely that the hyper-outsourced lean business model has led several of the larger social media platforms into an *efficiency trap*: blinded by the extraordinary gains in operational efficiency possible by well-tuned (and highly exploitative) post-Fordist lean platform structures coupled to the operation of multi-sided markets, many platform companies have rapidly scaled their input–output efficiency by 'leveraging lean', as it were. In doing so, they have experienced enormous growth due to positive network effects where more users bring on more producers, which in turn bring more users and so on. This, however, has led to considerable problems of legitimacy down the line. To see how and why, we will now briefly lay out one of the dominant approaches to platforms, namely the conceptualization of platforms as multisided markets.

Platforms as highly efficient organizations

Multi-sided marketplaces bring various users together through match-making operations (Evans and Schmalensee, 2016) such as recommender systems, rankings, content curation, advertisement programmes and subscriptions. Digital media platforms typically operate a largely advertisement-based model (Srnicek, 2017) built upon asymmetric pricing, where producers and users can upload and access content without direct remuneration from the platform, whereas advertisers must pay to display ads on the platform. In return, YouTube (and its parent company, Google) collects data on user behaviour and content characteristics to match ads with suitable content and relevant users. As we outlined in the previous section, the digital media platforms operating this type of multisided structure involve a truly staggering amount of audiovisual content being fed into the infrastructure for further distribution. This happens at zero cost at the point of acquisition in terms of labour remuneration. On the face of it, this looks ideal in terms of cost efficiency. By outsourcing production to actors that depend on, but are external to, the platform – the so-called 'creators' – YouTube and related platforms integrate elements from the lean approach that originated in the post-Fordist era but has continued in its purest form in platforms like Airbnb and Uber (Srnicek, 2017). The key value creation mechanism for this type of platform lies in the various matchmaking activities, and this is exactly where legitimacy rears its problematic head: creation of value depends directly on the platform's ability to attract sufficient commitments from *all* sides of the market and if the platform loses legitimacy in the eyes of any of the sides, the profitability of the platform will take a hit. Given the linkages between sides, this can quickly led to negative network effects.

In sum, the platform model has proved to be a highly efficient way to connect sides in multisided marketplaces, but it has also led to digital media platform companies struggling with legitimacy – in other words, they may run *efficient platform infrastructures*, but they are increasingly seen as *illegitimate platform companies*. Much of this tension originates in the attempt to run a largely lean business based on a traditional advertising platform model.

Three legitimacy problems for the digital media platforms

In the following, we illustrate the issues of legitimacy through three prototypical problems for digital media platforms. We use YouTube as a primary case, but we draw on supplementary cases throughout to illustrate the relevance of the argument to the platform more broadly. YouTube is the dominant video hosting service in the world that runs some of the most popular websites and mobile apps on the internet. Furthermore, the company has since 2006 been a part of Google (which is now a subsidiary of Alphabet) and is thus embedded in a larger organizational structure that affects efficiency as well as legitimacy, as we will see. We draw in other digital media platforms along the way to encompass a broader range of issues which is not covered by the YouTube case. In our discussion, we recapitulate the issues of efficiency and effectiveness and touch upon a strong trend in the business model of communication platforms, namely the move from an advertising platform towards an integrated system of brand-safe content and creator-driven e-commerce (for a detailed discussion, see Ørmen and Gregersen, 2022). Again, we formalize this trend as a combination of marketplace sides and legitimacy concerns, and we end with a view towards the competition between platforms and their battle for supremacy.

Problematic content

First, YouTube has faced concerns of legitimacy from both users, advertisers and regulators over various types of *problematic content*. These problems tend to be related to a range of topics, from various types of disinformation/misinformation, hate speech and discrimination, as well as violent and sexually explicit videos. All these types of content have been found on the platform and have led to issues of legitimacy when the platform gets called out for peddling such content. Importantly, these problems are typically not just seen as problems of *mere presence* but also problems of the *operational precedence* given by YouTube through the algorithmic curation of content of the platform. Academic researchers and journalists have thus argued that YouTube's recommendation algorithm amplifies politically problematic content, leading to allegations of radicalization by way of algorithmic curation (Roose, 2019) and YouTube being called out as 'an organ of radicalization' (Quinn, Blackall and Dodd, 2020).

These types of problematic content and the (mis)management of same are an obvious source of legitimacy problems for YouTube in the eyes of most users. The problem for YouTube, however, is not limited to users and their opinions. As is common for advertising-based revenue models, illegitimate content also directly threatens the cash flow tied to content. When problematic content became a public issue influential advertisers publicly threatened to pull their advertisements from the platform, a process referred to in the YouTube creator community as 'the Adpocalypse' (Kumar, 2019).

At face value this appears to be a standard challenge of information asymmetry, where a seller withholds crucial information from buyers, which would affect the market price if disclosed. In a seminal article, Akerlof (1970) shows how information asymmetry affects the sale of second-hand goods (for example, used cars) to such a degree that buyers instinctively assume that all goods are of worse quality than disclosed. This depresses prices overall and forces sellers of quality goods out of the market, since they cannot get an acceptable price, leaving only a market for lemons (used cars of bad quality). However, information asymmetry is not as straightforward when applied to the platform model. Whereas the salesperson in Akerlof's original example deliberately withholds information to sell used products for a higher price, platforms are not *withholding* information as much as they are *ignorant* of what they are selling. As the library of content grows and ad matching as well as price setting occurs algorithmically through recommender and auction systems, it becomes more and more difficult, if not downright impossible, to know what one is peddling. Thus, platforms must generate information before asymmetry can even exists.

This lack of information about their content is an existential threat to many platforms as they risk losing a major source of revenue due to advertiser migration. This, in turn, will make them lose the competitive edge that successful algorithmic matchmaking offers, namely positive network effects and economies of scale. Many celebrated cases in the business literature on platforms focus on such positive network effects (most prominently in Evans and Schmalensee, 2016; Parker, Van Alstyne and Choudary, 2016), although they do touch upon possible negative effects as well. An important point, however, is that the underlying mechanism of multi-threaded interconnection is itself agnostic as to whether the resulting effects are positive or negative. It is thus the very nature of the multisided market that makes for a precarious situation. Once important advertisers withdraw from the platform, it becomes less attractive for creators to create advertising-friendly content, which in turn makes for fewer viewers within the all-important verticals, which leads to the platform being less attractive for both creators and brands and so on. This threat of negative effects spinning out of control means that platforms often have to take drastic steps to reduce content concerns and restore legitimacy.

It is important to emphasize that the issue of problematic content for advertising-based platforms is not limited to user-generated content: A digital media platform faces the additional problem that *advertising content* can be deemed problematic. To get a sense of the scale of this problem, a recent transparency report (*Our 2021 Ads Safety Report* – Google, 2022) discloses that Google removed no fewer than 3.4 billion ads and restricted or blocked 1.7 billion web pages in 2021 for violating their policies.

In summary, the notion – one might say ideology – of brand-safety cuts across all sides in the marketplace as users, advertisers and content publishers do not wish to be connected to problematic content related to the other sides. This problem, however, is not restricted to the sides producing content or ads, nor to the matching issues arising from the platform structure. Other actors who are not at the outset identified as sides in the multi-sided market may find various aspects of the platform transactions problematic. Infrastructural platforms that control access for sectoral platforms to users (Dijck, Poell and Waal, 2018) can exercise power, for example, by imposing demands to moderate content. As banks and major credit card companies restricted services to YouPorn and OnlyFans due to concerns about illegal sexual content on the platforms (Nast, 2022), both platform companies initiated steps to remove troves of unverifiable profiles (in YouPorn's case) and sexually explicit content (in OnlyFans' case, albeit the platform soon reversed the decision). Likewise, Google and Amazon removed the social network service Parler from their hosting platforms (Play Store and Web Services, respectively) in response to Parler's role in the 2021 United States Capitol Attack.

Problematic users

The audience base for YouTube has also led to legitimacy problems. YouTube ostensibly serves an enormous audience which contains a very diverse set of niche audiences and communities, for example, science communication enthusiasts, music teachers, Asian-Americans, socialists and incels to name a few examples from the scholarly literature. The business model underlying this cornucopia of content is fundamentally based on extensive data-harvesting from the viewer side of the market to classify them as belonging to so-called content verticals and serve matching ad content. It has gradually become clear, however, that many avid YouTube viewers are children under the age of 13. As it is illegal under US law to collect personal data about children below the age of 13 without their parents' consent, the FTC fined YouTube $170 million for violating the Children's Online Privacy Protection Act (COPPA) and forced the platform to implement systems that ensure future compliance (Cohen, 2019). This has led to an increased focus on compliance on the parts of uploaders, who must declare whether their content is targeted at kids at the time of upload. In classic neo-liberalist fashion, this pushes problems of editorial control and responsibility downwards to the uploader. The problem, however, is that although YouTube may very well manage to transfer the responsibility in legal terms to the creator who uploads content, YouTube must still ensure that ads served to children are deemed safe for children in the eyes of parents and other parties – the legitimacy problem persists regardless of the legal side of things. This has led YouTube to build and launch a separate app for YouTube Kids where all advertisements 'must be pre-approved by YouTube's policy team prior to being served' (YouTube, nd). This clearly threatens the lean platform model since it requires more editorial control and human vetting of content as opposed to mass ingestion and subsequent algorithmic culling of content and ads.

Another problem related to the user side is the identity and nature of the individual users. One key issue is that of various types of fraudulent user behaviour such as fake accounts and bot activity. Studies have thus documented how click farms involving bots or human accounts sell large-scale user activity (traffic, engagement, comments and so on) to boost the popularity of social media profiles, websites or mobile apps (Vonderau, 2021). Since late 2017, Meta (formerly Facebook) has disclosed the amount of fake accounts they remove on a quarterly basis (Community Standards Enforcement | Transparency Center, nd). Again, the numbers are truly staggering: the company has had to cull app. 1.5 billion fake accounts per business quarter. Likewise, research suggests that a large part of the traffic on Twitter is generated or amplified by bots (Al-Sibai, 2022). Ironically, Elon Musk, whose acquisition of Twitter in 2022 involved a vow from Musk to strike down on automated traffic and bots, might himself have a large following of bots (Cuthbertson, 2022).

To assess the quality of its users, YouTube has outsourced the assessment to a third-party provider, DoubleVerify, which has achieved accreditation from the Media Rating Council in the US. In this way, YouTube can enhance legitimacy by giving away control over (some of) its media measurements. The main point is that users are not just users – if they are not of the right kind and quality, problems of legitimacy will follow.

Problematic practices

Third, and partly because of the previous two problems, the main subsidization model of the multisided market is vulnerable. Whereas advertisement has been lucrative for digital media platforms, many creators have struggled to establish a viable business based on this source of income alone (Cunningham and Craig, 2021). Instead, creators have cultivated attractive revenue streams that sidestep YouTube's monetization system. This involves branded content, sponsorships and direct sales to consumers through the creator's own ecosystem or agencies. This entails that many producers can be *on* YouTube but derive most of their income *off* the platform (Ørmen and Gregersen, 2022). As another example, publishers criticized the newsletter platform Substack for obfuscating the deals it makes with high-profile writers (Kafka, 2021) instead of publicly disclosing the terms. This resulted in creators disavowing Substack's publishing platform and finding alternatives (of which there are now several).

From a regulatory standpoint, the growth of more latent forms of advertisement (for example, content marketing, branded content) raise clear legitimacy concerns. Traditional advertisement is thus demarcated as paid-for content, but a main selling point of the novel forms of promotion is arguably to obfuscate such demarcation and offer marketing camouflaged as authentic content produced and distributed by creators. Although policies are in place to regulate influencer marketing in many countries and jurisdictions, these policies lag behind the laws for traditional advertisement both in clarity and coverage (The Digital, Culture, Media and Sport Committee, 2022). This leaves a grey zone of what is allowed on and condoned by digital media platforms, especially when dealing with vulnerable audiences such as children.

Platforms act as market makers (akin to brokerage firms in finance) that makes trade between sides possible (Wigand, 1997; 2020). In industries where there are few alternative marketplaces, this gives the dominant platform a near-monopoly. Several ongoing investigations and lawsuits accuse Apple of using its monopoly power in the iPhone marketplace (App Store) to demand high commission for in-app purchases (such as subscriptions) and for throttling alternative payment systems (Boffey, 2021). However, many platforms also offer solutions *in* the markets they operate. The European Union has criticized Apple for restricting access to the NFC technology for third-party apps, thereby giving preferential treatment to its own payment service Apple Pay (Evans, 2022).

Lastly, antitrust regulators have raised concerns about the ways advertisement-based platforms handle their internal ads auction system. Representatives from the advertisement industry and regulators alike have criticized Google for manipulating prices in the ads market and excluded competing ad exchanges to assert dominance (Koetsier, 2022). As Google controls one of the leading ad auction systems (Adx), demand-side platforms (DoubleClick) and supply-side platforms (Google Ads), the company has integrated access to all steps in ad auctions in most corners of the world. By integrating activities in the value chain vertically (as Google has done in the digital ad market) the company can attain high efficiency but at the risk of being faced with charges and lawsuits on monopolization and anti-competitive behaviour.

In short, digital media platforms like YouTube face legitimacy problems on all sides. Advertisers will withdraw and re-allocate funds elsewhere if they identify threats to their brand, producers will go elsewhere if they see better opportunities to thrive (financially and/or creatively) and political institutions might force platforms to police content, users, and monetization schemes.

Conclusion

As this chapter has demonstrated, digital media platform companies have emerged as operators of highly efficient matchmaking platforms which has allowed them to match content creators with advertisers and ordinary users at unprecedented scale. However, as our discussion of the three prototypical legitimacy problems has laid out, this efficiency may come at a cost. In short, the highly efficient algorithmic matchmaking of platforms has shown itself to be detrimental to their legitimacy in the eyes of attractive partners (such as high-profile content creators and brands) as well as concerned regulators. These legitimacy problems tend to arise when platforms commit themselves to achieving positive network effects by increasing the number of producers and consumers attached to the platform, all while keeping the production side of the transactions external to the firm. This minimal level of quality assurance then tends to create problems downstream.

From a cynical point of view, one might expect the digital media platform companies to simply double down on the raw efficiency of the network-effects driven business model, possibly with some deftly decoupled performativity in the style predicted by Meyer and Rowan (1977). This has clearly been part of the platform company playbook, as indicated by the Janus-faced approach of companies such as Alphabet/YouTube and Meta/Facebook where downright fraudulent behaviour has been combined with a sombre *mea culpa* in congressional hearings and elsewhere. There are, however, signs that platform companies are responding in a more complex manner. One response to these legitimacy problems is thus epitomized in the ideal of 'the creator', here exemplified through YouTube's public communication. The platform company portrays the creator as a small-scale producer of original content on a journey to develop an audience and earn money through the YouTube monetization system (see, for example, www.youtube.com/creators/). Through human and algorithmic management, YouTube regulates access to the platform's resources (notably content monetization) and cultivates content producers to be successful on the platform (efficiently managing their resources to build up a loyal fanbase) but more importantly, to act as brand ambassadors for YouTube (signalling effectiveness to key partners such as a large brands, advertisers and regulators). The ideal creator is dependent (Cutolo and Kenney, 2020) upon the platform to succeed.

To attract this ideal creator, platforms often acquire or commission production from established producers or aspiring creators willing to comply with brand-safe expectations. From the early days, YouTube has invested in acquiring content. Lately, YouTube has expanded these activities and now operates three separate $100 million funds: a Shorts fund, a Black Voices Fund and a Kids Fund. These funds are a continuation of an active content investment strategy that started with 'YouTube Original Channel Initiative' in 2010 and has continued in various instantiations (currently as YouTube Originals). The investments span from acquisitions of existing content to commissioning novel films and series. The addition of funds suggests a shift toward the cultivation of talent. For the Shorts fund, there is no upfront payment to creators. Instead, channels can qualify if they meet the standard criteria for monetization as well as produce sufficient engagement (https://blog.youtube/news-and-events/introducing-youtube-shorts-fund/). In that sense, it reads more like a competitive prize (Stark and Pais, 2021). The Black Voices Fund functions more like a product development facility (or 'incubator' as YouTube calls it), where selected candidates receive resources, support and training in making a living of YouTube. For the YouTube Kids Fund, it remains unclear who is eligible and under which conditions producers can apply for funding (https://blog.youtube/news-and-events/an-update-on-kids/). All funds run outside of YouTube Partner Program (YPP) as application or invite-only.

YouTube's activities within this field is thus reminiscent of yet another oldie-but-goodie, namely a traditional model from the cultural industries which emphasizes the role of the *editeur* (Miege and Garnham, 1979) or producer. The role of the editeur is to manage a group of potentially valuable creators and cultivate them to produce content that is culturally successful and commercially attractive. Essentially, the company does not pay these upcoming content creators but remains ever ready in the wings to claim a piece of the pie if a creator strikes gold on the big stage. Following Miege, YouTube's editeurship can be seen as an effort to operate a set of interconnected pools of potential creators, referred to as 'fish tanks' (Miege and Garnham, 1979), holding a properly cultivated creator population. To capitalize on their investment in talent, YouTube operates a range of spaces for monetary exchange between users supplementing the advertisement exchange. These include a site for influencer marketing that connects brands to producers as well as a market for digital goods and donations facilitating direct support from fans to producers (see Ørmen and Gregersen, 2022). Thus, YouTube is moving toward a *platform of marketplaces* diversifying the potential revenue streams instead of the more unitary marketplace platform focused on cross-subsidization described by Evans and Schmalensee (2016).

For a long time, YouTube was the only major media platform with a revenue-sharing model (the YPP). Now, platforms like Twitch, Roblox, Facebook, Instagram and TikTok run creator programmes modelled after the YPP with content and monetization tutorials, financial and legal support, as well as creator marketplaces. This development points to a growing isomorphism (DiMaggio and Powell, 1983; Caplan and boyd, 2018) in the way platforms institutionalize the ideal of the creator and thus balance the efficiency of the lean platform with the effectiveness of a trustworthy organization. Consequently, the platform model itself is transforming. Whereas the digital platform model previously was likened to an efficient market matching sellers and buyers (see, for example, Evans and Schmalensee, 2016), the current instantiations are more reminiscent of a mall connecting specific brands to select customers. In the latter case, the job of the platform is not to increase activity on all sides but rather to ensure customer flow into the most valuable boutiques, and this involves both lucrative brands as well as successful creators. This, in turn, means picking winners in the marketplace as well as designing moderation policies and recommendation systems to elevate trustworthy (and thus effective) content at the expense of the plethora of potentially problematic (and thus ineffective) content that is at the bottom of the fish tanks.

9

Player-Driven Economies and 'Money at the Margins': Game Items as Contingent Commodity Money

Anne Mette Thorhauge

In this chapter, I analyse the Steam platform and the third-party websites that utilize its infrastructure as a monetary network that transforms game items into units of transaction comparable to conventional money. I first address the way in which the business model of Steam has evolved from that of a storefront into that of a 'tangled market', integrating 'transactional affordances' across every corner of the platform. In extension of this I describe how this quest to integrate player-driven economies into the platform's revenue model has extended beyond the platform into a wider system of third-party websites where game items are traded, gambled and rewarded in ways that increase their status as units of transaction. I analyse this system as a 'monetary network' in Nigel Dodd's definition of the term and identify the specific roles of the Steam platform and third-party websites in enabling transactions, ensuring convertibility into state-issued currencies and harnessing emergent economic practices, in this way consolidating the platform's status as an alternative means of payment. I argue that Steam and the associated third-party websites can be considered a 'money game' residing at the margins of the global monetary system in the same manner as bitcoin (Hütten and Thiemann, 2017). In extension of this analysis, I discuss the characteristics of game items in comparison to other type of commodity money foregrounding their 'contingency' on the platform from which they originate.

Introduction

In this chapter I will discuss the Steam platform economy as a monetary network. The Steam platform has historically dominated the field of PC gaming, making up approximately 15 per cent of the global game market. At the time of writing, the platform features more than 58,000 games and mods of which approximately 13,000 are being played by at least one player at the time of writing. It was established as a digital storefront in 2003, and since then it has been augmented in several ways. Communication and interaction features have been added which has widened the functioning of the platform from that of a storefront to that of a social network and entertainment platform (Werning, 2019). Yet, as a social network and an entertainment platform Steam's business model differs considerably from other entertainment platforms such as Facebook and YouTube. These platforms, which have received the bulk of attention in critical platform studies (Gillespie, 2010; Van Dijck et al, 2018; Burgess, 2021), base their business models on the multi-sided market of advertising, providing content to users and user attention to advertisers. Indeed, the emphasis on advertising among large social networks is so comprehensive that the role of advertisers is often included as platforms constituencies (Gillespie, 2010) and part of platform logics (Burgess, 2021), and the intensive collection of users' data for the purpose of segmentation and advertising has given rise to worries about a new era of 'surveillance capitalism' (Zuboff, 2015; 2019). In contrast to this, the Steam platform directly rejects advertisement as a revenue model and foregrounds its micro-transaction system as a preferred alternative. This is an entirely different type of platform economy. Indeed, the platform's historic development can be interpreted as a strategic expansion of economic transactions beyond the context of the storefront, such as the introduction of player-trading, the Steam community market and paid mods in the Steam community workshop (Joseph, 2018), effectively including players and player-driven economies in the platform's revenue model (Thorhauge, 2023). In the subsequent sections I will describe the different contexts of economic exchange on the Steam platform and how these extend onto the wider internet. In extension of this I will discuss the different ways items rooted in Steam-based game titles are integrated as goods, tokens, prizes and even salaries, making up what can be defined as a 'monetary network' (Dodd, 1994) at the intersection between the Steam platform and economic practices on the wider internet. I describe this as a monetary network in Nigel Dodd's definition of this term and highlight the different points in this network where game items are made convertible into conventional currencies, enhancing their status as units of transaction and commodity money. Game items as units of transaction, however, remain tied to the platform on which they originate, and in my discussion I will address whether this makes them different from other types of commodity money. In order to conduct this analysis, I will first address the notion of money as a social and institutional arrangement.

Money as social and institutional arrangements

Money is notoriously difficult to define. A range of possible approaches exist which may possess a certain explanatory power in their respective contexts yet fail to account for the phenomenon of money in its entirety (Dodd, 1994). In classic economic theory money has either been defined as a commodity with particular capabilities or with reference to its functions in the economy (Ingham, 2013; Lehdonvirta and Castronova, 2014). Popular accounts of commodity money typically describe them as an evolution from everyday goods over precious metals to fiat money, culminating with bitcoin and cryptocurrency as its utopian fulfilment (Eich, 2019). In accordance with this line of thought, objects with certain characteristics such as their fungibility, divisibility, transportability, countability, recognizability, durability and so on (Lehdonvirta and Castronova, 2014: 179–82) are more useful in the process of exchange. However, as Nigel Dodd (1994) points out, the attempt to identify money by way of such physical characteristics is analytically insufficient, as it does not explain why some objects do indeed achieve the status of money while others don't. Alternatively, money can be defined in extension of the functions it serves in the economy such as media of exchange, stores of value and units of account. Money facilitates trade, stores value over time and serves as a standard measure of value (Lehdonvirta and Castronova, 2014: 179–82). However, this functionalist approach only explains what money *does*, not what it *is* (Ingham, 2013) and specific forms of money do not necessarily fulfil all of these functions simultaneously (Dodd, 1994). While a functionalist account of money surely foregrounds the importance of money in the economy, it does not bring us closer to the *ontology of money*. In the field of economic sociology emphasis has been put on money as social and institutional arrangements, foregrounding the role of states and banks in the creation and maintenance of 'money of account'. According to Ingham (2013), and contrary to popular beliefs that primitive commodity money has 'evolved' into money of account, money 'is always an abstract claim or credit whose "moneyness" is conferred by money of account' (Ingham, 2013: 49). Even in ancient Babylon commodity money was backed by a system of account, supported by a local political authority. In this approach to money, emphasis is neither on the physical characteristics of money nor on its functions but on the institutional arrangements that endow diverse objects with their status as money in order to make them serve certain functions in the economy, typically with a particular emphasis on the role of states and banks in this process. Nigel Dodd criticizes Ingham's emphasis on state and sovereignty in the definition of money however, and points out that it reduces money to state-issued currencies (Dodd, 2005). He emphasizes the 'diversification of money' including local forms of money that are not necessarily issued by a state or political authority. Indeed, while the political and institutional arrangements associated with state-issued money has allowed us to equal money primarily with national currencies from the end of the 1970s to the financial crisis (Eich, 2019), the fundamental distrust in the global financial system entailed by this historical event brought about a surge of cryptocurrencies and 'data-monies' that do not rely on states and banks. Bitcoin has been explained as 'commodity money without gold, fiat money without state and credit money without debt' (Bjerg, 2016) and can in this way be defined through a double disintermediation from bank and states (Dodd, 2018), the two key institutions in Ingham's definition of money. Technically this is done by replacing the authority of the state and the money lending power of the bank with the 'distributed ledger' made possible by blockchain technologies. This double disintermediation is tied to the tech-utopian idea that bitcoin can 'remove politics from the production and management of money altogether' (2018: 8). However, as Dodd points out, this is an illusion since bitcoin relies on a great deal of social organization and surely involves both a great deal of trust and a considerable centralization of power with those who control the network and computer programs (Dodd, 2018; Eich, 2019). Indeed, the overwhelming focus on the algorithmic aspects of cryptocurrencies has overshadowed the social, institutional and, indeed, political processes that are involved in their creation and maintenance. For instance, Hütten and Thiemann define bitcoin as a 'money game' and describe its relation vis-à-vis other monetary systems and legal frameworks as a historic development from confrontation to horizontal and vertical integration (Hütten and Thiemann, 2017). This development has ensured bitcoin a place 'at the margins' of the global monetary system by 'weaving itself into the dominant money games'(Hütten and Thiemann, 2017: 25). Indeed, much of this historical development has less to do with the specific programmed properties of cryptocurrencies and more to do with general institutional and political rearrangements. Nigel Dodd's notion of 'monetary networks' is very useful for analysing and explaining these arrangements. With this concept, Dodd emphasizes 'the network of social relationships that make [economic] transactions possible' rather than the object exchanged or the exchange relationship itself (Dodd, 1994: xxiii). Instead of assigning the nature of money to its historical institutions or its physical or programmed properties we must include the entire social network that makes economic transactions possible by enabling transactions, assigning value to goods, translating value into units of transaction, and so on. Dodd assigns five analytical properties to economic networks including a standardized system of account, information about the network's spatial and temporal properties, legalistic information and, finally, expectations regarding other actors' behaviour. He proposed this framework in 1994 and for some reason does not give it much attention in later publications. However, it is very useful for analysing money independently of banks and states without succumbing to an overly materialistic or functionalistic perspective. In the subsequent sections I will apply this framework to the Steam platform economy to explain how specific aspects of the Steam platform architecture have enabled the emergence of a monetary network that does not rely on blockchain technologies and mining, yet still establishes what can be defined as a 'local money' that thrives at the margins of the wider economic system. In extension of this I will discuss the specific role of the Steam platform in this monetary network and in the production of a possibly new species of 'contingent commodity money'.

Steam's tangled markets: expanding the scope of economic transactions

The Steam platform was introduced as a download client for the game Counterstrike in 2003. In the following years it managed to attract enough game publishers and gamers to become a regular storefront, in fact, the dominating storefront in the market of PC gaming (Thorhauge, 2023). In addition to its growth in numbers, Steam introduced new features that expanded its business model in distinctive ways: the monetization of playbour and the expansion of the scope of economic transactions. As concerns the first, the strategic inclusion and involvement of so-called 'modding communities', have been part of the platforms' strategy from the beginning. Modding refers to the activity of modifying games, either in the form of simple add-ons or through 'total conversions' (Postigo, 2007). Indeed, Counterstrike is itself such a 'total conversion' and the engine on which it is built was made freely available to modders from the beginning while licensed to commercial actors (Kerr, 2017). In this way player active player contributions have been key to the Steam platform from the introduction of the Steam community (2007) and player reviews (2013) to the introduction 'paid mods' (2015) giving community mod makers the opportunity to *earn money doing what they love* and taking a 30 per cent share in the process (see Joseph, 2018). This (relatively controversial) design choice is part of a more general strategy of expanding the scope of economic transactions on the platform which can also be detected in the promotion of the 'microtransaction system' that allows game publishers to sell items in-game by way of the Steam API, as well as the introduction of player-trading and the Steam community market (2012). In the latter, players can list items from specific game titles insofar game publishers have chosen to make them marketable. In this way the Steam community market can be defined as a 'secondary market' (Lehdonvirta and

Castronova, 2014) for game items. Because of this development, the Steam platform as of today features several 'markets', or contexts of economic exchange beyond the storefront. Players can buy games from publishers in the store and buy additional items in the games, exchange items by way of their inventories, trade items in the market, buy player-created items in the workshop or upload their own, sharing the sales with the publisher and the platform owner. However, these economic transactions do not only take place on the Steam platform. Economic transactions extend beyond the platform to the wider internet in the form of trading sites, gambling sites and other kinds of economic practices.

Powered by Steam, not affiliated with Valve corporation: economic practices beyond the Steam platform

In the periphery of Steam exists a wider system of third-party websites that thrive on Steam's player-driven economies (Thorhauge, 2022; 2023) and transform them into different types of business. These websites are often obscure in terms of their status and purposes, and it is difficult to keep a stable record of them because they disappear and reappear in new versions. One important reason for this volatility is that they are often in conflict with regulatory frameworks such as national gambling regulation. Furthermore, some of these sites are direct scams that are primarily put in place to deprive users of their items without offering them any value in return. A more systematic examination of the business models emerging in extension of Steam-based player-trading discloses a variety of interconnected businesses that transform game items into *goods* that can be bought and sold, *prizes* that can be won, *tokens* that can be wagered and even *rewards* that can be earned.

Thus, quite a few sites make it possible to trade game items from game titles beyond the Steam community market such as cs.deals. On these sites, players can buy or sell items using either their Steam wallet or their credit card by logging in with their Steam account. Thus, game items take the role as virtual goods that can be sold at a certain prize.

On another group of websites game items are included as tokens and prizes. Some of these sites have specialized in 'lootboxes', that is, boxes containing unknown game items. Customers pay for opening these boxes and, if they are lucky, the revealed content may exceed the original investment in terms of value. One example is csgocases.com. In these contexts, game items take the role as prizes that can be won for money. Other websites go full circle and allow customers to use game items as tokens that can be wagered to earn other game items in classic casino games such as blackjack and roulette, see for example daddyskins.com. On these websites game items take the role of tokens and prices and function in the same manner as conventional currencies such as euro or dollars do in traditional casinos. A final group of websites impart different types of 'micro-work' with game items or Steam gift cards representing one among several possible compensations. Users can answer surveys, watch videos, recommend content to their friends, and get game items and other virtual goods in return. These websites seem to work independently of the Steam platform architecture. Yet, they are important in the context of this analysis because they represent yet another way of integrating game items into economic transactions. In combination, these websites make up an alternative and somewhat clandestine system of businesses that contribute to the Steam platform economy by increasing the demand for game items on the platform, but also consolidating the status of the Steam platform as an economic infrastructure and game items as units of transaction. In extension of Otto's analysis in this volume, they can be seen as 'shadow intermediaries' 'between platforms facilitating the tools, frameworks and publishing stores for building app and data infrastructures on the one end, and the customers and users on the other' (p 89). While the intermediaries in Otto's analysis concerns app developers within fully legal markets, the basic principle remains the same: the platform offers the tools, frameworks and stores while much of the work is done by third parties.

In the introduction I point out that the Steam platform economy differs considerably from other social networks and entertainment platforms. One key characteristic is the rejection of advertisement as a revenue model and, conversely, the strong promotion of microtransactions as an alternative. The Steamworks documentation clearly express that no limits are put on the way individual publishers choose to integrate this feature in their gameplay, which strongly indicates that micro-transactions represent a key business emphasis from the perspective of the platform owner. The websites mentioned above do not seem to base their functionality directly on the microtransaction system, however. Most of the websites ask players to log onto Steam, make their profile public and share their trade link, to enable the website to send items to their account or withdraw items from their account.

In this way, it seems to be users' ability to exchange items between their inventories that form the technological backbone and transactional affordances (see Manzerolle's chapter in this volume) that enable these third-party websites. Obviously, the Steam terms of service do state that earning money from game items on Steam in this manner is not allowed, otherwise Valve could potentially be held responsible for the gambling phenomena arising in association with the platform. Yet, the enforcement of this condition is half-hearted at best and quite a few of these third-party websites state that they are 'Powered by Steam. Not affiliated with Valve Corp'.

As long as third-party websites use the player trading feature rather than the Steam community market as the key functionality for exchanging items, Valve does not profit directly from these exchanges. Whereas Valve earns a share of all transactions taking place by way of the micro-transaction system and the Steam community market, the direct exchange of items between players' inventories is effectively a kind of 'barter' that does not involve a monetary exchange and thus cannot be 'taxed' by the platform. Still Valve has an indirect economic interest in these exchanges, as the existence of 'secondary markets' increase the total value of the market (Lehdonvirta and Castroniova, 2014) and also increases the demand for game items (Thorhauge and Nielsen, 2021) which may, among other things, be purchased by way of the micro-transaction system. Additionally, a more far-fetched strategic aim may concern the status of the Steam platform as the key transaction mechanism in a wider monetary network. In their chapter on Alibaba in this volume, Yuan and Zhang explain how the platform spawns the Ant group, one of the most valuable technology companies in the world, on the basis of its Alipay mobile payment service. Similarly, Lana Swartz observes how large platform companies such as Facebook and Apple are currently orienting themselves toward payment and economic transactions as a new lucrative business domain (Swartz, 2020). From these perspectives, Steam's key role in a monetary network constituted across a plethora of diverse third-party websites may represent an alternative and somewhat more subtle expansion into fintech (see also Thorhauge, 2023).

The Steam platform as a monetary network and a social-financial technology

In the beginning of this chapter, I introduce Nigel Dodd's notion of 'monetary networks' as a useful framework for analysing this phenomenon (Dodd, 1994). Instead of defining money by way of its material properties or by way of the institutional arrangements that characterize the dominant system of national currencies, Dodd addresses money as that entire network that makes economic transactions possible in the first place. He singles out five analytical properties of this network: a standardized system of account, information about the networks' extension in time and space, legalistic information and expectations regarding other actors' behaviour. These analytical properties can to various degrees be applied to the network of economic transactions emerging in relation to the Steam platform turning the platform into a key exchange mechanism and game items into units of transaction.

Depending on the level of analysis, the standardized system of account can either be ascribed directly to the management of digital rights accomplished by the Steam platform architecture, or more indirectly to the game items' convertibility into dominant state-issued currencies. As concerns the first, the 'Steam wallet' and 'the Steam inventory' effectively keeps track of Steam credits and game items identifying which users have which credits and items at their disposal at a certain point in time. The Steam platform architecture does not allow users to withdraw credit from their Steam wallet and in this way Valve can be said to at least officially confine the exchange of game items (and their value in terms of Steam credits) to the context of the platform. However, the Steam community market's facilitation of player trading on the platform using state-issued currencies as conversion factors, is a first important step in the translation of informal player economies into conventional market value at a symbolic level. As concerns the second, third-party trading sites directly offer users the option of converting the somewhat fictional monetary value of Steam-based game items into actual monetary value. Or, put differently, while the Steam platform offers the exchange mechanism and the units of exchange, these third-party websites effectively transport them into wider economic practices on the internet, increasing their convertibility into conventional currencies in the process. These individual steps of translation from fictive game economy over a platform-based economy to wider economic practices, entails that game items exchanged on the Steam platform are effectively integrated into the systems of account represented by the dominant monetary systems. In this way it effectively exists at the margins of the dominant money games in the same way as bitcoin does (Hütten and Thiemann, 2017).

As concerns information about spatial and temporal properties Nigel Dodd, writing in 1994, may point to information about the geographic territory. Geographic territory in the form of a nation state issuing and safeguarding the relative stability of its currency is surely what has been associated with money in recent historical times and used as a guiding principle in the assessment of a given currency's stability and expected use. Yet, as the rise of cryptocurrencies bear witness to, national territory should be seen as a variable rather than a given as concerns the constitution of money. In the case of the Steam platform as a nexus in a wider monetary network the information about spatial and temporal properties as well as expectations with regard to the actions of others are defined by the practices of the gaming community. For instance, it is more likely that a certain game item can be exchanged with someone playing the same game and thus appreciates its value, just as the historical properties of a game and the size and relative stability of its gaming community hint to how likely it is that the investment is valid in the future. While this is surely a less stable foundation as compared to that of a central bank, we should not forget that gaming communities may rise to a size and a stability that exceeds that of several national currencies. Indeed, back in 2001 Castronova published a working paper analysing *Norrath*, the game-world of *Everquest* (released by Sony Online Entertainment in 1999), as a national economy, complete with estimations of nominal hourly wages, GNP per capita and a currency with an exchange rate above that of the yen and the lira at the time (Castronova, 2001). Similarly, the exchange of gold from *World of Warcraft* into dollars has given rise to a whole business of 'goldfarming' at the intersection between the fictional game economy and the wider economic system (Lehdonvirta and Castronova, 2014; Liboriussen, 2015). From this perspective certain game economies are in practice more stable and predictable than those of a nation in crisis and may serve as alternative sources of information about the monetary network's spatial and temporal properties.

Finally, as concerns legalistic information, this is where the Steam platform architecture becomes an important factor. As the repeated use of the expression 'powered by Steam, Not affiliated with Valve Corp' indicates, the economic exchange of game items taking place beyond the platform from a strictly legal perspective takes place in a limbo. By way of its EULA Valve, the owner of the Steam platform, has officially disenfranchised any legal responsibility regarding these exchanges, and in cases of scams and fraud happening beyond the platform, users surely have little legal protection. Moreover, most of the sites I have been able to locate are registered in territories notorious for a limited enforcement of national and international law, such as Curacao. In this way, the Steam platform economy as a monetary network surely displays a very limited level of legal information (and enforcement). At the same time, much of what is usually assigned to the role of states and legal frameworks, is in practice undertaken by the platform itself, such as handling property rights and defining the rules of transactions (Fligstein, 1996; 2001) much like the blockchain in term of cryptocurrencies. The Steam inventory effectively defines property rights in terms of who possesses which items at certain points in time, just as rules assigned to items on the platform define whether and when they can be traded and listed in the market. In this way the platform architecture itself can to some degree be said to define and automate part of what is otherwise handled by national legal systems. Of course, we should not succumb to the 'tech-utopia' of certain cryptocurrency advocates and believe that the platform can entirely replace the social and political organization of money (Dodd, 2018; Eich, 2019), yet, it can serve to ensure a basic level of digital property right and rules of transaction that enable the exchange of game items beyond the platform.

In this way, the economic practices emerging on and beyond the Steam platform in extension of the platform architecture and the way third-party developers use this for alternative forms of business can be meaningfully interpreted as a monetary network turning game items into units of transaction and the Steam platform into an exchange mechanism in a wider monetary network. This monetary network is only partly constituted by the platform architecture. Its full functionality rests on a diverse and socially embedded transactional network across several websites and contexts of exchange. And while bitcoin and other cryptocurrencies have been introduced with somewhat confrontational statements (Hütten and Thiemann, 2017) this network goes under the radar. This may either be due to its emergent nature or due to a deliberate attempt to avoid regulation. As compared to bitcoins, it resides in an even farther margin of the dominant economic system where a range of economic actors invest a great deal of creativity into transforming its affordance into ways of making a business.

Contingent commodity money?

In my analysis I have addressed how the business model of the Steam platform involves a strategic expansion of the scope of economic transactions on as well as beyond the platform. Game items from different game titles are bought, collected and gifted between players in a range of contexts of the Steam platform in extension of what is made possible by the platform architecture. By featuring a secondary market strategy in the form of the Steam community market, game items from specific Steam game titles can be traded between players using a 'Steam wallet', enhancing these items' status as commodities as well as their symbolic equation with monetary value in terms of state-issued currencies. And by way of third-party trading sites, the game items figure next to credit cards and cryptocurrencies on various trading and gambling sites beyond the Steam platform effectively functioning as units of exchange. From the perspective of the Steam platform these extra-platform activities can be regarded as just another way of increasing the general size of its market and thus the demand for game items. However, it may also serve the strategic aim of building a monetary network based on the active contributions and avid trading of the Steam-based gaming communities. From this perspective, the transactional communities (Swartz, 2020), and their practices at the intersection between Steam and the wider internet can be analysed as an emerging monetary network in extension of Nigel Dodd's definition of this term. Unlike bitcoin and other cryptocurrencies this monetary network is not organized around a blockchain system, but it may represent yet another path into the endeavour of making money at the margins, once the monopolies of the state and the banking systems have been broken, potentially turning the Steam platform into a means of payment beyond the level of its player-driven economies. Dodd refers to Goodhart's law that states that 'as soon as an instrument or assets is publicly defined as money ... substitutes will be produced for purposes of evasion' (Dodd, 1994: xx). This evasion may concern direct political regulation, and it may concern practical obstacles such as the way the Steams platform hinders the use of Steam credit beyond the platform. In any case, the emergence of substitutes is not a consequence of the digital nature of Steam-based game items; substitutes are features of monetary systems at any historical point in time. The primary and potentially important difference between the Steam platform and local monies in a wider historical perspective rather concerns the way the specific units of transaction, that is, the game items, remain tied to the player-driven economies in which they originate, and that the platform inventory remains the only possible 'bank account' in which they can be stored. The game items only exist in extension of the game platform. They are what Nieborg and Poell define as 'contingent commodities' (Nieborg and Poell, 2018), deeply intertwined with and defined by the platforms. Nieborg and Poell introduce the notion of 'contingent commodities' in the context of cultural production on digital platforms, emphasizing how diverse cultural products such as games and news are increasingly shaped by the business logics of the platforms on which they are distributed. In this analysis, their notion of 'contingent commodities' is relatively rhetoric or figurative, and the cultural products in question remain the intellectual property of their diverse creators. However, Daniel Joseph aptly demonstrates how game items are in a very direct sense contingent on their platforms, they remain the property of the game platform which players may access and enjoy but never download and fully own (Joseph, 2020). This may be the primary and paramount difference contemporary digital platforms (and blockchain systems) make in the domain of financial technologies, that is, not the inclination to create new money but rather the contingent nature of this money. Of course, it can be argued that state-issued currencies are also the 'property' of the central bank and that you can for the same reason never fully own a dollar bill or a euro bill. Yet, it is the moneyness if these objects, so to say, rather than their material existence as such that depends on the central banks, while the existence of game items as digital objects (and of cryptocurrencies, indeed) is a direct function of their programmed systems from which they cannot be separated. While states and banks confer the moneyness of traditional money, the Steam platform defines the very digital existence of game units as such, and the wider monetary network endows them with the status as units of transaction.

Conclusion: platforms and the production of money

Ingham (Ingham, 2013) points out that much classic economic theory builds on the idea that money is a neutral commodity, a 'veil' that covers what can basically be boiled down to a barter economy (Samuelson, 1973, cited in Ingham, 2004). In doing so, economic theory fails to explain and take into consideration the way money is created and distributed in society. He points out that power in societies does not only relate to the possession and quantity of money but also to the *production* of money in the first place, with the state and the banking system as key institutions in question. Bitcoin's 'double disintermediation' from state and banks (Dodd, 2018) in the wake of the financial crisis breaks with equation of money with state-issued currency that has remained common sense since the end of the 1970s (Eich, 2019) and in the contemporary landscape a plethora of cryptocurrencies and related money-forms such as Steam-based game items compete for the status as money. Many of these phenomena are accompanied with simplistic ideas that programmed systems can entirely replace the social and institutional arrangements involved in the creation of money and on an utterly naïve trust in the integrity of the code and the people that control it. This is obviously not tenable. However, the introduction of programmed systems into the production of money makes a difference after all, since the introduction of 'exchange mechanisms with extended memories' whether in the form of blockchain systems or gaming platforms do imply that part of what was formerly undertaken by institutions is now automated in programmed systems. Moreover, it shifts ownership toward those who control the code. A programmed system cannot by itself produce money; this depends on the wider monetary network of which it is part and, ultimately, its position in the wider financial system. Yet, its relative power in the monetary network may be larger as compared to traditional means of money production.

In terms of the Steam platform, the transformation of game items into units of transaction happens 'under the radar' in a monetary network composed of active gaming communities, 'shadow' intermediaries and the Steam platform architecture. Unlike bitcoin, which was introduced with somewhat confrontational statements vis-à-vis the existing monetary system, this monetary network remains low profile in the far outskirts of the monetary systems, and so does the role of the Steam platform architecture in the continuous reproduction of this specific money form. This may be due to the emergent nature of this phenomenon, but it may also be a strategic choice of Valve, the owner of the Steam platform, in the attempt to avoid regulation as stated by Goodhart's law.

10

After the Attention Economy: A Postdigital Anthropology of the Future

Morten Axel Pedersen

Introduction

Over recent years, Big Tech and social media platforms have been increasingly scrutinized as part of the 'techlash', which first gained traction in critical data studies (for example, boyd and Crawford, 2012; Zuboff, 2019) and among artists (for example, Cramer, 2015; Bridle, 2018), but has now become part of mainstream scientific, public and political discourse in the US[1] and the EU, where calls for regulation of platform capitalism is becoming the norm across party lines and divisions.[2] Concurrently, a new concept has found its way into the critical theoretical vocabulary of certain social science and humanities scholars, namely 'postdigital'. As the editor of *Postdigital Science and Education* states in the journal's mission statement:

> We are increasingly no longer in a world where digital technology and media is separate, virtual, 'other' to a 'natural' human and social life. This has inspired the emergence of a new concept—'the postdigital'— which ... is gaining traction in a wide range of disciplines including but not limited to the arts. (Jandrić et al, 2018: 893)

Now, apart from its explicit cultural–aesthetic purchases and dimensions (for example, art theorists using the postdigital to denote art that self-consciously mixes digital and non-digital materials, as discussed in, for example, Alexenberg, 2014), the concept 'is also deeply economic and political' (Jandrić et al, 2018: 894). In that sense, the postdigital can be seen to supplement concepts mobilized by Marxist-inspired economic sociologists and anthropologists, such as 'embeddedness' (Polanyi, 1944; Gregory, 1982) and 'fetishization' (Taussig, 1980; Spyer, 1997), as discussed in this volume's Introduction and several of the individual chapters.

So, how can the postdigital foster novel theorizations of platform capitalism and digital markets? For Florian Cramer, one advantage of this concept is that it opens up for an 'approach to digital media that no longer seeks technical innovation or improvement, but *considers digitization as something that has already happened* and thus might be further reconfigured' (2015; emphasis added). But that is not all. As illustrated in various blogposts explicitly using this concept,[3] in addition situating digitalization in the past, the postdigital also enables us to ask about, theorize and speculate about what *might come after* platforms and platform capitalism. Unlike, say, the concept of embeddedness and cognate political economical terms, postdigitality is thus an explicitly historical concept, in that notions of temporality – past, present and future – are built directly into it. But there are also downsides to that. As pointed about with respect to 'postsocialism' (Humphrey, 2002), 'post-concepts' risk losing their power if they refer to directly to particular time-and space-bound entities, such as Soviet state communism and its collapse. To be sure, the postdigital faces a similar risk. Like other post-concepts, which, after a spike in popularity, turned out to be either too vague to have any real descriptive or analytical purchase, or (which is not necessarily the same thing, on which more below) to be too historically specific to have durably value. Of course, just like 'postsocialism', the postdigital does need be able to capture what is going on in the current moment (such as the current techlash). But that is not a sufficient. If the concept is to have purchase beyond its present (perhaps already past) hype, it needs to be, first, sufficiently narrowed down and explicated as a concept (that is, better defined), and second, put into analytical use on concrete potential future that reaches beyond the now. In what remains of this paper, I shall attempt to address these two criteria in turn.

Below, I first compare the concept of the postdigital to the concept of postmodernity. Invoking Lyotard, I argue that it is too simplified to conceive of the postdigital condition as one that is less digitalized than its digital predecessor. Rather, for the concept to have real analytical purchase, we need to think of it as denoting something that is simultaneously more *and* less digitized than what came before. In that sense, it resembles postmodernism. In the same way that the postmodern condition took the form of phenomena, practices and discourses that in some ways were more, and in other ways less, modern than modernism, so also the postdigital can be theorized as a *mutation of the digital*. In fact, as I then go on to suggest, there are grounds for speculating that global tech, including its two most fundamental pillars of platform capitalism and digital attention economy, is about to undergo such a postdigital transformation as a result of the dual pressure exerted on this business model by, on the one hand, rapid developments in artificial intelligence (AI) and ever increasing political and legal regulation on the other.

From postmodernity to postdigitality

Postdigitality, Cramer writes:

> should not be understood here in the same sense as postmodernism ... but rather in the sense of post-punk (a continuation of punk culture in ways which are somehow still punk, yet also beyond punk); post-communism (as the ongoing social-political reality in former Eastern Bloc countries); post-feminism ... [and] postcolonialism ... as postcolonial practices in a communications world taken over by a military-industrial complex made up of only a handful of global players. (2015: 13, 21)

It is precisely the approach towards the meaning of postdigitality that I shall also adopt here. But, unlike Cramer, I don't want to dismiss the concept of postmodernism to reach this point. On the contrary, as I am now going to argue, vital lessons can be heeded from the manner in which this concept was introduced and used by Lyotard (1984) and other postmodernist icons.

Just to convey from the onset that I am no (ordinary) postmodernist myself, let me begin by making a decidedly non-postmodernist move, namely by tracing this concept back to its origins, that is, Lyotard and his essay on *The Postmodern Condition* (1984). As Lyotard writes, 'I define postmodern as incredulity toward metanarratives ... Each of us lives at the intersection of many of these' (1984: xxiv). Before elaborating on why I believe that this oft-cited quotation is value for my present purposes, let me highlight something that has to my knowledge received (too) little attention in discussions about *The Postmodern Condition*, namely that it was written as a commentary to the then nascent digital age. As Lyotard writes, 'It is reasonable to suppose that the proliferation of information-processing machines is having, and will continue to have, as much of an effect on the circulation of learning as did advancements in human circulation (transportation systems) and later, in the circulation of sounds and visual images (the media)' (Lyotard 1984, cited in Lessem, et al 2013: 288). So, could we go as far as saying that Lyotard 'foresaw' digital age? Certainly, he had prescient sense of what the increasing power and use of 'information-processing machines' would have on the imbrication between power and knowledge. As he put it, '[w]e can predict that anything in the constituted body of knowledge that is not translatable in this [digital] way will be abandoned and that the direction of new research will be dictated by the possibility of its eventual results being translatable into computer language' (1984: 4).[4]

Yet, as Aylesworth notes (2015), Lyotard's conception of the relationship between modernism and postmodernism is not *only* linear and historical in the sense the latter is imagined taking over from the former as time progresses. Rather, their mutual imbrication is conceived of as more than linear, on could perhaps say, as trans-temporal (Holbraad and Pedersen, 2009). In the words of Aylesworth, neither Lyotard nor his peers thus 'suggest[ed] that postmodernism is an attack upon modernity or a complete departure from it. Rather, its differences *lie within modernity itself*, and postmodernism is a continuation of modern thinking in another mode' (2015; emphasis added). It is exactly this understanding of the 'post' prefix I take to be so germane for the edited volume as a whole – the notion that the phenomenon thus designated was always *already latently present* before it came into being, in potential. After all, as Aylesworth continues in an apt formulation, something can 'become modern only if it is first postmodern, for postmodernism is not modernism at its end but in its nascent state'.

This, then, is the lesson and insight that I want to heed from Lyotard and his postmodernist (and poststructuralist) peers – that far from necessarily representing concepts that are imprisoned within a specific historical moment, notion that deploy the prefix 'post' instead holds the potential to complicate overly easy periodizations. Much like, say, postmodernist art represented an intensification of certain stylistic traits that were already present or dormant in modern art, so also the postdigital may be theorized as the product of a simultaneous transformation, where certain features and dynamics that have become closely associated with 'the digital' shall undergo a further intensification, acceleration and radicalization, whereas others will contract, slow down or wither away.

I thus find myself in agreement with Mark Carrigan (2020), who, in a recent blogpost, writes that, contrary to what many think, the current moment in history is not (only) charactered by 'a disenchantment with digital technology'. In fact, he suggests, 'we can ... see an *intensification* of our enchantment with technology, one which the conceptual structure of the post-digital is ill equipped to capture'. With respect to the latter statement, however, I beg to differ. It thus seems to me that, once freed from its '1–1 mapping' into our current historical moment, it becomes not just possible but potentially productive in both an empirical and a theoretical sense, to 'think of the post-digital as an ontological orientation and methodological attitude' (Carrigan, 2020). Crucially, however, these particular and productive 'conceptual affordances' (Holbraad, 2013) of the postdigital can only be elicited by using in a more-than-historical, empirical sense. Only when we cease to conceive of it as denoting a period or position space and time can the postdigital be repurposed as a *theoretical* concept, whose value lies in its capacity to temporalize otherwise too presentist conceptions of the digital.

After the digital attention economy

So, how might the concept of the postdigital allow us to theorize platform capitalism? In keeping with my overarching point that the concept and the state of the postdigital should not be conceived of in opposition to the digital but as a mutation of the digital condition, I shall suggest there are indications that the global platform economy itself is now beginning to undergo such a postdigital transformation. Specifically, I here wish to pinpoint one development in the tech economy, which can both be seen as an harbinger of a broader conceptual, cultural and political-economic shift in terms of what 'the digital' means – and what it does – for social life. Elements of this transformation have in the making for some years (after all, as the contributions to this volume offers a powerful testament to, the platform economy is characterized by incremental, ongoing changes and not sudden or even radical revolutions). Nevertheless, in light of recent developments and discourses, there is reason to believe that all these minor and scattered changes are now in the process of coming together and effectuating a major rupture.

The candidate I would like to identify for such a postdigital transformation is the 'digital attention economy' (Wu, 2016; Williams, 2018; Otto, this volume). As several anthropologists have argued, the human attention over the last decade or so has served as a 'floating signifier' around which a plethora of moral discourses, political imaginaries and cultural anxieties pertaining to digital markets generally and platform capitalism in particular has congealed (Schull, 2014; Pedersen et al, 2021). While the evidence is still inconclusive as to whether social media platforms are 'addictive' or not (Orben and Przybylski, 2019), an increasing number of politicians, thought leaders and snake oil merchants have acted *as if* this is the case (think, for example, of the Danish prime minister's recent vilification of the smartphone as one of the 'biggest problems of our time' or the bombastic claims and scaremongering made by organizations such as the Center for Humane Technology). Indeed, as part of the wider techlash that has swept through (especially) the Western world since Cambridge Analytica, Russian troll farms and so on, a moral panic has broken out in these and other highly digitized countries (such as China[5]) revolving around the alleged dangers of smart phone use to everything from the psychological well-being of our children to the future of democracy if not mankind as whole. While these discourses are varied in form and content, it is no exaggeration to say that the 'digital attention economy' has played a central role in many of them, either as a floating signifier that explicitly can be attached to and integrated into virtually any dystopian scenario of unhinged digitalization and surveillance capitalism galore or as a tacit cultural and political imaginary that has come to undergird core techlash rationales, including the widespread assumption (popularized first via behavioural economics and subsequent pop/ular scientific works) that the attention plays a 'bottle-neck' or 'flashlight' function in human neuro-cognitive processes (Williams, 2018).

Yet, arguably, the digital attention economy has now peaked. Irrespective of whether the techlash crowd's scaremongering holds true,[6] the business model undergirding the digital attention economy – and platform capitalism more generally – is today under increasing strain. Beginning with the General Data Protection Regulation (GDPR) and other attempts by the EU to reign in and protect its citizens from Big Tech (including both anti-trust lawsuits filed by the Commission and upcoming AI legislation), governments' across the world, including federal and state US governments as well as autocratic regimes in China and elsewhere, have passed laws and imposed regulation targeting of some of more extreme and sinister aspects and ramifications of the surveillance capitalism such as digital disinformation, negative effects on children's' and adolescents' well-being, and so forth. But that is not all. I would argue that, in addition to these politically, legally and culturally derived limitations imposed in the digital attention economy, we are also in the midst of a deeper structural transformation of the *source of value commodified* by Big Tech. Predominantly driven (as such shifts often are) by discoveries in fundamental science and resulting technical innovations, what is at issue, I shall now suggest, is nothing but the replacing of the human attention and the associated logic and imaginary of information-processing scarcity with a different economic logic, whose modus of operandi does not turn on a *lack* of cognitive resources and capacity to process information but their *abundance*.

Perhaps not surprisingly, the scientific/technological innovation that I have in mind to is large language models, such as the Generative Pre-trained Transformer (GPT) models that have caused so much stir since the release of Chat GPT3 in late 2022. Without pretending to possess the expertise or time (let alone space, as in word length) necessary to discuss the multifarious political-economic impact of this new frontier in Big Tech, I wish here to home in a one specific such dimension, namely the potential ramifications of the rapidly increasingly commercialization and proliferation of large language models on platform capitalism and its signature business model of digital attention economy/surveillance capitalism, as discussed above. Incidentally, I am not alone in thinking that recent developments in AI might portent a sea change in the political-economy of digital data. In a Substack entry from earlier this year (which has more recently inspired a podcast about the same topic), tech entrepreneur Alistair Croll asks[7]: 'With the attention economy in full swing—and possibly even waning—what comes next? When AI and tools like ChatGPT … are abundant and cheap, what becomes scarce? If information consumes our attention, what does AI consume?' With reference to the Godfather of attention economy, Nobel Prize winner Herbert Simon, Croll goes on to suggest that:

> The Internet has given us a shortage of *directed attention* we can spend, but AI is now making *attending to* something cheap and easy ... In a world where calculators did the math, understanding the problem was what mattered. In a world where search knew all the facts, choosing the right facts mattered ... If Herbert Simon were with us today, I think he'd consider *priority*, *outcome*, or *novelty* worthwhile candidates for the economy that follows attention. An abundance of AI attending to things will create a poverty of prioritization, tangible outcomes, and algorithm-defying novelty. If you're a startup, how are you building towards one of those economies?

This speculation has a lot of things going for it. In particular, I like the way in which Simon's litmus test for an attention economy (that what it consumes is scarce human cognitive capacity) is repurposed to speculate about new forms of scarcity – and thus value, capital and profit – in the age of AI capitalism. By asking the question, 'what does AI consume', Croll compels us to imagine what digital capitalism might become after the digital attention economy. In this potential postdigital future, I venture, it will not just be the ultimate resources of scarcity (that is, attention) that will differ from today. More fundamentally, it will a political economy in which existing limitations to cognitive capacity and 'human bottlenecks' in information-processing will have disappeared! Freed from the burden of having to economize with their attention (since many processes of attentional selection internal to their cognitive apparatus will, on this particular speculation, be delegated to AI chatbots), humans will be free to spend their time doing ... what? 'Prioritize' which 'outcomes' are most 'novel'?

I am less convinced with this second part of Croll's prognosis about what comes after the digital attention economy and about the nature of postdigital capitalism (and society) more generally. 'Novelty', after all, seems to the one resource that society is never going to run out of, alongside with its close cousin of lying. Indeed, one of the more sinister (if not misanthropic lessons from the information/digital/big data age is that it has only *enhanced* the human propensity for bullshit, as evidenced from ongoing discussions about post-truth society, fake news, echo-champers and so forth. As can be gauged from recent discussions about the future of intellectual property rights, and the future of creativity write large, in the age of large language models, there is every reason to believe that postdigital society is going to be saturated with AI-based creations (narratives, images, music and not to forget research). Far from being the ultimate scarce resource, then, it is more likely that subjects of the postdigital age will be suffering from a *novelty abundance*. To paraphrase

Donald Trump, we are going to be so tired from new AI creations that we are going to be wishing, begging even, for it to stop.

But if it is not 'novelty' (or attention' let alone 'information') that is going be the ultimate scarce resource (as well as source of value and profit) in the future postdigital age, what then? What, in Simon's terms, will the postdigital political economy 'consume'? Here, I would like to propose a candidate that is diametrically opposed to not only 'novelty' but also to 'creativity' and 'innovation', which have since the nineteenth century been celebrated (especially in Western contexts) for being uniquely human capacities. I have in mind the notion of *repetition* as well as associated concepts such as 'replication' and 'sameness', which (traditionally especially in Buddhist contexts but also in scientific discussions about Open Science and validity more generally) have been linked to ideas and imaginaries about timelessness, transparency and truth (Turner, 1982; Open Science Collaboration, 2015; Pedersen, 2016). While I acknowledge that this sounds like an unsexy candidate to take over from 'attention' as the limited resource coveted by tech investors, thought leaders and politicians, there are, I believe, sound technical reasons for believing that it might nevertheless turn out to as good a bet as any. At issue is the fact that, because they are stochastic models (or, in less friendly terms, 'parrots') machine learning algorithms including large language models are seldom able to produce the same output twice, even if they have received identical inputs (including, with GPT models, so-called prompts) (Schreiner, 2023; Uddin, 2023). Unlike a traditional machine, which mindlessly (as it were) executes the same instruction over and over again and therefore is unable to produce much (if any) novelty, statistical machines are remarkably good at generating new, 'optimized' outputs, but at the cost of being correspondingly bad at producing what traditional machines are so good at, namely perfect copies. To be sure, the so-called parameter temperature of large language models can be set a low level, which 'will result in more predictable output, while a higher temperature will result in more random output'. However, because of their stochastic nature, the fact remains that 'responses are indeterministic/non-predictable … mean[ing] that you will get a slightly different response every time you call the API'.[8]

One can, against this (admittedly speculative) background make the following – to many people probably farfetched and for still more people undoubtedly chilling – prophesy regarding what I take to be the incipient postdigital economy and, more generally, postdigital era. Having relegated to AI so many of the competencies that used to be distinctly human, including several of the capacities traditionally associated with intelligence, the inhabitants of future societies will come to celebrate – and potentially also commodify and commercialize – those very aspects and dimensions of material and symbolic production that are beyond the reach of AI-powered creativity. That is, the perfectly self-similar – and therefore also (and rather crucially when it comes to the future of science and research processes more generally), perfectly *transparent* – repetitions and replications of the same. Somewhat paradoxically (and frightening), then, as the machines of the future will increasingly become like the humans of the past, so also the humans of the future will start resembling the machines of the past!

Conclusion

By way of conclusion, let's return to the concept of the postdigital. As my above discussion of platform capitalism and attention economy hopefully made clear, the postdigital imaginary enabled me to make certain diagnoses and predictions about present and future digital economies, which would otherwise have been difficult or perhaps impossible to make. Specifically, it allowed me to ask what might come after the digital attention economy with a view to speculative about emergent scarce resources and new forms of commercial, cultural and political capital in a future AI-driven tech economy. Nonetheless, as I also argue with my co-editors in this volume's Introduction, it should be kept in mind that attempts to squeeze political-economic phenomena like 'the platform' or 'the digital attention economy' into the conceptual straitjacket of rigid periodizations will result in oversimplified generalizations, which do not take into account the vagaries, contingencies and particularities of actually existing, always embedded, digital economies. To mitigate against this risk, anyone who ended up using the concept of the postdigital in their work (or as a description of their own work, in the case of for instance artists) will be well-advised to keep in mind that, more than denoting a historical period with a beginning and an end, the theoretical purchase of this and other 'post-concepts' lies in their capacity to transcend the suffocating prison of linear time and hence allowing speculative anthropologists to elicit latent future potentials from present phenomena and dynamics.

With these words of warning in mind, I should like close this afterword with an unapologetically linear prediction about the future of platform capitalism. As a consequence of the dual (legal-political and technological-economic) pressure exerted on the hitherto so successful business model of the digital attention economy, I suggest, for quintessentially 'surveillance capitalist' firms such as like Meta and Alphabet thrive, they will need to become less dependent, financially, technologically and branding-wise on social media platforms like Facebook, Instagram and YouTube. In their stead, new and distinctly postdigital infrastructures for the algorithmically based production, augmentation and commodification of social life will become the new frontier for the imbrication between labour, capital, data and time. As part of this ever-increasing regulation and still decreasing potential for growth, 'the attention' will recede into the background as both a core commodity and as a floating signifier capturing the wider cultural, political and social anxieties of our time. However, this new postdigital condition will not be characterized by a reduction let alone a disappearance of the digital interfaces and machine learning algorithms designed with the purpose of partaking and intervening in basic cognitive, affective and social processes. On the contrary, the capacity for computationally augmenting and automating knowledge domains traditionally considered uniquely human will only grow with the development of ever more sophisticated and ubiquitous AI systems.

Notes

[1] As one Atlantic subheading goes, 'Facebook is acting like a hostile foreign power. It is time we treated it like that' (www.theatlantic.com/magazine/archive/2021/11/facebook-authoritarian-hostile-foreign-power/620168/?utm_campaign=the-atlantic&utm_medium=social&utm_source=facebook).

[2] www.politico.com/news/2021/06/15/big-tech-house-antitrust-changes-494506; https://www.politico.com/news/2021/06/23/gop-infighting-big-tech-crackdown-495605

[3] In two blogposts entitled, respectively, 'Planning the exodus from platform realism' and 'The possibilities of the post-platform school', artist Ben Grosser (https://networkcultures.org/blog/2021/06/29/platform-realism/) and a group of school researchers (https://data-smart-schools.net/2021/07/01/the-possibilities-of-the-post-platform-school/) thus critically discuss some of the problems arising from the infusion of platform-capitalism into educational contexts and postdigital possibilities for overcoming these in the future.

[4] Consider also this, rather prescient observation, in light of for example, Starlink and Twitter: 'It is conceivable that the nation-states will one day fight for control of information, just as they battled in the past for control over territory, and afterwards for control of access to and exploitation of raw materials and cheap labor ... Suppose, for example, that a firm such as IBM is authorized to occupy a belt in the earth's orbital field and launch communications satellites or satellites housing data banks. Who will have access to them? Who will determine which channels or data are forbidden? The State? Or will the State simply be one user among others? (1984: 5–6).

[5] As recently reported in *Time Magazine*, China's cyberspace regulator is proposing to 'combat smart phone addiction' by 'requiring providers of smart devices to have a 'minor mode' that would limit usage by those under the age of 18 to at most two hours' (https://time.com/6301185/china-smartphone-addiction-children-limit/).

[6] To clarify: my reservations about the techlash discourse is directed specifically towards exaggerated if not downright unsubstantiated claims about people's alleged 'addiction' to digital devises and similar (and even more dubious) arguments about the supposedly 'damages' to children's brains as a result of smart phone use.

[7] https://acroll.substack.com/p/what-comes-after-the-attention-economy

[8] https://anjireddy-kata.medium.com/ai-fundamentals-building-a-chatbot-using-open-ai-chat-gpt-apis-a32efcba3e32; see also https://community.openai.com/t/a-question-on-determinism/8185

References

Adams, J.T. (1922) 'On the term "British Empire"', *The American Historical Review*, 27(3): 485–9. https://doi.org/10.2307/1837801.

AIR (1975) The Statesman Ltd and Ors vs The Fact Finding Committee. Cal 14, Available from: https://indiankanoon.org/doc/1256778/ [accessed 11 March 2024].

Akerlof, G.A. (1970) 'The market for "lemons": Quality uncertainty and the market mechanism', *The Quarterly Journal of Economics*, 84(3): 488–500. https://doi.org/10.2307/1879431.

Al-Sibai, N. (2022) 'Twitter bots love Tesla: Elon Musk is pledging to destroy them', *Futurism*, [online] 3 May, Available from: https://futurism.com/twitter-bots-researcher-interview [Accessed 16 May 2022].

Alami, I. and Dixon, A.D. (2020) 'The strange geographies of the "new" state capitalism', *Political Geography*, 82: 102237.

Albarrán-Torres, C. (2018) *Digital Gambling: Theorizing Gamble-Play Media*. Routledge.

Albarrán Torres, C. and Goggin, G. (2014) 'Mobile social gambling: Poker's next frontier', *Mobile Media and Communication*, 2(1): 94–109. https://doi.org/10.1177/2050157913506423.

Alexenberg, M. (2014) *The Future of Art in a Postdigital Age: From Hellenistic to Hebraic Consciousness*. Palgrave.

Alibaba.com (2016) 'Alibaba issues 2016 fiscal year report, making plans for its four main businesses', 阿里巴巴发布2016财报 全力布局四大业务. [online], Available from: https://activities.alibaba.com/alibaba/exporter/promotion/info-6.php [Accessed 15 February 2024].

Aliresearch.com (2020) 'The history of "rural Taobao": How the internet changed the rural areas', "农村淘宝"进化史：互联网如何改变乡村. [online], Available from: www.aliresearch.com/ch/information/informationdetails?articleCode=89262863042088960andtype=%E6%96%B0%E9%97%BB [Accessed 20 June 2023].

Aliresearch.com (2021) 'The list of Taobao villages in 2021 has been released, and the number of Taobao villages across the country has exceeded 7,000', 2021年淘宝村名单出炉 全国淘宝村数量已突破7000. [online], Available from: www.aliresearch.com/ch/informat ion/informationdetails?articleCode=256317657652006912andtype= %E6%96%B0%E9%97%BBandadcode=andvillageCode=andvillageYear=andi tem=%E6%B7%98%E5%AE%9D%E6%9D%91 [Accessed 20 June 2023].

Amazon (nd) 'Introducing Amazon Halo', Amazon.com, [online], Available from: www.amazon.com/gp/product/B07QK955LS?pf_rd_r=D9MWFK 17YZV2NVFW00V8andpf_rd_=edaba0ee-c2fe-4124-9f5d-b31d6b1bf bee#faq [Accessed 29 August 2020].

Ames, M. (2019) *The Charisma Machine: The Life, Death, and Legacy of One Laptop Per Child*. MIT Press.

Aneez, Z., Chattapadhyay, S., Parthasarathi, V. and Kleis Nielsen, R. (2017) *Indian News Media and the Production of News in the Age of Social Discovery*. Reuters Institute for the Study of Journalism.

Aneez, Z., Neyazi, T.A., Kalogeropoulos, A. and Kleis Nielsen, R. (2019) *India Digital News Report*. Reuters Institute for the Study of Journalism, Oxford.

Ang, Peng Hwa and Pramanik, A. (2008) 'By the industry, of the industry, for the industry: The possibilities and limits of self-regulation of Indian broadcasting', Paper presented at International Seminar 'Contours of Media Governance' organized by the Centre for Culture, Media and Governance with IDRC. Jamia Millia Islamia. New Delhi (8–10 December).

Ang, Y.Y. (2016) *How China Escaped the Poverty Trap*. Cornell University Press.

Anwar, S.T. (2017) 'Alibaba: Entrepreneurial growth and global expansion in B2B/B2C markets', *Journal of International Entrepreneurship*, 15: 366–89.

Apperley, T. and Parikka, J. (2015) 'Platform studies' epistemic threshold', *Games and Culture*, 13(4): 349–69. https://doi.org/10.1177/1555412015616509.

Arrow, Kenneth J. (2015) *Economic Welfare and the Allocation of Resources for Invention*. Princeton University Press.

Athique, A. (2019) 'Digital emporiums: Platform capitalism in India', *Media Industries Journal*, 6(2).

Athique, A. and Parthasarathi, V. (2020) 'Platform economy and platformization', in A. Athique and V. Parthasarathi (eds) *Platform Capitalism in India*. Palgrave Macmillan, pp 1–19.

Aylesworth, G. (2015) 'Postmodernism', in *The Stanford Encyclopedia of Philosophy*, Available from: https://plato.stanford.edu/entries/postmodern ism/ [Accessed 9 February 2024].

Babe, R. (1995) *Communication and the Transformation of Economics: Essays in Information, Public Policy, and Political Economy*. Routledge.

Babe, R. and Comor, E. (2018) 'Introduction to political economy in the modern state', in H. Innis (ed) *Political Economy in the Modern State*. University of Toronto Press, pp IX–XLVI. https://doi.org/10.3138/9781487518905.

REFERENCES

Bailey, N. (1759) *An Universal Etymological Dictionary*, 17th edn, with considerable improvements. Printed for T. Osborne, C. Hitch and L. Hawes, B. Dod, J. Hinton, John Rivington, and 16 others in London.

Balnaves, M. and O'Regan, T. (2010) 'The politics and practice of television ratings conventions: Australian and American approaches to broadcast ratings', *Continuum: Journal of Media and Cultural Studies*, 24(3): 461–74.

Banerjee, A. (2023) 'Alibaba's breakup lifts hopes China's regulatory winter is thawing', Reuters [online], Available from: www.reuters.com/technology/alibabas-hong-kong-shares-set-open-up-15-split-up-plans-2023-03-29/ [Accessed 9 February 2024].

Beckert, J. (2009) 'The social order of markets', *Theory and Society*, 38(3): 245–69.

Beddeleem, M. (2020) 'Recoding liberalism: Philosophy and sociology of science against planning', in D. Plehwe, Q. Slobodian and P. Mirowski (eds) *The Nine Lives of Neoliberalism*. Verso, pp 21–45.

Bennett, T. and Dodsworth, F. (2013) 'Habit and habituation', *Body and Society*, 19(2–3): 3–29.

Bermejo, F. (2009) 'Audience manufacture in historical perspective: From broadcasting to Google', *New Media and Society*, 11(1–2): 133–54.

Bernard, P. (2018) 'CallMiner named a leader in AI-fueled speech analytics', CallMiner [online] 25 June, Available from: https://callminer.com/blog/named-a-leader-ai-speech-analytics [Accessed 6 July 2023].

Beverungen, A., Mirowski, P., Nik-Khah, E. and Schröter, J. (2019) *Markets* (Illustrated edn). Meson Press.

Bhatia, G. (2016) *Offend, Shock, or Disturb: Free Speech under the Indian Constitution*. Oxford University Press.

Bhattacharya, A. (2017) 'Amazon's Alexa heard her name and tried to order up a ton of dollhouses'. Quartz [online] 7 January, Available from: https://qz.com/880541/amazons-amzn-alexa-accidentally-ordered-a-ton-of-dollhouses-across-san-diego/ [Accessed 6 July 2023].

Bickerton, C, and Invernizzi Accetti, C. (2021) *Technopopulism: The New Logic of Democratic Politics*. Oxford University Press.

Birch, K., Chiappetta, M. and Artyushina, A. (2020) 'The problem of innovation in technoscientific capitalism: Data rentiership and the policy implications of turning personal digital data into a private asset', *Policy Studies*, 41(5): 468–87.

Birch, K., Cochrane, D.T. and Ward, C. (2021) 'Data as asset? The measurement, governance, and valuation of digital personal data by Big Tech', *Big Data and Society*, 8(1): 205395172110173. https://doi.org/10.1177/20539517211017308.

Bjerg, O. (2016) 'How is bitcoin money?', *Theory, Culture and Society*, 33(1): 53–72.

Blanke, T. and Pybus, J. (2020) 'The material conditions of platforms: Monopolization through decentralization', *Social Media + Society*, 6(4): 205630512097163. https://doi.org/10.1177/2056305120971632.

Bloomberg (2021, 11 July) China's Attacks on Tech Are a Losing Strategy in Cold War II. https://www.bloomberg.com/opinion/articles/2021-07-11/china-s-attacks-on-didi-alibaba-are-losing-strategy-in-cold-war-against-u-s

Boffey, D. (2021) 'Apple accused of breaking EU law over App Store sales fees', *The Guardian*, [online] 30 April, Available from: www.theguardian.com/technology/2021/apr/30/apple-eu-law-app-store-iphone-ipad-music-streaming [Accessed 16 May 2022].

Bogost, I. and Montfort, N. (2009) 'Platform studies: Frequently questioned answers', Paper presented at the Digital Arts and Culture Conference, Irvine, California, 12–15 December 2009. http://pdf.textfiles.com/academics/bogost_montfort_dac_2009.pdf.

Böhm, S. and Land, C. (2012) 'The new "hidden abode": Reflections on value and labour in the new economy', *The Sociological Review*, 60(2): 217–40. https://doi.org/10.1111/j.1467-954X.2012.02071.x.

Bohn, D. (2019) 'Google Assistant will soon be on a billion devices, and feature phones are next', *The Verge* [online] 7 January, Available from: wwwtheverge.com/2019/1/7/18169939/google-assistant-billion-devices-feature-phones-ces-2019 [Accessed 6 July 2023].

Bolin, G. (2011) *Value and the Media: Cultural Production and Consumption in Digital Markets*. Ashgate.

Bolin, G. and Velkova, V. (2020) 'Audience-metric continuity? Approaching the meaning of measurement in the digital everyday', *Media, Culture and Society*, 42(7–8): 1193–209.

Bovens, M. (2007) 'Analysing and assessing accountability: A conceptual framework', *European Law Journal*, 13(4): 447–68.

Bowles, S., Kirman, A. and Sethi, R. (2017) 'Fredrich Hayek and the market algorithm', *Journal of Economic Perspectives*, 31(3): 215–230.

boyd, d. and Crawford, K. (2012) 'Critical questions for big data: Provocations for a cultural, technological, and scholarly phenomenon', *Information, Communication and Society*, 15(5): 662–79.

Braudel, F. (1982) *On History*. University of Chicago Press.

Braudel, F. (1992) *Civilization and Capitalism, 15th–18th Century*, Vol II: The Wheels of Commerce. University of California Press.

Bridle, J. (2018) *New Dark Age. Technology and the End of the Future*. Verso.

Bruell, A. (2018) 'Fraudulent web traffic continues to plague advertisers, other businesses', *Wall Street Journal*, [online] 11 February, Available from: www.wsj.com/articles/fraudulent-web-traffic-continues-to-plague-advertisers-other-businesses-1522234801 [Accessed 6 July 2023].

Bryan, D. and Rafferty, M. (2006) 'Financial derivatives: The new gold?', *Competition & Change*, 10(3): 265–82.

REFERENCES

Buchanan, J. (1991) *Economics and the Ethics of Constitutional Order.* University of Michigan.

Burgess, J. (2021) 'Platform studies', in S. Cunningham and D. Craig (eds) *Creator Culture: An Introduction to Global Social Media Entertainment.* New York University Press, pp 21–38.

Business Wire (2018) 'Clarabridge unveils new updates to the Clarabridge Banking solution'. Businesswire.com [online], Available from: https://www.businesswire.com/news/home/20181107005148/en/Clarabridge-Unveils-New-Updates-to-the-Clarabridge-Banking-Solution [Accessed 9 February 2024].

Buzzard, K.S.F. (2002) 'The peoplemeter wars: A case study of technological innovation and diffusion in the ratings industry', *Journal of Media Economics*, 15(4): 273–91.

Cainiao.com (2024) [online], Available from: https://www.cainiao.com/

Callminer. (nd) 'How Ai improves the customer experience', Callminer.com [online], Available from: www.technoreports.info/resourcefiles/HOW_AI_IMPROVES_THE_CUSTOMER_EXPERIENCE.pdf [Accessed 24 August 2020].

Callon, M. (1998) 'Introduction: The embeddedness of economic markets in economics', *The Sociological Review*, 46(1_suppl): 1–57.

Caplan, R. and boyd, d. (2018) 'Isomorphism through algorithms: Institutional dependencies in the case of Facebook', *Big Data and Society*, 5(1). https://doi.org/10.1177/2053951718757253.

Caprotti, F. and Liu, D. (2022) 'Platform urbanism and the Chinese smart city: The co-production and territorialisation of Hangzhou City Brain', *GeoJournal*, 87(3): 1559–73.

Caraway, B. (2011) 'Audience labor in the new media environment: A Marxian revisiting of the audience commodity', *Media Culture Society*, 33(5): 693–708.

Carey, J.W. (1988) *Communication as Culture: Essays on Media and Society* (Rev. ed.). Routledge.

Carrier, J. (2018) 'Moral economy: What's in a name', *Anthropological Theory*, 18(1): 18–35.

Carrigan, M. 2020. 'Some critical thoughts about the post-digital', [online], Available from: https://markcarrigan.net/2020/12/02/some-critical-thoughts-about-the-post-digital/

Castronova, E. (2001) 'Virtual worlds: A first-hand account of market and society on the cyberian frontier', Available from: https://papers.ssrn.com/sol3/papers.cfm?Abstract_id=294828 [Accessed 9 February 2024].

Chadha, K. (2012) 'Twitter as media watch-dog? Lessons from India's Radia tapes scandal', *Global Media and Communication*, 8(2): 171–76.

Chadwick, A. (2013) *The Hybrid Media System: Politics and Power.* Oxford University Press.

Chakrabarty, D. (2007) *Provincializing Europe: Postcolonial Thought and Historical Difference – New Edition*. Princeton University Press.

Chen, A. (2019) 'Why companies want to mine the secrets in your voice', *The Verge* [online] 14 March, Available from: www.theverge.com/2019/3/14/18264458/voice-technology-speech-analysis-mental-health-risk-privacy [Accessed 7 July 2023].

Chhotray, V. (2011) *The Anti-politics Machine in India: State, Decentralization and Participatory Watershed Development*. Anthem Press.

Clark, D. (2016) *Alibaba: The House That Jack Ma Built*. Ecco/ HarperCollins Publishers.

Coffey, S. (2001) 'Internet audience measurement', *Journal of Interactive Advertising*, 1(2): 10–17.

Cohen, J.E. (2017) 'Law for the platform economy', *U.C. Davis L. Rev*, 51: 133–204.

Cohen, K. (2019) 'YouTube channel owners: Is your content directed to children?', *Federal Trade Commission Business Blog*, [online] 22 November, Available from: www.ftc.gov/news-events/blogs/business-blog/2019/11/youtube-channel-owners-your-content-directed-children [Accessed 3 November 2021].

Cohn, B.S. (1996) *Colonialism and Its Forms of Knowledge: The British in India*. Princeton University Press.

Community Standards Enforcement | Transparency Center (nd) [online], Available from: https://transparency.fb.com/data/community-standards-enforcement/fake-accounts/facebook/ [Accessed 16 May 2022].

Comor, E. (2001) 'Harold Innis and "The bias of communication"', *Information, Communication and Society*, 4(2): Article 2. https://doi.org/10.1080/713768518.

Craig, S. (2010) 'Daniel Starch's 1928 survey: A first glimpse of the US radio audience', *Journal of Radio and Audio Media*, 17(2): 182–94.

Crain, M. (2021) *Profit Over Privacy*. University of Minnesota Press.

Cramer, F. (2015) 'What is "post-digital"?', In D.M. Berry and M. Dieter (eds) *Postdigital Aesthetics: Art, Computation and Design*. Palgrave Macmillan, pp 12–26.

Crawford, K. and Calo, R. (2016) 'There is a blind spot in AI research', *Nature*, 538: 311–13, Available from: https://doi.org/10.1038/538311a [Accessed 6 July 2023].

Culpepper, P.D. and Thelen, K. (2019) 'Are we all Amazon Primed? Consumers and the politics of platform power', *Comparative Political Studies*, 53(2). https://doi.org/10.1177/0010414019852687.

Cunningham, S. and Craig, D. (eds) (2021) *Creator Culture: An Introduction to Global Social Media Entertainment*. New York University Press.

Curran, D. and Smart, A. (2021) 'Data-driven governance, smart urbanism and risk-class inequalities: Security and social credit in China', *Urban Studies*, 58(3): 487–506.

REFERENCES

Cuthbertson, A. (2022) 'More than half of Elon Musk's Twitter followers are fake', *The Independent*, [online] 2 May, Available from: www.independent.co.uk/tech/elon-musk-twitter-followers-fake-spambot-b2069527.html [Accessed 16 May 2022].

Cutolo, D. and Kenney, M. (2021) 'Platform-dependent entrepreneurs: Power asymmetries, risks, and strategies in the platform economy', *Academy of Management Perspectives*, 35(4): 584–605.

Dagiral, É. and Khetrimayum, M.S. (2020) 'Governance and accountable citizenship through identification infrastructures: Database politics of Copernicus (France) and National Register of Citizens (India) Science', *Technology and Society*, 25(3): 368–85.

Dansk Industri (2021) "Digitalisering Der Flytter Danmark." Dansk Industri [online], Available from: www.danskindustri.dk/DownloadDocument?id=209253anddocid=211425 [Accessed 9 June 2022].

Dao, S., Zhiqiu, Y., Tran, Ly., Phan, P., Huynh, T. and Le, T. (2022) 'An analysis of vocal features for Parkinson's disease classification using evolutionary algorithms', *Diagnostics (Basel)*, 12(8): 1980. https://doi.org/10.3390/diagnostics12081980.

Das, B. and Parthasarathi, V. (2011) 'Media research and public policy: Tiding over the rupture', in R. Mansell and M. Raboy (ed) *Handbook on Global Media and Communication Policy*. Wiley-Blackwell, pp 243–60.

Dasika, A. (2018) 'Voice first systems: The future of interaction?', *Digital Leaders* [online] 5 July, Available from: https://digileaders.com/voice-first-systems-future-interaction/ [Accessed 6 July 2023].

Daub, A. (2020) *What Tech Calls Thinking: An Inquiry into the Intellectual Bedrock of Silicon Valley*. Farrar, Straus and Giroux.

Daubs, M.S. and Manzerolle, V.R. (2016) 'App-centric mobile media and commoditization: Implications for the future of the open web', *Mobile Media and Communication*, 4(1): 52–68. https://doi.org/10.1177/2050157915592657.

Davis, M. and Xiao, J. (2021) 'De-Westernizing platform studies: History and logics of Chinese and US Platforms', *International Journal of Communication*, 15: 103–22.

De Kloet, J., Poell, T., Guohua, Z. and Yiu Fai, Chow (2019) 'The platformization of Chinese society: Infrastructure, governance, and practice', *Chinese Journal of Communication*, 12(3): 249–56.

del Nido, J.M. (2021) *Taxis vs Uber: Courts, Markets, and Technology in Buenos Aires*. Stanford University Press.

Diakopoulos, N. and Koliska, M. (2017) 'Algorithmic transparency in the news media', *Digital Journalism*, 5(7): 809–28.

Digitaliseringspartnerskabet (2021) Visioner Og Anbefalinger Til Danmark Som et Digitalt Foregangsland. Digitaliseringsstyrelsen, Available from: https://fm.dk/media/25226/visioner-og-anbefalinger-til-danmark-som-et-digitalt-foregangsland_digitaliseringspartnerskabet_a.pdf [Accessed 9 February 2024].

Dijck, J. van, Poell, T. and Waal, M. de (2018) *The Platform Society*. Oxford University Press.

DiMaggio, P.J. and Powell, W.W. (1983) 'The iron cage revisited: Institutional isomorphism and collective rationality in organizational fields', *American Sociological Review*, 48(2): 147–60. https://doi.org/10.2307/2095101.

Dodd, N. (1994) *The Sociology of Money: Economics, Reason and Contemporary Society*. Polity Press.

Dodd, N. (2005) 'Reinventing monies in Europe', *Economy and Society*, 34(4): 558–83.

Dodd, N. (2014) *The Social Life of Money*. Princeton University Press.

Dodd, N. (2018) 'The social life of Bitcoin', *Theory, Culture and Society*, 35(3): 35–56.

Draper, N. and Turow, J. (2019) 'The corporate cultivation of digital resignation', *New Media and Society*, 2(8): 1824–39.

Duncan, J. and Reid, J. (2013) Towards a measurement tool for the monitoring of media diversity and pluralism in South Africa: A public-centred approach. *Communicatio*, 39(4): 483–500.

Duus, K. (2022) 'Reconfiguring work: Examining moral economies relating to digital platform work in Brussels', Paper presented at the European Association of Social Anthropology, 26 July, Belfast.

Dyer-Witheford, N. (2014) 'App Worker', in P.D. Miller and S. Matviyenko (eds) *The Imaginary App*. MIT Press, pp 125–42.

Edge (2014) 'Reinventing society in the wake of big data: A conversation with Alex (Sandy) Pentland', [online], Available from: www.edge.org/conversation/reinventing-society-in-the-wake-of-big-data [Accessed 9 February 2024].

Eich, S. (2019) 'Old utopias, new tax havens: The politics of Bitcoin in historical perspective', *Regulating Blockchain: Techno-social and Legal Challenges*. Oxford University Press, pp 85–96.

Eisenstein, E.L. (1993) *The Printing Revolution in Early Modern Europe*. Cambridge University Press.

Erhvervsministeriet (2021) *Redegørelse Om Danmarks Digitale Vækst*. Erhvervsministeriet. https://em.dk/media/14173/redegoerelse-om-danmarks-digitale-vaekst-2021_endelig2.pdf [Accessed 9 June 2022].

Erickson, P. (2015) *The World the Game Theorists Made*. University of Chicago Press.

Evans, D.S. and Schmalensee, R. (2016) *Matchmakers: The New Economics of Multisided Platforms*. Harvard Business Review Press.

Evans, J. (2022) 'EU accuses Apple of market abuse with NFC and Apple Pay', *Computerworld* [online], Available from: www.computerworld.com/article/3658858/eu-accuses-apple-of-market-abuse-with-nfc-and-apple-pay.html [Accessed 16 May 2022].

Ferdinand, P. (2016) 'Westward ho—The China dream and "One Belt, One Road": Chinese foreign policy under Xi Jinping', *International Affairs*, 92(4): 941–57.

Ferguson, J. (2006) *Global Shadows: Africa in the Neoliberal World Order*. Duke University Press.

Fligstein, N. (1996) 'Markets as politics: A political-cultural approach to market institutions', *American Sociological Review*, 61(4): 656–73. https://doi.org/10.2307/2096398.

Fligstein, N. (2001) *The Architecture of Markets*. Princeton University Press.

Forbes.com (2000, 24 July) 'B2B For The Little Guys', Forbes [online], Available from: www.forbes.com/global/2000/0724/0314096a.html?sh=37e0fd433545 [Accessed 8 March 2024].

Fourcade, M. and Kluttz, D.N. (2020) 'A Maussian bargain: Accumulation by gift in the digital economy', *Big Data and Society*, 7(1). https://doi.org/10.1177/2053951719897092.

Fourcade, M. and Healy, K. (2017) 'Seeing like a market', *Socio-Economic Review*, 15(1): 9–29.

Frank, T. (2002) *One Market under God: Extreme Capitalism, Market Populism, and the End of Economic Democracy*. Vintage.

Freedman, D. (2014) 'Metrics, models and the meaning of media ownership', *International Journal of Cultural Policy*, 20(2): 170–85.

Frenken, K. and Fuenfschilling, L. (2020) 'The rise of online platforms and the triumph of the corporation', *Sociologica*, 14(3): 101–13.

Frieden, R. (2008) 'Academic research and its limited impact on telecommunications policy making', *International Journal of Communication*, 2, 421–28.

Fuchs, C. (2012) 'Dallas Smythe today: The audience commodity, the digital labour debate, Marxist political economy and critical theory', *TripleC: Communication, Capitalism and Critique*, 10(2): 692–740.

Fuchs, C. (2022) *Digital Capitalism*. Routledge.

Fuller, M. (2008) *Software Studies: A Lexicon*. MIT Press.

Gao, X. (2020) 'State-led digital governance in contemporary China', in *State Capacity Building in Contemporary China*. Springer Nature Singapore, pp 29–45.

Garnham, N. (1990) *Capitalism and Communication: Global Culture and the Economics of Information*. SAGE Publications.

Gawer, A. (2014) 'Bridging differing perspectives on technological platforms: Toward an integrative framework', *Research Policy*, 43(7): 1239–49.

Geertz, C. (1960) 'The Javanese Kijaji: The Changing Role of a Cultural Broker', *Comparative Studies in Society and History*, 2: 228–49.

Gerbner, G. (1973) 'The teacher image and the hidden curriculum', *American Scholar*, 42(1): 42–71.

Gibbons, T. (2015) 'Active pluralism: Dialogue and engagement as basic media policy principles', *International Journal of Communication*, 9: 1382–99.

Gillespie, T. (2010) 'The politics of "platforms"'. *New Media and Society*, 12(3): 347–64. https://doi.org/10.1177/1461444809342738.

Gillespie, T. (2014) 'The relevance of algorithms', in T. Gillespie, P. Boczkowski and K. Foot (eds) *Media Technologies*. MIT Press, pp 167–94.

Gillespie, T. (2018) *Custodians of the Internet: Platforms, Content Moderation, and the Hidden Decisions That Shape Social Media*. Yale University Press.

GoI (1954) *Report of the Press Commission*. Government of India.

GoI (1975) *Report of the Fact Finding Committee on Newspaper Economics*. Government of India.

Google (2022) 'Our 2021 ads safety report' [online], Available from: https://blog.google/products/ads-commerce/ads-safety-report-2021/ [Accessed 16 May 2022].

Gorman, L. and McLean, D. (2003) *Media and Society in the Twentieth Century*. Blackwell Publishing.

Gorwa, R. (2019) 'What is platform governance?', *Information, Communication and Society*, 22(6): 854–71.

Granovetter, M. (1985) Economic action and social structure: The problem of embeddedness. *American Journal of Sociology*, 91(3): 481–510.

Greeven, M. (2023) 'Alibaba's restructuring is a chance for a fresh start', [online], Available from: https://asia.nikkei.com/Opinion/Alibaba-s-restructuring-is-a-chance-for-a-fresh-start [Accessed 9 February 2024].

Gregory, C. (1982) *Gifts and Commodities*. Cambridge University Press.

Hann, Chris. (2016) 'The moral dimension of economy: Work, workfare, and fairness in provincial Hungary', Working paper 174. Halle, Germany: Max Planck Institute for Social Anthropology.

Hardt, M. and Negri, A. (2004) *Multitude: War and Democracy in the Age of Empire*. Penguin Press.

Hargittai, E. and Marwick, A. (2016) '"What can I really do?" Explaining the privacy paradox with online apathy', *International Journal of Communication* 10: 3737–57.

Hartford, K. (2005) 'Dear Mayor: Online communications with local governments in Hangzhou and Nanjing', *China Information*, 19(2): 217–60.

Helberger, N. (2005) *Controlling Access to Content: Regulating Conditional Access in Digital Broadcasting*. Vol. 15. Kluwer Law International [Thesis, fully internal, Universiteit van Amsterdam].

Helberger, N. (2012) 'Exposure diversity as a policy goal', *Journal of Media Law*, 4: 65–92.

Helberger, N. (2019) 'On the democratic role of news recommenders', *Digital Journalism*, 7(8): 1–20.

Helmond, A. (2015) 'The platformization of the web: Making web data platform ready', *Social Media+ Society*, 1(2): 2056305115603080.

Herrigel, G. (2010) *Manufacturing Possibilities: Creative Action and Industrial Recomposition in the United States, Germany, and Japan*. Oxford University Press.

Hesmondhalgh, D. (2019) *The Cultural Industries* (4th edn). SAGE Publications.

Hobbis, G. and Hobbis, S.K. (2022) 'Beyond platform capitalism: critical perspectives on Facebook markets from Melanesia', *Media, Culture and Society*, 44(1): 121–40.

Hobbis, S.K. and Hobbis, G. (2020) 'Non-/human infrastructures and digital gifts: The cables, waves and brokers of Solomon Islands internet', *Ethnos*, October: 1–23. https://doi.org/10.1080/00141844.2020.1828969.

Hoffman P.H., Lutz, C. and Ranzini, G. (2016) Privacy cynicism: A new approach to the privacy paradox. *Cyberpsychology: Journal of Psychosocial Research on Cyberspace*, 10(4): 7, Available from: http://dx.doi.org/10.5817/CP2016-4-7 [Accessed 6 July 2023].

Holbraad, M. (2013) 'Can the thing speak?', Open Anthropology Cooperative Press, *Working Papers Series*, 7(1). http://openanthcoop.net/press/http://openanthcoop.net/press/wp-content/uploads/2011/01/Holbraad-Can-the-Thing-Speak.pdf.

Holbraad, M. and Pedersen, M.A. (2017) *The Ontological Turn: An Anthropological Exposition*. Cambridge: Cambridge University Press.

Hong, Y. (2017) 'Networking China: The digital transformation of the Chinese economy', Urbana [online], Available from: www.proquest.com/docview/2375962116?pq-origsite=gscholarandfromopenview=true [Accessed 6 July 2023].

Hong Kong Exchange News (2020) Ant Group, Available from: https://web.archive.org/web/20201020200428/https://www1.hkexnews.hk/app/sehk/2020/102484/documents/sehk20082500535.pdf

Hufton, O. (1986) 'Fernand Braudel', *Past and Present*, 112(1): 208–13.

Humphrey, C. (2002) 'Does the category "postsocialist" still make sense?', in C.M. Hann (ed) *Postsocialism: Ideals, Ideologies and Practices in Eurasia*. Routledge, pp 12–28.

Hütten, M. and Thiemann, M. (2017) 'Moneys at the margins: From political experiment to cashless societies', in M. Campbell-Verduyn (ed) *Bitcoin and Beyond*. Routledge, pp 25–47.

Ingham, G. (2013) *The Nature of Money*. John Wiley and Sons.

Innis, H.A. (1995) *Staples, Markets, and Cultural Change: Selected Essays of Harold Innis* (Centenary edn). McGill-Queen's University Press.

Innis, H.A. (2007) *Empire and Communications*. Dundurn.

Innis, H.A. (2008) *The Bias of Communication* (2nd edn). University of Toronto Press.

Innis, H.A. (2018) *Political Economy in the Modern State*. University of Toronto Press.

Innis, H.A. (2015) *Harold Innis's History of Communications: Paper and Printing – Antiquity to Early Modernity*. Rowman & Littlefield.

Jackson, J. (2016) 'Facebook inflated video viewing times for two years', *The Guardian*, [online] 23 September, Available from: www.theguardian.com/media/2016/sep/23/facebook-video-viewing-times-ad-agencies-metric [Accessed 8 March 2024].

James, D. (2011) 'The return of the broker: Consensus, hierarchy, and choice in South African land reform', *Journal of the Royal Anthropological Institute*, 17: 318–38.

Jandrić, P., Knox, J., Besley, T., Ryberg, T., Suoranta, J. and Hayes, S. (2018) 'Postdigital science and education', *Educational Philosophy and Theory*, 50(10): 893–99. https://doi.org/10.1080/00131857.2018.1454000.

Jeffrey, R. (1994) 'Monitoring newspapers and understanding the Indian state', *Asian Survey*, 34(8): 748–63.

Jenkins, Jr, H. (2018, 14 August) 'Google and the search for the future', *Wall Street Journal*, [online], Available from: www.wsj.com/articles/SB1000 142 4052748704901104575423294099527212 [Accessed 25 October 2018].

Jensen, C.B. and Blok, A. (2013) 'Techno-animism in Japan: Shinto cosmograms, actor-network theory, and the enabling powers of non-human agencies', *Theory, Culture and Society*, 30(2): 84–115.

Jia, L. and Winseck, D. (2018) 'The political economy of Chinese Internet companies: Financialization, concentration, and capitalization', *International Communication Gazette*, 80(1): 30–59.

Jiang, Y., Zhang, L. and Jin, Y. (2021) 'China's e-commerce development and policy relevance,' in M. Smeets, *Adapting to the Digital Trade Era: Challenges and Opportunities*, WTO Chairs Programme, pp 140–57, Available from: https://www.wto.org/english/res_e/publications_e/adtera_e.htm

Joseph, D. (2018) 'The discourse of digital dispossession: Paid modifications and community crisis on steam', *Games and Culture*, 13(7): 690–707.

Joseph, D. (2020) 'Battle pass capitalism', *Journal of Consumer Culture*, 21(1): 68–83. https://doi.org/10.1177/1469540521993930

Joseph, G. and Nathan, D. (2019, 30 January) 'Prisons across the US are quietly building databases of incarcerated of incarcerated people's voice prints', *Appeal* [online] 30 January, Available from: https://theappeal.org/prisons-across-the-u-s-are-quietly-building-databases-of-incarcerated-peoples-voice-prints/ [Accessed 6 July 2023].

Juniper Research (2017, 26 September) 'Ad fraud to cost advertisers $19 billion in 2018, representing 9% of total digital advertising spend', *Business Wire*, [online] 26 September, Available from: www.businesswire.com/news/ home/20170926005177/en/Juniper-Research-Ad-Fraud-Cost-Advertisers-19 [Accessed 9 February 2024].

Just, N. and Latzer, M. (2017) 'Governance by algorithms: Reality construction by algorithmic selection on the internet', *Media, Culture and Society*, 39(2): 238–58.

Kafka, P. (2021) 'Substack writers are mad at Substack: The problem is money and who's making it', Vox [online], Available from: www.vox.com/recode/22338802/substack-pro-newsletter-controversy-jude-doyle [Accessed 16 May 2022].

REFERENCES

Khan, L.M. (2018) 'Sources of tech platform power', *Georgetown Law Technology Review*, 325–34.

Karppinen, K. (2012) *Rethinking Media Pluralism*. Fordham University Press.

Kazin, M. (2017) *The Populist Persuasion: An American History*. Cornell University Press.

Keane, M. and Yu, H. (2019) 'A digital empire in the making: China's outbound digital platforms', *International Journal of Communication*, 13: 4624–41.

Kearns, M. and Roth A. (2019) *The Ethical Algorithm*. Oxford University Press.

Keller, M.H. (2018) 'The flourishing business of fake YouTube views', *New York Times*, [online] 11 August, Available from: www.nytimes.com/interactive/2018/08/11/technology/youtube-fake-view-sellers.html [Accessed 8 March 2024].

Kenney, M. and Zysman, J. (2016) 'The rise of the platform economy', *Issues in Science and Technology*, 32(3): 61.

Kenney, M. and Zysman, J. (2020) 'The platform economy: Restructuring the space of capitalist accumulation', *Cambridge Journal of Regions, Economy and Society*, 13(1): 55–76. https://doi.org/10.1093/cjres/rsaa001.

Kerr, A. (2017) *Global Games: Production, Circulation and Policy in the Networked Era*. Taylor & Francis.

Kittler, F. (2009) 'Towards an ontology of media', *Theory, Culture and Society*, 26(2–3): 23–31. https://doi.org/10.1177/0263276409103106.

Kjøsen, A.M. (2016) *Capital's Media: The Physical Conditions of Circulation*. Electronic Thesis and Dissertation Repository. https://ir.lib.uwo.ca/etd/4156

Koetsier, J. (2022) 'Google antitrust: The 14 most explosive allegations', *Forbes*, [online] 4 February, Available from: www.forbes.com/sites/johnkoetsier/2022/02/04/google-antitrust-the-14-most-explosive-allegations/ [Accessed 16 May 2022].

Kong, S.T. (2019) 'E-commerce development in rural China', in L. Song, Y. Zhou, and L. Hurst (eds) *The Chinese Economic Transformation*. Australia National University Press, pp 129–41.

Kordzadeh, N. and Ghasemaghaei, M. (2021) 'Algorithmic bias: Review, synthesis, and future research directions', *European Journal of Information Systems*, 31(3): 388–409, Available from: https://doi.org/10.1080/0960085X.2021.1927212 [Accessed 6 July 2023].

Kounine, A. (2019) '5 things you need to know about the voice-activated future of marketing,' *Marketing Insider* [online] 20 February, Available from: www.mediapost.com/publications/article/332219/5-things-you-need-to-know-about-the-voice-activate.html [Accessed 6 July 2023].

Krippner, G and Alvarez, A.S. (2007) 'Embeddedness and the intellectual projects of economic sociology', *Annual Review of Sociology*, 33: 219–40.

Kumar, S. (2019) 'The algorithmic dance: YouTube's Adpocalypse and the gatekeeping of cultural content on digital platforms', *Internet Policy Review*, 8(2). https://doi.org/10.14763/2019.2.1417.

Kusimba, S, Kunyu, G. and Gross, E. (2018) 'Social networks of mobile money in Kenya', in B. Maurer, S. Musaraj and I.V. Small (eds) *Money at the Margins: Global Perspectives on Technology, Financial Inclusion, and Design* (Vol. 6): Berghahn Books, pp 179–99.

Laghate, G. (2020) 'TRPs: Built on houses of cards?', *Times of India*, [online] 12 October, Available from: https://timesofindia.indiatimes.com/india/trps-built-on-houses-of-cards/articleshow/78610546.cms [Accessed 13 July 2021].

Lai, S. and Flensburg, S. (2020) 'A proxy for privacy uncovering the surveillance ecology of mobile apps', *Big Data and Society*, 7(2): 205395172094254. https://doi.org/10.1177/2053951720942543.

Langley, P. and Leyshon, A. (2017) 'Platform capitalism: The intermediation and capitalization of digital economic circulation,' *Finance and Society*, 3(1): 11–31. https://doi.org/10.2218/finsoc.v3i1.1936.

Langley, P. and Rodima-Taylor, D. (2022) 'FinTech in Africa: An editorial introduction', *Journal of Cultural Economy*, 15(4): 387–400. https://doi.org/10.1080/17530350.2022.2092193.

Latour, B. (2005) *Reassembling the Social: An Introduction of Actor-Network-Theory*. Oxford University Press.

Lee, C.S. (2019) 'Datafication, dataveillance, and the social credit system as China's new normal', *Online Information Review*, 43(6): 952–70.

Lehdonvirta, V. and Castronova, E. (2014) *Virtual Economies: Design and Analysis*. MIT Press.

Lessem, R., Schieffer, A. and Rima, S.D. (2013) *Integral Dynamics Political Economy, Cultural Dynamics and the Future of the University*. Routledge.

Li, A.H. (2017) 'E-commerce and Taobao villages: A promise for China's rural development?', *China Perspectives*, 2017(2017/3): 57–62.

Li, W. and Li, C. (2022) 'Analysis of the internationalization strategy of cross-border e-commerce enterprises: The case of Alibaba group', *iBusiness*, 14(4): 270–83.

Liboriussen, B. (2015) 'Amateur gold farming in China: "Chinese ingenuity"', *Independence, and Critique. Games and Culture*, 11(3): 316–31. https://doi.org/10.1177/1555412015598603.

Lin, Y. (2017) 'The courses and policy environment of e-commerce development in China', *Journal of Social Science Research*, 11(2): 2364–73.

Lindquist, J. (2015) 'Brokers and brokerage, anthropology of', in *International Encyclopedia of the Social and Behavioral Sciences*, Elsevier, pp 870–74. https://doi.org/10.1016/B978-0-08-097086-8.12178-6.

Lingel, J. (2020) *An Internet for the People*. Princeton University Press.

Liu, S. and Avery, M. (2021) *Alibaba: The Inside Story Behind Jack Ma and the Creation of the World's Biggest Online Marketplace*. HarperCollins Publishers Ltd.

Loubere, N. (2017) 'China's internet finance boom and tyrannies of inclusion', *China Perspectives*, 2017(2017/4): 9–18.

Luo, X. (2018) 'In China's Taobao villages, e-commerce is one way to bring new jobs and business opportunities to rural areas', [online], Available from: https://blogs.worldbank.org/eastasiapacific/china-s-taobao-villages-e-commerce-one-way-bring-new-jobs-and-business-opportunities-rural-areas [Accessed 9 February 2024].

Ma, L., Christensen, T. and Zheng, Y. (2023) 'Government technological capacity and public–private partnerships regarding digital service delivery: Evidence from Chinese cities', *International Review of Administrative Sciences*, 89(1): 95–111.

MacKenzie, D. (2006) *An Engine, Not a Camera: How Financial Models Shape Markets*. Cambridge, MA: MIT Press.

Mackenzie, A. (2018) '48 million configurations and counting: Platform numbers and their capitalization', *Journal of Cultural Economy*, 11(1): 36–53.

Lyotard, J.-F. (1984) *The Postmodern Condition: A Report on Knowledge*. University of Minnesota Press.

Manzerolle, V. (2010) 'Mobilizing the audience commodity: Digital labour in a wireless world', *Ephemera: Theory and Politics in Organization*, 10(4): 455–69. https://scholar.uwindsor.ca/communicationspub/5.

Manzerolle, V. and Daubs, M. (2021) 'Friction-free authenticity: Mobile social networks and transactional affordances', *Media, Culture and Society*, 43(7): 1279–96. https://doi.org/10.1177/0163443721999953.

Manzerolle, V. and Kjøsen, A. (2012) 'The communication of capital: Digital media and the logic of acceleration', *TripleC*, 10(2): 214–29.

Manzerolle, V. and Wiseman, A. (2016) 'On the transactional ecosystems of digital media', *Communication and the Public*, 1(4): 393–408. https://doi.org/10.1177/2057047316679418.

Martin, J. (1976) 'What should we do with a hidden curriculum when we find one?', *Curriculum Inquiry*, 6(2): 135–51.

Martin, R. (2015) *Knowledge Ltd: Toward a Social Logic of the Derivative*. Temple University Press.

Marwick, A. and Hargittai, E. (2018) 'Nothing to hide, nothing to lose? Incentives and disincentives to sharing information with institutions online', *Information, Communication and Society*, 22(12): 1697–13. https://doi.org/10.1080/1369118X.2018.1450432.

Marx, K. (1976) *Capital: Volume 1: A Critique of Political Economy*. Penguin Publishing Group.

Maton, K. (2008) 'Habitus', in M. Grenfell (ed) *Pierre Bourdieu: Key Concepts*. Routledge, pp 48–64.

Mattelart, A. (1996) *The Invention of Communication*. University of Minnesota Press.

Mattelart, A. (2000) *Networking the World, 1794–2000* (1st edn). University of Minnesota Press.

McCormick, J. (2019) 'What AI can tell from listening to you', *Wall Street Journal*, [online] 1 April, Available from: www.wsj.com/articles/what-ai-can-tell-from-listening-to-you-11554169408 [Accessed 6 July 2023].

McGuigan, L. and Manzerolle, V. (2015) ' "All the world's a shopping cart": Theorizing the political economy of ubiquitous media and markets', *New Media and Society*, 17(11): 1830–48. https://doi.org/10.1177/1461444814535191.

McKelvey, F. and Hunt, R. (2019) 'Discoverability: Toward a definition of content discovery through platforms', *Social Media + Society*, 5(1): 2056305118819188.

McMorrow, R. (2023) 'Alibaba plans to split into six in radical overhaul', [online], Available from: www.ft.com/content/41defa45-5ca5-479d-aef7-9edfbb21b73c [Accessed 9 February 2024].

Medappa, K. (2022) 'Chasing targets, making life: An ethnographic study of platform-based cab drivers and food delivery workers in Bengaluru, India', PhD dissertation, Department of Development Studies, University of Sussex.

Meier, L.M. and Manzerolle, V.R. (2019) 'Rising tides? Data capture, platform accumulation, and new monopolies in the digital music economy', *New Media and Society*, 21(3): 543–61. https://doi.org/10.1177/1461444818800998.

Meyer, J.W. and Rowan, B. (1977) 'Institutionalized organizations: Formal structure as myth and ceremony', *American Journal of Sociology*, 83(2): 340–63. https://doi.org/10.1086/226550.

Miege, B. and Garnham, N. (1979) 'The cultural commodity', *Media, Culture and Society*, 1(3): 297–311. https://doi.org/10.1177/016344377900100307.

Mirowski, P. (2009) 'Postface: Defining neoliberalism', in Philip Mirowski, Dieter Plehwe (eds) *The Road from Mont Pelerin: The Making of the Neoliberal Thought Collective*. Harvard University Press, pp 417–55.

Mirowski, P. and Somefun, K. (1998) 'Markets as evolving computational entities', *Journal of Evolutionary Economics*, 8: 329–56.

Moore, P.V. and Joyce, S. (2020) 'Black box or hidden abode? The expansion and exposure of platform work managerialism', *Review of International Political Economy*, 27(4): 926–48.

Morgan, E. (1989) *Inventing the People: The Rise of Popular Sovereignty in England and America*. Norton.

Moriuchi, E. (2019) ' "Social credit effect" in a sharing economy: A theory of mind and prisoner's dilemma game theory perspective on the two-way review and rating system', *Psychology and Marketing*, 37(5): 641–62.

Morozov, E. (2019) 'Digital socialism? The calculation debate in the age of big data'. *New Left Review*, (116): 33–67.

Murray, D. (1930) *Chapters in the History of Bookkeeping, Accountancy and Commercial Arithmetic*. Jackson, Wylie and Co.

Mäki, U. (ed) (2001) *The Economic World View: Studies in the Ontology of Economics*. Cambridge University Press.

Nakamoto, S. (2008) *Bitcoin: A Peer-to-Peer Electronic Cash System*, Available from: https://bitcoin.org/bitcoin.pdf [Accessed 2 February 2024].

Napoli, P.M. (2003) *Audience Economics: Media Institutions and the Audience Marketplace*. Columbia University Press.

Napoli, P.M. (2005) 'Audience measurement and media policy: Audience economics, the diversity principle, and the local people meter', *Communication Law and Policy*, 10(4): 349–82.

Napoli, P.M. (2011a) *Audience Evolution. New Technologies and the Transformation of Media Audiences*. Columbia University Press.

Napoli, P.M. (2011b) 'Exposure diversity reconsidered', *Journal of Information Policy*, 1: 246–59.

Napoli, P.M. and Karaganis, J. (2007) 'Toward a federal data agenda for communications policymaking', *CommLaw conspectus*, 16: 53–96.

Napoli, P.M. and Napoli, A.B. (2019) 'What social media platforms can learn from audience measurement: Lessons in the self-regulation of "black boxes"', *First Monday*, 24(12).

Nash, J. (2001) 'Globalization and the cultivation of peripheral vision', *Anthropology Today*, 17(4): 15–22.

Nast, C. (2022) "XXX-Files: Who torched the Pornhub palace?", *Vanity Fair* [online], Available from: www.vanityfair.com/style/2022/01/xxx-files-who-torched-the-pornhub-palace [Accessed 16 May 2022].

Naughton, B. (2020) 'Chinese industrial policy and the digital Silk Road', *Asia Policy*, 15(1): 23–40.

Naughton, B. (2021) *The Rise of China's Industrial Policy, 1978 to 2020*. Universidad Nacional Autónomica de México, Facultad de Economía. https://ucigcc.org/publication/the-rise-of-chinas-industrial-policy-1978-to-2020/

Navaro-Yashin, Y. (2002) *Faces of the State: Secularism and Public Life in Turkey*. Princeton University Press.

Nee, V. (2010) 'Bottom-up economic development and the role of the state: A focus on China', *Sociologica*, 4(1): 1–12.

Negri, A. (1999) *Insurgencies. Constituent Power and the Modern State*. University of Minnesota Press.

Nettels, C. (1933) 'British payments in the American Colonies, 1685–1715', *The English Historical Review*, 48(190): 229–49.

Nieborg, D.B. and Helmond, A. (2019) 'The political economy of Facebook's platformization in the mobile ecosystem: Facebook Messenger as a platform instance', *Media, Culture and Society*, 41(2): 196–218.

Nieborg, D.B. and Poell, T. (2018) 'The platformization of cultural production: Theorizing the contingent cultural commodity', *New Media and Society*, 20(11): 4275–92.

Nik-Khah, E. (2020) 'On skinning a cat: George Stigler on the marketplace of ideas', In D. Plehwe, Q. Slobodian and P. Mirowski (eds) *The Nine Lives of Neoliberalism*. Verso, pp 46–69.

NYU Langone Health. (2018) 'Harnessing voice recognition software to screen for post traumatic stress disorder', *NYU Langone Health News Hub* [online], Available from: https://nyulangone.org/news/harnessing-voice-recognition-software-screen-post-traumatic-stress-disorder [Accessed 6 July 2023].

Oliver, C. (1991) 'Strategic responses to institutional processes', *Academy of Management Review*, 16(1): 145–79. https://doi.org/10.5465/amr.1991.4279002.

Olma, S. (2014) 'Never mind the sharing economy: Here's platform capitalism', [online], Available from: https://networkcultures.org/mycreativity/2014/10/16/never-mind-the-sharing-economy-heres-platform-capitalism/ [Accessed 16 January 2022].

Open Science Collaboration (2015) 'Estimating the reproducibility of psychological science', *Science*, 3: 49. https://doi.org/10.1126/science.aac4716.

Orben, A. and Przybylski, A.K. (2019) 'The association between adolescent well-being and digital technology use', *Nature Human Behaviour*, 3: 173–82.

Ørmen, J. and Gregersen, A. (2022) 'Towards the engagement economy: interconnected processes of commodification on YouTube', *Media, Culture and Society*, 45(2): p 01634437221111951. https://doi.org/10.1177/01634437221111951.

Parikka, J. (2014) 'Cultural techniques of cognitive capitalism: Metaprogramming and the labour of code', *Cultural Studies Review*, 20(1). https://doi.org/10.5130/csr.v20i1.3831.

Parker, G., Van Alstyne, M. and Choudary, S.P. (2016) *Platform Revolution: How Networked Markets Are Transforming the Economy and How to Make Them Work for You* (1st edn). W.W. Norton and Company.

Parthasarathi, V. and Athique, A. (2020) 'Market matters: Interdependencies in the media economy', *Media, Culture and Society*, 42(3): 431–48.

Parthasarathi, V. and Raghunath, P. (2023) 'Expanding horizons of media bazaars: Topography of the DME in India', in T. Flew, J. Holt and J. Thomas (eds) *Handbook of the Digital Media Economy*. SAGE Publications, pp 361–84.

Parthasarathi, V. and Simran, A. (2020) 'Rein and laissez faire: The dual personality of media regulation in India', *Digital Journalism*, 8(6): 797–819.

Parthasarathi, V., Amanullah, A. and Koshy, S. (2016) 'Digitalization as formalization: A view from below', *International Journal of Digital Television*, 7(2): 155–71.

Peck, J. (2021) 'On capitalism's cusp', *Area Development and Policy*, 6(1): 1–30. https://doi.org/10.1080/23792949.2020.1866996.

Peck, J. and Phillips, R. (2021) 'The platform conjuncture', *Sociologica*, 14(3): 73–99. https://doi.org/10.6092/ISSN.1971-8853/11613.

REFERENCES

Pedersen, M.A. (2016) 'Moving to remain the same: An anthropological theory of nomadism', in P. Charbonnier, G. Salmon and P. Skafish (eds) *Comparative Metaphysics: Ontology after Anthropology*. Rowman and Littlefield, pp 221–46.

Pedersen, M.A, Albris, K. and Seaver, N. (2021) 'The political economy of attention', *Annual Review of Anthropology*, 50: 309–25.

Perrin, P. (2018) 'Demanding a better ad experience: Why one in four internet users say no to ads', *eMarketer* [online] 4 December 4, Available at https://content-na1.emarketer.com/demanding-a-better-ad-experience [Accessed 6 July 2023].

Peters, J. Durham (2015) *The Marvelous Clouds: Toward a Philosophy of Elemental Media*. Chicago: University of Chicago Press, Available from: https://doi.org/10.7208/9780226253978

http://go.utlib.ca/cat/10120439) Chicago, IL: The University of Chicago Press.

Petersen, R.F.J. (2018) 'Regeringens digitale vækstmotor udnævner første adm. direktør', *Iwatch,* [online] September 21, Available from: https://itwatch.dk/ITNyt/Politik/article10883633.ece [Accessed 29 June 2023].

Pfeffer, J. and Salancik, G.R. (1978) *The External Control of Organizations: A Resource Dependence Perspective*. Harper and Row.

Philips (2022) 'Why are you still typing? Dictation is seven-times faster', *Philips Speechlive*, [online] 1 September, Available from: www.speechlive.com/us/blog/why-are-you-still-typing-dictation-is-seven-times-faster/ [Accessed 6 July 2023].

Picard, R.G. (2011) 'Economic approaches to media policy', in Robin Mansell and Marc Raboy (ed) *The Handbook of Global Media and Communication Policy*. Wiley-Blackwell, pp 353–65.

PaPlantin, J.-C., Lagoze, C., Edwards, P.N. and Sandvig, C. (2018) 'Infrastructure studies meet platform studies in the age of Google and Facebook', *New Media and Society*, 20(1): 293–310. https://doi.org/10.1177/1461444816661553.

Plantin, J.C. and Punathambekar, A. (2019) 'Digital media infrastructures: Pipes, platforms, and politics', *Media, Culture and Society*, 41(2): 163–74.

Plantin, J.C. and De Seta, G. (2019) 'WeChat as infrastructure: The techno-nationalist shaping of Chinese digital platforms', *Chinese Journal of Communication*, 12(3): 257–73.

Platana, D. and Pempus, B. (2023) 'What is a prop bet?', *Forbes*, [online] 8 March, Available from: www.forbes.com/betting/guide/prop-bet/ [Accessed 26 June 2023].

Polanyi, K. (1944) *The Great Transformation: The Political and Economic Origins of Our Time*. Farrar and Rinehart.

Pollman, E. and Barry, J.M. (2016) Regulatory entrepreneurship. *Southern Californian Law Review*, 90: 383–448.

Postigo, H. (2007) 'Of mods and modders: Chasing down the value of fan-based digital game modifications', *Games and Culture*, 2(4): 300–13.

Quinn, B., Blackall, M. and Dodd, V. (2020) 'YouTube accused of being "organ of radicalisation"', *The Guardian*, [online] 2 March, Available from: www.theguardian.com/technology/2020/mar/02/youtube-accused-of-being-organ-of-radicalisation [Accessed 16 May 2022].

Ravenelle, A. (2019) *Hustle and Gig: Struggling and Surviving in the Sharing Economy*. University of California Press.

Reuters (2018, 8 May) 'Alibaba buys Rocket Internet's Pakistan ecommerce platform Daraz', Reuters [online], Available from: www.reuters.com/article/idUSASO0004IL [Accessed 9 February 2024],

Reuters (2021, 20 April) 'China's Alibaba invests $350 mln in capital increase to Turkey's Trendyol trade registry', Reuters [online], Available from: www.reuters.com/world/middle-east/chinas-alibaba-invests-350-mln-capital-increase-turkeys-trendyol-trade-registry-2021-04-20/ [Accessed 9 February 2024].

Riofrancos, T. (2020) *Resource Radicals: From Petro-Nationalism to Post-Extractivism in Ecuador*. Duke University Press.

Roberts, S. (2018) 'Digital detritus', *First Monday* 23:3 [online] 5 March, Available from: https://firstmonday.org/ojs/index.php/fm/article/view/8283 [Accessed 6 July 2023].

Rochet, J.C. and Tirole, J. (2003) 'Platform competition in two-sided markets', *Journal of the European Economic Association*, 1(4): 990–1029.

Roose, K. (2019) 'The making of a YouTube radical', *The New York Times*, [online] 8 June, Available from: www.nytimes.com/interactive/2019/06/08/technology/youtube-radical.html [Accessed 16 May 2022].

Rosenblat, A. (2018) *Uberland: How Algorithms Are Rewriting the Rules of Work*. University of California Press.

Ross, A. and Nieborg, D. (2021) 'Spinning is winning: Social casino apps and the platformization of gamble-play', *Journal of Consumer Culture*, 21(1): 84–101. https://doi.org/10.1177/1469540521993931.

Rubin, B.F. (2020) 'Amazon sees Alexa devices more than double in just one year', CNET [online], Available from: www.cnet.com/news/amazon-sees-alexa-devices-more-than-double-in-just-one-year/ [Accessed 6 July 2023].

Samuelson, P. (1973) *Economics*, 9th edn. McGraw-Hill.

Schaps, D.M. (2004) *The Invention of Coinage and the Monetization of Ancient Greece*. University of Michigan Press.

Schor, J. (2021) *After the Gig: How the Sharing Economy Got Hijacked and How to Win It Back*. California University Press.

Schüll N.D. (2014) *Addiction by Design: Machine Gambling in Las Vegas*. Princeton University Press.

Schreiner, M. (2023) 'Stochastic parrot or world model? How large language models learn', The Decoder [online], Available from: https://the-decoder.com/stochastic-parrot-or-world-model-how-large-language-models-learn/ [Accessed 9 February 2024].

Schroter, J. (2019) 'Money determines our situation', in A. Beverungen, P. Mirowski, E. Nik-Khah and J. Schröter (eds) *Markets: In Search of Media*. Meson Press, pp 71–111.

Seaford, R. (2004) *Money and the Early Greek Mind: Homer, Philosophy, Tragedy*. Cambridge University Press. https://doi.org/10.1017/CBO9780511483080

Seaver, N. (2019) 'Knowing algorithms', in Janet A. Vertesi and David Ribes (eds) *DigitalSTS: A Field Guide for Science and Technology Studies*. Princeton University Press, pp 412–22.

Shapiro, T. (2016) 'How emotion-detection technology will change marketing', HubSpot [online] 17 October, Available from: https://blog.hubspot.com/marketing/emotion-detection-technology-marketing [Accessed 6 July 2023].

Sheehan, J. and Wahrman, D. (2015) *Invisible Hands: Self-Organization and the Eighteenth Century*. University of Chicago Press.

Shen, H. (2018) 'Building a digital Silk Road? Situating the internet in China's Belt and Road initiative', *International Journal of Communication*, 12: 19.

Shen, H. (2021) *Alibaba: Infrastructuring Global China*. Routledge.

Shi, W. and Ye, M. (2021) 'Chinese capital goes global: The Belt and Road initiative and beyond', *Journal of East Asian Studies*, 21(2): 173–92.

Sims, C. (2017) *Disruptive Fixation: School Reform and the Pitfalls of Techno-Idealism*. Princeton University Press.

Sinha, A. and Basu, A. (2019) 'The politics of India's data protection ecosystem', *Economic and Political Weekly*, 54(49). www.epw.in/engage/article/politics-indias-data-protection-ecosystem.

Smythe, D. (1977) 'Communications: Blindspot of Western Marxism', *Canadian Journal of Political and Social Theory*, 1(3): 1–27.

Sohn-Rethel, A. (2021) *Intellectual and Manual Labour: A Critique of Epistemology* (M. Sohn-Rethel, Trans.) Haymarket Books.

Spector, R. (2013) 'Serious about Siri', *Brandeis Magazine* [online], Spring, Available from: www.brandeis.edu/magazine/2013/spring/inquiry/siri.html [Accessed 6 July 2023].

Spencer, A.S. and Kirchhoff, B.A. (2006) 'Schumpeter and new technology based firms: Towards a framework for how NTBFs cause creative destruction', *International Entrepreneurship and Management Journal*, 2(2): 145–56.

Spyer, P (ed). (1997) *Border Fetishisms. Material Objects in Unstable Spaces*. Routledge.

Srnicek, N. (2017) *Platform Capitalism*. Polity.

Stabrowski, F. (2017) '"People as businesses": Airbnb and urban micro-entrepreneurialism in New York City', *Cambridge Journal of Regions, Economy and Society*, 10(2): 327–47.

Stanford University (2016) 'Smartphone speech recognition can write text messages three times faster than human typing', *Stanford News* [online] 24 August, Available from: https://news.stanford.edu/2016/08/24/stanford-study-speech-recognition-faster-texting/ [Accessed 6 July 2023].

Stark, D. and Pais, I. (2021) 'Algorithmic management in the platform economy', *Sociologica*, 14(3): 47–72. https://doi.org/10.6092/issn.1971-8853/12221.

State Council (2005) Several Opinions on Accelerating the Development of Electronic Commerce, Available from: https://www.gov.cn/gongbao/content/2005/content_63341.htm

Stone, B. (2013) *The Everything Store: Jeff Bezos and the Age of Amazon*, Random House.

Strathern, M. (1988) *The Gender of the Gift*. Cambridge University Press.

Swan, E. (2000) *Building the Global Market: A 4000 Year History of Derivatives* (1st edn). Springer.

Swartz, L. (2020) *New Money: How Payment Became Social Media*. Yale University Press.

Taneja, H. and Mamoria, U. (2012) 'Measuring media use across platforms: Evolving audience information systems', *International Journal on Media Management*, 14(2): 121–40.

Taneja, H. (2013) 'Audience measurement and media fragmentation: Revisiting the monopoly question', *Journal of Media Economics*, 26(4): 203–19.

Taussig, M. (1980) *The Devil and Commodity Fetishism in South America*. The University of North Carolina Press.

Taylor, C. (2004) *Modern Social Imaginaries*. Duke University Press.

The Digital, Culture, Media and Sport Committee (2022) *Influencer culture: Lights, camera, inaction?* Parliamentary Copyright House of Commons 2022: House of Commons: Digital, Culture, Media and Sport Committee, Available from: https://committees.parliament.uk/publications/22107/documents/164150/default/ [Accessed 9 February 2024].

The Economist (2021, 14 August) Xi Jinping's assault on tech will change China's trajectory, Available from: https://www.economist.com/leaders/2021/08/14/xi-jinpings-assault-on-tech-will-change-chinas-trajectory

Thelen, K. (2018) 'Regulating Uber: The politics of the platform economy in Europe and the United States', *Perspectives on Politics*, 16(4): 938–53.

Thomas, K. (1987) 'Numeracy in early modern England: The Prothero lecture', *Transactions of the Royal Historical Society*, 37: 103–32. https://doi.org/10.2307/3679153.

Thompson, E.P. (1971) 'The moral economy of the English crowd in the eighteenth century', *Past and Present*, 50: 76–136.

Thomson, G. (1972) *The First Philosophers*. Lawrence and Wishart.

Thorhauge, A.M. (2022) *The Steam Platform Economy: From Retail to Player-Driven Economies. New Media & Society*, 14614448221081401.

Thorhauge, A.M. (2023) *Games in the Platform Economy: Steam's Tangled Markets*. Bristol University Press.

Thorhauge, A.M. and Nielsen, R. (2021) 'Epic, steam, and the role of skin-betting in game (platform) economies', *Journal of Consumer Culture*, 21(1): 52–67.

Thurman, N. (2014) 'Newspaper consumption in the digital age', *Digital Journalism*, 2(2): 156–78.

Tkacz, N. (2014) *Wikipedia and the Politics of Openness*. University of Chicago Press.

TRAI (2020) *Recommendations on Review of Television Audience Measurement and Rating System in India*, New Delhi (28 April).

Troullinou, P. (2017) 'Exploring the subjective experience of everyday surveillance: the case of smartphone devices as means of facilitating "seductive" surveillance', PhD dissertation, Open University, Available from: https://oro.open.ac.uk/52613/2/thesis_PT_library_submission.pdf [Accessed 9 February 2024].

Tse, E. (2016, 5 April) The Rise of Entrepreneurship in China. *Forbes*, Available from: https://www.forbes.com/sites/tseedward/2016/04/05/the-rise-of-entrepreneurship-in-china/?sh=3ce552c23efc

Tubaro, P. (2021) 'Disembedded or deeply embedded? A multi-level network analysis of online labour platforms', *Sociology*, 55(5). https://doi.org/10.1177/0038038520986082.

Turner, V. (1982) 'Images of anti-temporality: An essay in the anthropology of experience', *The Harvard Theological Review*, 75(2): 243–65.

Turow, J. (2005) 'Audience construction and culture production', *Annals of the American Academy of Political and Social Science*, 597(January): 103–21, Available from: www.jstor.org/stable/25046064 [Accessed 6 July 2023].

Turow, J. (2011) *The Daily You*. Yale University Press.

Turow, J. (2021) *The Voice Catchers*. Yale University Press.

Turow, J., Draper, N. and Hennessy, M. (2015) 'The tradeoff fallacy', [online], Available from: http://dx.doi.org/10.2139/ssrn.2820060 [Accessed 6 July 2023].

Turow, J., Lelkes, Y., Draper, N. and Waldman, A. (2023) 'Americans cannot consent to companies' use of their data', *International Journal of Communication*, 17(2023): 1–20, published online in July 2023.

Uddin, M.S. (2023) 'Stochastic parrots: A novel look at large language models and their limitations', [online], Available from: https://towardsai.net/p/machine-learning/stochastic-parrots-a-novel-look-at-large-language-models-and-their-limitations [Accessed 9 February 2024].

Valcke, P. (2011) 'A European risk barometer for media pluralism: Why assess damage, when you can map risk?', *Journal of Information Policy*, 1: 185–216.

Van Dijck, J. (2014) 'Datafication, dataism and dataveillance: Big data between scientific paradigm and ideology', *Surveillance and Society*, 12(2): 197–208. https://doi.org/10.24908/ss.v12i2.4776.

Van Dijck, J., Poell, T. and De Waal, M. (2018) *The Platform Society: Public Values in a Connective World*. Oxford University Press.

van Doorn, N. (2020) 'A new institution on the block: On platform urbanism and Airbnb citizenship', *New Media and Society*, 22(10): 1808–26.

Verint (nd) 'Speech analytics transcription accuracy', Verint.com [online] Was available from: www.verint.com/wp-content/uploads/speech-analytics-transcription-accuracy-white-paper-english-us.pdf [Accessed 18 May 2019].

Vilar, P. (2011) *A History of Gold and Money: 1450–1920* (J. White, Trans.). Verso.

Vonderau, P. (2021) 'Questioning the content supply model: A provocation', in P. McDonald, C. Brannon Donoghue and T. Havens (eds) *Digital Media Distribution: Portals, Platforms, Pipelines*.: New York University Press, pp 126–42.

Vrankulj, A. (2013) 'Beyond Verbal launches, closes funding round to decode human emotions from voice data', BiometricUpdate.com, [online], Available from: www.biometricupdate.com/201305/beyond-verbal-launches-closes-funding-round-to-decode-human-emotions-from-voice-data [Accessed 6 July 2023].

Wadhwa, V. (2011) What we really need to fear about China. *The Washington Post*, Available from: https://www.washingtonpost.com/national/on-innovations/what-we-really-need-to-fear-about-china/2011/09/14/gIQAPrMy0K_story.html

Wadhwa, V. (2013) LinkedIn: Chinese Can Innovate—But China Can't, Available from: https://www.linkedin.com/pulse/20131114180931-8451-chinese-can-innovate-but-china-can-t

Walsh, S. (2021) *The Gig Is Up*. Dowgoof Pictures.

Wang, J. (2017) '"Stir-frying" internet finance: Financialization and the institutional role of financial news in China', *International Journal of Communication*, 11: 22.

Wang, J. and Doan, M.A. (2019) 'The Ant empire: Fintech media and corporate convergence within and beyond Alibaba', *The Political Economy of Communication*, 6(2): 25–37.

Wang, Y. (2015) 'The rise of the "shareholding state": Financialization of economic management in China', *Socio-Economic Review*, 13(3): 603–25.

Webster, J.G. (1990) 'The role of audience ratings in communications policy', *Communications and the Law*, 12(2): 59–72.

REFERENCES

Webster, J.G. (2014) *The Marketplace of Attention: How audiences take shape in a Digital Age*, MIT Press.

Wei, Y.D., Lin, J. and Zhang, L. (2020) 'E-commerce, Taobao villages and regional development in China', *Geographical Review*, 110(3): 380–405.

Welch, C. (2023) 'Inside Amazon's canceled plan to make Halo a fitness success', *The Verge*, [online] 1 May, Available from: www.theverge.com/2023/5/1/23704825/amazon-halo-canceled-features-ai-training-apple-watch [Accessed 6 July 2023].

Werning, S. (2019) 'Disrupting video game distribution: A diachronic affordance analysis of Steam's platformization strategy', *Nordic Journal of Media Studies*, 1(1): 103–124.

Whyte, J. (2019) *The Morals of the Market: Human Rights and the Rise of Neoliberalism*. Verso.

Wigand, R.T. (1997) 'Electronic commerce: Definition, theory, and context', *The Information Society*, 13(1): 1–16. https://doi.org/10.1080/019722497129241.

Wigand, R.T. (2020) 'Whatever happened to disintermediation?', *Electronic Markets*, 30(1): 39–47. https://doi.org/10.1007/s12525-019-00389-0.

Williams, B.O.B. and Johnson, R.G. (2005) 'Ready reckoners', *IEEE Annals of the History of Computing*, 27(4): 64–80.

Williams, J. (2018) *Stand Out of Our Light. Freedom and Resistance in the Attention Economy*. Cambridge University Press.

Wolf, E. (1956) 'Aspects of group relations in a complex society: Mexico', *American Anthropologist*, 58, 1065–78.

Wu, T. (2016) *The Attention Merchants: The Epic Struggle to Get Inside Our Heads*. Knopf.

Wu, Y., Zhang, W., Shen, J., Mo, Z. and Peng, Y. (2018) 'Smart city with Chinese characteristics against the background of big data: Idea, action and risk', *Journal of Cleaner Production*, 173, 60–66.

Yates, L. (2021) *The Airbnb 'Movement' for Deregulation: How Platform-Sponsored Grassroots Lobbying is Changing Politics*. Manchester: University of Manchester.

YouTube (nd) 'Advertising on YouTube Kids', YouTube Help. [online] Available from: https://support.google.com/youtube/answer/6168681 [Accessed 3 November 2021].

Yue, H. (2017) 'National report on e-commerce development in (China', Inclusive and Sustainable Industrial Development Working Paper Series WP17, 6. UNIDO. www.unido.org/sites/default/.

Zervas, G., Proserpio, D. and Byers, J.W. (2021) 'A first look at online reputation on Airbnb, where every stay is above average', *Marketing Letters*, 32: 1–16.

Zhang, L. (2020a) 'When platform capitalism meets petty capitalism in China: Alibaba and an integrated approach to platformization', *International Journal of Communication*, 14: 21.

Zhang, L. (2020b) 'Putting ant under the microscope', Sixth Tone, [online], Available from: www.sixthtone.com/news/1006422/putting-ant-under-the-microscope [Accessed 9 February 2024].

Zhang, L. and Chen, J.Y. (2022) 'A regional and historical approach to platform capitalism: The cases of Alibaba and Tencent', *Media, Culture & Society*, 44(8): 1454–72.

Zhang, L. and Yuan, E.J. (2022) 'Entrepreneurs in China's "Silicon Valley": State- led financialization and mass entrepreneurship/innovation', *Information, Communication and Society*, 26(2): 286–303. https://doi.org/10.1080/1369118X.2022.2155486.

Zhao, J. (2015) '2 billion for rural e-commerce: Special funds are used to build logistics' 20亿攻坚农村电商：专项资金用于建物流 http://finance.sina.com.cn/china/20150515/050722186128.shtml [Accessed 15 February 2024].

Zhao, Y. (2010) 'China media colloquium | for a critical study of communication and China: Challenges and opportunities', *International Journal of Communication*, 4: 8.

Zheng, Y. and Huang, Y. (2018) *Market in State: The Political Economy of Domination in China*. Cambridge University Press.

Ziewitz, M. (2016) 'Governing algorithms: Myth, mess, and methods', *Science, Technology, and Human Values*, 41(1): 3–16.

Zuboff, S. (2015) 'Big Other: Surveillance capitalism and the prospects of an information civilization', *Journal of Information Technology*, 30(1): 75–89. https://doi.org/10.1057/jit.2015.5.

Zuboff, S. (2019) *The Age of Surveillance Capitalism: The Fight for a Human Future at the New Frontier of Power*. Profile Books.

Index

References to endnotes show both the page number and the note number (72n3).

A

ABC (Audit Bureau of Circulation) 59, 61, 63
accumulation 5, 17, 18, 24, 32, 91
Adobe 4, 78
advertising
  ad blocking and 78
  apps and 88
  currency 68
  data and 62, 63, 65, 67, 70, 72, 77
  government 69
  media and 7, 53, 59, 60, 63, 66, 68, 70, 72
  platforms and 5, 10, 11, 34, 91, 128, 131–4, 135–8, 141, 146
  services 7
  voice intelligence and 82, 85–6
Affectiva 79
affordances
  capitalism and 13, 36
  conceptual 156
  connectivity and 13, 17, 33
  platforms and 17–18, 33, 36, 44, 54, 103, 150
  transactional 17–18, 20–3, 33–5, 140, 146
AI (artificial intelligence) 75, 76, 79, 82, 87, 120, 155, 158–60, 161, 162
Airbnb 6, 38, 39, 42, 44, 47, 50, 51, 131
Alexa 75, 76
algorithms
  audience and 54, 63, 64–5, 71, 72n3
  capitalism and 1
  cryptocurrencies and 143
  data and 70, 79–80, 109
  digital markets and 58
  history 19
  machine learning 160, 162
  platforms and 54, 55, 64–5, 109, 125, 132–3, 135, 137
  social media and 57
  trade and 29
  Uber and 47
  voice intelligence and 79–80, 86

Alibaba 15, 108–10, 111–26
Alphabet 16n3, 88, 89, 90, 91, 94, 96, 132, 137, 161
aMAP 61, 62, 63, 68
Amazon 1, 7, 8, 10, 16n3, 22–3, 47, 49, 74–6, 81–2, 85, 134
Ant group 108, 123, 147
anthropology 3
APIs (Application Programming Interfaces) 4, 100, 144, 160
Apple 16n3, 73, 74, 75, 76, 82, 85, 88, 90, 91, 94, 136
apps
  advertising and 78, 135
  data and 100–106, 146
  developers 14, 88–92, 94–6, 98–9, 103, 146
  economy 90, 92, 93
  market 14, 93–4, 99
  privacy policy 84
  voice intelligence and 73–4, 76
Archytas 27
Argentina 39, 40, 42, 44, 45, 48, 50
Atari 4
audience
  commodity 70
  construction of 79, 86
  development of 137
  enumeration 14, 55, 59, 63, 67, 70, 72, 74
  measurement 14, 53–6, 57–8, 59–62, 64–5, 67–8, 71–2, 73–4
  markets and 73
  media 54–6, 58, 68
  news 53–6, 58, 61, 66, 69, 72
  platforms and 54
  targeting of 77, 82
  voice intelligence and 73–4, 77
  vulnerable 136

B

Baidu 75, 123
Bank of America 82

189

BARC (Broadcast Audience Research Council) 63, 68, 69, 70, 72n2
Bennett, Tony 83
Big Tech 2, 3, 10, 88–90, 94, 107n3, 120–1, 153, 158
biometrics 14, 55, 73, 75, 81, 86
bitcoin *see* cryptocurrencies
Bixby 76
Blanke, Tobias 91, 105
blockchains 34–5, 143–4, 149, 150–2
Bourdieu, Pierre 82–3
Braudel, Fernand 5, 6–8, 28, 90
BRI (Belt and Road Initiatives) 112, 120, 121–2
brokers 88–90, 92, 94, 99, 103, 105
Buchanan, James 19

C

Calo, Ryan 81
capital 2, 82
capitalism
　connectivity and 22
　contemporary 126
　data 1
　definition 20
　digital 110
　global 109, 110, 111
　history of 7, 13
　market 3
　media and 13, 24–5, 35
　monopoly and 2
　needs of 18
　platform
　　affordances and 34
　　conceptions 9
　　infrastructure and 18
　　markets and 13, 20, 21–2, 157
　　media and 21–2, 24, 35, 36
　　monopolies and 33
　　new type 5, 8
　　postdigital and 154, 157–8, 161
　　regulation of 153
　　research on 2, 19, 23, 91, 106
　　rethinking of 12–13
　　rise of 13
　　situatedness 9
　power and 7
　surveillance 1, 10, 91, 141, 158, 161
Carey, James 31, 32
China 2, 15, 75, 108–26, 157, 162n5
Clarabridge 79
Cognito 75
commodification 5
commodities 19, 23, 24, 26, 28, 30, 31, 34, 70, 141–2, 144, 150, 151, 162
communication 2, 28, 31–2, 109
computing systems 4
Comscore 66, 67, 69
connectivity 17–18, 20–1, 22, 23, 33, 35, 36

COVID-19 8, 109
Craigslist 39, 46, 49
Cramer, Florian 154, 155
Crawford, Kate 81
Croll, Alistair 158–9
cryptocurrencies 3, 33, 34, 35, 142, 143, 148, 149, 150, 151–2

D

data
　authoritarianism and 2
　brokers 62–3, 66, 90, 94, 99
　collection
　　app developers and 95–6, 98, 101–2, 104, 105
　　concerns about 93
　　digitized 1, 70
　　financial services and 123
　　media and 60, 62–3, 67
　　platforms and 10–11, 88–9, 131, 141
　　prices and 47
　　supermarkets 84
　　voice intelligence and 76–8
　extraction of 91, 92
　generation of 57
　infrastructure 117
　markets 14, 104, 105
　mining 77, 120
　ownership of 71
　privacy 71, 82
　production of 33
　protection 71, 93, 102
　providers 61, 67, 68, 70
　sources 71
　synchronization 96
　transparency 71
　use of 84
　valuing of 103, 105
DeFi (decentralized finance services) 35
del Nido, Juan M. 13–14, 39, 40, 42, 44, 47, 48, 50
Denmark 14, 50, 51, 88, 89, 90–5, 99–103, 105–6
derivatives 13, 18, 30–1, 32, 33, 35
digital resignation 74–5, 84–6
digital technologies 2, 3, 109, 117
digitization 8, 93–4, 115, 117, 120, 154
diversity 56, 66
Dodd, Nigel 15, 140, 141, 142–4, 147, 148
Dodsworth, Francis 83
dotcom bubble 8, 10, 13, 115
Draper, Nora 84

E

Easterbrook, Tom 28
eBay 115
Echo 76, 82
e-commerce 108, 112–18, 121, 123, 125, 128, 132

INDEX

economy
  attention 1, 3, 158–9, 161
  global 2, 10, 112, 125, 157
  digital 108, 112, 125, 157–8, 161
  media 68–71
  online 69–71
  platform 2, 3, 5, 17, 34, 40, 44, 51, 55, 65, 71, 92, 112, 124, 128, 141, 144, 157
  political 2, 3, 13, 17
  surveillance 3
  theory 19
Ecuador 43
empowerment 38, 39, 45
enumerative accountability 53, 55, 57–8, 60–1, 66–7, 69–71, 72, 79
Europe 16n2, 19, 28, 75, 93, 99, 102, 136, 158
exchange abstraction 18, 23, 24, 26, 34, 35
exploitation 3, 13, 91

F

Facebook (Meta)
  Big Tech 107n3
  entertainment 141
  fake accounts 135
  financial services and 147
  foundation 6
  media and 59, 69–70, 77, 128, 137, 138, 161
  ordinary lives and 49
  parent company Meta 106n2, 107n3
  research on 39
Factiva 74
FanDuel 50
Ferguson, James 39–40
FFCN (Fact Finding Committee on Newspaper Economics) 60
Firebase 96–8, 99, 100, 101, 102, 104

G

gaming 4, 15, 32, 33, 50, 104, 140–1, 144–52
GDPR (General Data Protection Regulation) 99, 102, 104, 158
Geertz, Clifford 92
Gerbner, George 85
globalization 121
Google
  advertising and 134, 136
  Alphabet and 106n1
  Analytics 96
  Big Tech and 107n3, 113
  Cloud 4
  data protection and 101, 103
  media and 69–70
  monopolization and 1
  role 38
  voice intelligence and 74, 75–6, 77, 81, 82, 85
  YouTube and 131, 132

GPTs (Generative Pre-trained Transformers) 158, 160
Greco, Jerome 86
Greece 25–7
Gregersen, Andreas 15
Grotius, Hugo 43, 49, 52

H

habituation 74–5, 82–3, 85, 86
Halo 81
Hangzhou 120
Harris Committee 68, 69
hidden curriculum 74–5, 85, 86
Hulu 70

I

ICT (information and communication technology) 109, 110, 113, 114, 117, 119
India 14, 39, 40, 43, 54–6, 58–9, 60–3, 67–9, 70–2
infrastructures
  connectivity and 18, 22, 29
  digital 35, 93, 110, 119, 121–2
  economic 146
  global 2
  history 19
  institutional 60
  junctions 92
  material 3, 101
  media 3, 21
  monopolization and 1
  outsourcing of 90
  perspectives 54
  platforms as 125, 127, 132, 134
  postdigital 161
  service 89
  state-controlled 113–14, 117, 122
  technical 8, 103
  technological 25
Innis, Harold 21, 22, 27–9
Instagram 6, 46, 128, 138, 161
Intel 4
Intellectual and Manual Labor: A Critique of Epistemology (Alfred Sohn-Rethel) 18
interface 4, 18, 33
intermediaries 70, 88, 90, 92, 105, 146
internet
  attention and 159
  data and 78
  early days 56, 64, 73
  finance 123–4
  industry 108, 110, 112–14, 117, 119, 122–4
  marketing 78
  platforms 6, 77
  regulations 67
  surveillance and 84
  technology and 8, 123
  wider 141, 145, 150

191

J

Jackson, Philip 85
Japan 2
Joseph, Daniel 151

K

Katz, James 83
Kittler, Friedrich 21, 25

L

Latour, Bruno 103
LexisNexis 74
Leybourn, William 19–20
LG 85
Lindquest, Johan 89
Locke, John 43, 49
Lyft 43, 44
Lyotard, Jean–François 154–6

M

Ma, Jack 109, 110, 113, 122
Manzerolle, Vincent 13, 33, 34, 71, 90, 105
markets
  anti- 5, 7
  capitalism and 1, 3, 24
  changes 17, 20, 110
  data 14, 104, 105
  derivatives and 30–1
  digital
    audiences and 57–8, 66
    development of 36
    discussion on 1, 71
    dynamics of 64
    ecosystem of 13
    enumeration and 72
    local 2, 12
    platforms and 12, 13
    political economy of 2, 3
    postdigital and 154
    practices 13
    regulation of 7
  free 15
  global 31, 113
  local 14, 15, 26, 28, 29, 93, 98, 104, 105
  media and 14, 35, 63, 64–6, 72, 128
  money and 25–6
  monopolization of 1
  multi-sided 4, 5, 15, 128–9, 131, 133, 141
  platforms and 4–5, 17–18, 22, 65, 109, 125
  practices 109
  prices and 28–9, 32
  secondary 144–5
  systems 14
  transactions 20–1, 29
Martin, Randy 30, 31–2
Marxism 3, 5, 17, 21, 22, 23, 24
Mechanical Turk 46
media
  advertisement and 7

  capitalism and 13, 20–1, 24–5
  companies 71
  digital 8, 18, 21, 128, 131
  economic theory and 19, 21
  financial 23–4, 28
  India 59–62
  labour 71
  markets and 14, 35, 63, 65–6
  platforms and 13–15, 21, 54, 55, 58–9, 63, 65, 79, 132, 134, 136–7
  policy 55, 56, 58, 62
  social 23, 33, 34, 57
  studies 3, 13–15, 17, 18, 21, 25, 31
  transformations 29–30, 31
  see also economy: media; news
Meta *see* Facebook
Microsoft 4, 5, 16n3
monetary networks 15, 140–4, 147–9, 150–2
money
  arrangements 142
  capitalism and 13, 18, 24–5
  commodities and 24, 141–2, 144, 150
  communication and 23
  concept of 3
  definition of 142–3, 147
  history 25–7
  platforms and 24
  prices and 25, 28, 30
  production of 151–2
  transactions and 15, 22
Monocle 88, 89, 90, 92–3, 94–6, 98–9, 100, 101–5
monopolization 1, 2, 10, 13, 33, 70, 105, 109, 117, 136
Morency, Louis-Philippe 80
MRC (Media Ratings Council) 69

N

Nakamoto, Satoshi 35
Naughton, Barry 115
neoliberalism 37, 38, 42, 46, 61
Netflix 49, 66
news 53–5, 56, 58–9, 60–2, 65–6, 71–2
NICE 75
Nielsen 61, 62, 63, 67, 68, 70
NRS (National Readership Survey) 63

O

Ørmen, Jacob 15
Otto, Eva Iris 13, 14, 39
overall economic framing 5, 37

P

Parthasarathi, Vibodh 14, 74, 79
Pentland, Alex 77
personalization 14, 73, 74–5, 78–9
Platform for Purchasers, A (William Leybourn) 19–20
platformization 109, 110, 124–5

INDEX

platforms
 access to data 10
 advertising and 11, 133–4
 categories 5
 companies
  as operators 6
  data and 34, 88–94, 96, 98, 99, 101–6, 119
  financial services and 147
  governments and 15
  growth of 116, 119
  legitimacy 15, 127–8, 131–2, 137
  markets and 4
  media and 6
  monopolization 1, 2
  physical location 10
  politics and 50–1
 concept 3–5, 7–8
 defence of 39
 definitions 19–20, 128
 development 1, 2, 6–8, 13–14, 19, 37, 46
 digital 20, 22, 33, 73, 109–10, 112, 124, 131, 132, 134, 136–7, 151
 entertainment 141
 gaming 140–1, 144–52
 impact of 36
 intermediaries and 92
 legitimacy 127–37
 local 39, 90, 98
 markets and 4–5, 17–18, 22, 65, 104, 109, 125
 media and 13–14, 15, 21, 54, 55, 58, 59, 63, 65, 79, 132, 134, 136–7
 mobile 33
 moderation 77
 monopoly and 2, 10, 13, 33, 105, 109, 136
 multinational 88, 92, 93
 news and 53, 65
 popularity 2, 6
 power 2, 10, 11, 13, 15
 privacy agreements 71
 productivity 4, 5, 6
 provincialization of 9–10, 12–16
 regulation of 8
 responsibilities 6
 social imaginaries and 40, 41–2, 43
 society 2, 11
 studies on 1, 4, 6, 10, 11–12, 106, 141
 terms of service 71
 use of term 6, 35
 see also capitalism: platform; digital markets: platforms and; economy: platform; prices: platforms and
postdigitality 153–6, 157–60, 161–2
Postmodern Condition, The (Jean-François Lyotard) 155
postmodernity 155–6
Press Commission 60
prices
 capitalism and 7, 13, 18

commodities 19, 30, 31
 derivatives and 30–1
 history 26, 27–9, 31–2
 platforms and 21, 30, 47
privacy 71, 74, 82, 84
production 8, 13, 20, 22, 23, 24, 25, 26, 30, 32
Pybus, Jennifer 91, 105
Pythagoras 27

R

RDT (resource dependence theory) 15, 129–30
reconfigurations 64
Reddit 46
resignation *see* digital resignation
resources 15, 29, 35
RNI (Registrar of Newspapers for India) 60, 61, 63
Roberts, Sarah 83–4

S

Samsung 76, 82, 85
Schaps, David 26
Schmidt, Eric 77–8
Seaford, Richard 26–7
Silicon Valley 10, 12, 15, 34, 106, 110
Simon, Herbert 159, 160
Siri 73, 75, 76
SkinBeauty 95–6, 98, 100, 101–4
smart speakers *see* voice intelligence
SMEs (small and medium-sized enterprises) 112, 113–14, 122
social imaginaries 37–8, 39–42, 43–4, 45, 50–1
social media 23, 33–4, 38, 57, 69, 84, 131, 135, 153, 157, 161
social synthesis 18, 22–3, 24, 26, 27
sociology 3
Sohn-Rethel, Alfred 18, 22–3, 24, 26, 27, 31
Spotify 81
Steam 15, 104, 140–1, 144–52
strategic discourse 4, 6, 11, 37
STS (science and technology studies) 3
surveillance 1, 3, 10, 14, 71, 74–5, 82–4, 86, 91, 120, 141, 157–8, 161
Swartz, Lana 23–4, 26, 28, 33–4

T

Taobao 112, 114–15, 116, 117–19, 125
Taskrabbit 46
Taylor, Charles 40–1, 42, 43, 45, 49
technopopulism 52
Tencent 75, 123
Thomson, George 27
Thorhauge, Anne Mette 15, 104
TikTok 6, 77, 128, 138
TRAI (Telecommunications Regulatory Authority of India) 67, 68, 69
transactions
 communities 24, 26, 29, 34, 36, 150

costs 109
data and 22, 33
digital media and 18, 21
economic 15, 141, 143, 144–7, 150
enumeration of 64
exchange abstraction 22–3
facilitation of 17, 18
gaming and 140–52
market 20–1, 25, 29
media 36
money and 27
online 118, 122
platforms and 15, 17, 24, 33–4
problems 134
services 114
simultaneous 54
value of 19, 116
see also affordances: transactional
Troullinou, Pinelopi 82, 83
Turow, Joseph 13, 14
TV ratings 56, 61–4, 67–8, 69–70, 72n2
Twitter 6, 38, 39, 43, 46, 77, 135

U

Uber 6, 38, 39, 42, 44, 45, 47, 48, 49, 50, 51, 131

Unity 4
universalism 12, 37, 39
USA 10, 15, 32, 50–1, 54, 63, 67–9, 73–6, 79, 82, 84, 86, 134

V

Valve 146–8, 149, 152
voice intelligence 73–85, 86–7

W

Wales, Jimmy 46
WhatsApp 6, 77
Wikipedia 39, 45, 46, 49
Wolf, Eric 92
WTO (World Trade Organization) 113

X

Xi Jinping 121

Y

YouTube 6, 15, 38, 46, 70, 77, 91, 128, 131–3, 134–8, 141, 161
Yuan, Elaine J. 15, 94, 106

Z

Zhang, Lin 15, 94, 106